Copyright © 2024 by Welbon Omar S.

All rights reserved. This book or any portion thereof may not be reproduced or used in any manner whatsoever without the express written permission of the publisher, except for the use of brief quotations in a book review or scholarly journal.

GreenBooks Publishing
1 Gateway Center, Suite 2600
Newark, NJ 07102
www.greenbookspublishing.company.site

First Edition

ISBN: 9798884004382

This work is non-fiction. The accounts and cases are based on the author's experiences and research. Any resemblance to actual persons, living or dead, or actual events is coincidental.

Book design by Wilmington Graphic Design LLC

Printed in the United States of America

Part of the "Mind Your Own Business" series, this third installment follows "Secrets to Creating a Successful Brand in 2020" and "Maximizing Your Reach," providing further insights into developing and sustaining strong business relationships and brand identity through customer and client prioritization.

First Printing, 2024

This book is dedicated to the entrepreneurs that work long hours, early mornings, late nights, and put their blood sweat and tears into their business, hone their skills, focus on sharpening their craft, and constantly seek the evolution of their offerings to enhance their customer's experience and support their client's journey. To these souls who work on perfecting their patience daily. I admire you.

Also to Naeem, Mateena, Yusra, Bilaal, Nahlah, and Madinah, for affording me the quiet moments to compile this work, I love you all. To Lailah, I love you. Thank you for supporting me in my craft.

Foreword by Welbon Omar Salaam:
Setting the Stage for Strategic Success

In business the distinction between clients and customers sometimes gets blurred. This convergence has left many businesses grappling with a strategic dilemma: whom to prioritize and how to engage effectively. Hi. My name is Welbon Omar Salaam and as we embark on this journey through this book, I invite you to explore the nuanced dynamics of today's business environment with me.

My encounter with this dilemma was not merely academic but born from the trenches of real-world business challenges. Several years ago, our company stood at a crossroads, faced with stagnating growth and an increasingly disengaged customer base. It was during this period of introspection and analysis that the realization dawned upon us—the traditional division between clients and customers was not just outdated but detrimental to our growth strategy. This epiphany was the catalyst for a transformative shift in our approach, leading us to innovate and implement systems that not only distinguished between the two groups but also leveraged their unique dynamics for mutual benefit.

This book is a distillation of those lessons learned, a guide designed to navigate the complex interplay between client and customer engagement. Through in-depth analysis, practical advice, and real-world examples, we will unravel the strategies that can propel businesses to new heights. From mastering affiliate systems to cultivating a vibrant referral ecosystem, our journey will equip you with the tools necessary for success in the contemporary market.

As we turn the pages, remember that the goal is not just to differentiate between clients and customers but to understand the profound impact that this distinction can have on your business strategy. It is my sincere hope that this book serves as a beacon, guiding you towards innovative solutions and strategic mastery. Together, let us redefine the boundaries of business success, embracing the dual approach to client and customer engagement as a cornerstone of our growth strategies.

Introduction

Chapter 1 delves into the heart of a pivotal issue facing today's businesses: the strategic dilemma between prioritizing clients or customers. This chapter aims to lay the groundwork for understanding the essential differences between these two groups, their unique needs, and how these distinctions impact business strategies. Through a blend of analytical insight and practical examples, we will explore the consequences of this dilemma and set the stage for a comprehensive approach to engaging with both demographics effectively.

The Essence of the Dilemma

At the core of this strategic dilemma is the nuanced understanding of who clients and customers are. Customers are typically seen as the end-users of a product or service, often engaging in one-off transactions or short-term interactions. In contrast, clients are usually involved in longer-term, more personalized relationships with a business, often requiring tailored solutions and a deeper level of engagement. The challenge for businesses lies in navigating these relationships simultaneously, optimizing their strategies to cater to both without compromising the quality of engagement or diluting their brand value.

Impact on Business Strategy

The decision to focus on clients or customers profoundly affects every aspect of a business strategy, from product development and marketing to sales and customer service. Opting for a client-centric approach might necessitate a higher investment in relationship management and customized solutions. Conversely, a customer-focused strategy could require a broader appeal, scalable processes, and a robust transactional system. Businesses often find themselves oscillating between these approaches, seeking the elusive balance that maximizes growth and sustainability.

Setting the Stage for Dual Engagement

This chapter will not only highlight the strategic implications of this dilemma but also introduce the concept of dual engagement. Recognizing that businesses need not choose between clients and customers but can instead cultivate a harmonious strategy that embraces both, we will begin to outline the principles of this balanced approach. By understanding the intrinsic value and potential of each group, businesses can craft a comprehensive strategy that leverages the strengths of both client and customer relationships, setting the foundation for the detailed strategies and systems discussed in subsequent chapters.

As we proceed, keep in mind that the goal of this exploration is to empower businesses to make informed strategic decisions, fostering growth and stability in a rapidly changing market landscape.

Chapter 1 Pre-Breakdown: Straight Talk

Section 1.1: Cutting Through the BS

Forget the fluff. It's about knowing the difference between spamming the market and actually giving a darn about your clients. Some companies get it, diving deep into what their clients need and customizing their approach. The result? Better retention and more money in the bank. We've seen tech firms and financial advisors turn their game around by actually listening to their clients. Bottom line: personal touch = personal profit.

Section 1.2: The Customer Maze

Customers go through a jungle of choices from the moment they hear about you to the aftertaste of their purchase. We're talking about making every step count. Look at the big dogs – e-commerce giants and tech moguls who've mastered the art of keeping customers hooked with personalized experiences. They use every tech trick in the book – AI, big data, AR – to make shopping not just easy but almost psychic.

Section 1.3: Tough Calls

Here's where it gets real. Balancing between keeping your clients feeling like VIPs and not ignoring the crowd. It's about where to put your money and your people. Do you amp up your digital game for the masses or train your team to give the personal touch? There's no free lunch. Each choice has its price and its payoff.

Section 1.4: The Hybrid Hustle

It's about being smart – serving up personalized experiences without losing the efficiency of mass marketing. We're breaking down how to segment your audience, integrate your services, and customize your marketing without turning your operations into a circus. Real-life examples? A consumer electronics company splitting its focus to cater to tech heads and the average Joe, and a financial firm blending advisory services with digital efficiency.

Section 1.5: Blueprint for Bifocal Engagement

Diving into dual engagement means balancing on a tightrope. You need a plan that spells out how to charm both clients and customers without dropping the ball. We're laying out the steps from identifying your audience to rolling out the red carpet for them, all while keeping an eye on the numbers to make sure you're not just busy but effective.

Section 1.6: Tech to the Rescue

Tech isn't just for nerds; it's the secret sauce for dual engagement. We're reviewing the heavy hitters – CRM systems, analytics tools, digital marketing platforms – that make juggling clients and customers a breeze. Whether it's Salesforce for the big players or HubSpot for the up-and-comers, the right tech can make or break your strategy.

Section 1.7: No Time for Second Guessing

It's go time. The market waits for no one, and if you're going to master the art of dual engagement, you need to roll up your sleeves and dive in. We've got a checklist that's all business –

from segmenting your market to picking the right tech and keeping your team sharp. It's not about being everywhere at once but about being right where you need to be.

Let's Get to Work:
- **Audit Your Strategy:** What's working, and what's just noise? Cut the latter.
- **Know Your People:** Who are your clients and customers? Get specific or go home.
- **Pick Your Weapons:** Not all tech is created equal. Choose what gets you results.
- **Train Like You Mean It:** Your team's savvy is your secret weapon. Sharpen it.
- **Listen Hard:** Feedback isn't just noise; it's gold. Dig into it.
- **Watch the Scoreboard:** If you're not measuring, you're guessing. Stop that.
- **Evolve or Die:** The market changes. Your strategy should too.

Buckle up. It's going to be a wild ride, but for those ready to get real about engaging clients and customers, the rewards are worth it. Let's do this.

Chapter 1
Buckle up, nerds! Time to READ.

Section 1.1:
The Strategic Dilemma

Understanding the Core Differences

The landscape of business strategy and client engagement is marked by a critical distinction between generalized market approaches and the nuanced, tailored strategy of client-specific engagement. Central to this dichotomy is the understanding of who the clients are—entities or individuals seeking not just products or services, but advice, solutions, and a partnership that understands and meets their unique needs.

Businesses that recognize and act upon the core differences between broad market tactics and client-centric strategies position themselves advantageously in today's competitive marketplace. This section delves into the essence of what it means to truly engage with clients, offering an in-depth analysis complemented by case studies, expert insights, and statistical evidence that underline the efficacy of a personalized approach.

Expanded Analysis: Successful Case Studies

A compelling illustration of this principle is seen in the journey of a technology firm that transitioned from a one-size-fits-all product offering to a customized solution provider. Through interviews with the firm's leadership and analysis of their strategy overhaul, key factors emerged. The firm's client retention rates soared by 35% within the first year post-implementation of tailored solutions, a testament to the value of understanding and addressing specific client needs.

Further evidence is provided by a financial advisory firm that prioritized client relationships over sheer transaction volume. By incorporating expert advice into their service delivery, they not only enhanced client satisfaction but also saw a 25% increase in annual revenue, driven by both retention and referrals. These case studies are buttressed by insights from industry experts who emphasize the transformative impact of a client-focused approach on business outcomes.

In synthesizing detailed case studies, expert insights, and statistical data, this section underscores the strategic dilemma businesses face in the modern market. It advocates for a shift towards understanding and leveraging the core differences in client engagement, highlighting the profound benefits of adopting a client-centric approach in fostering sustainable business growth and client satisfaction.

Section 1.2: Customers: Pursuing Products and Services

In-Depth Examples: Navigating the Customer Journey

The journey of a customer, from initial awareness to post-purchase engagement, is intricate and varies significantly across different industries. This section provides detailed walkthroughs of customer journey maps from companies renowned for their exceptional service or product offerings, showcasing how a deep understanding of the customer journey can drive unparalleled success.

A standout example is a leading e-commerce giant, which has meticulously crafted its customer journey to ensure convenience, speed, and satisfaction at every touchpoint. By analyzing extensive customer data and feedback, the company continuously refines its user experience, resulting in a highly personalized shopping experience that anticipates customer needs and preferences.

Another example is a global tech company known for its innovative consumer electronics. The customer journey map here highlights the seamless integration of product discovery, in-store experiences, online support, and community engagement, facilitated by cutting-edge technology and a customer-first approach. These examples are complemented by discussions on how continuous feedback loops and customer data analysis are leveraged to innovate and improve product and service offerings.

Technological Solutions:
Enhancing the Customer Experience

The transformation of the customer experience through technology is profound and multifaceted. This section delves into specific technologies that have revolutionized how companies engage with their customers, enhancing every stage of the customer journey.

One notable innovation is the use of artificial intelligence in personalizing customer interactions. Detailed screenshots and diagrams illustrate how AI-powered chatbots and recommendation engines operate, providing a behind-the-scenes look at the technology that enables companies to offer personalized advice and product suggestions at scale.

Furthermore, the application of big data analytics in understanding customer behavior is explored through visuals of analytics dashboards. These tools allow businesses to derive actionable insights from vast amounts of customer data, informing product development, marketing strategies, and customer service improvements.

The use of augmented reality (AR) in retail is another technological advancement highlighted. Diagrams and screenshots show how AR apps let customers visualize products in their own space before making a purchase, significantly enhancing the decision-making process and increasing customer satisfaction.

By providing in-depth examples of customer journey maps and elaborating on the technological solutions that have transformed the customer experience, this section illustrates the dynamic interplay between customer needs, market trends, and technological innovation. It underscores the importance of a customer-centric approach in product and service development, reinforced by a commitment to continuous improvement and technological advancement.

Section 1.3: Strategic Implications of the Dilemma

Decision-Making Challenges

Navigating the strategic dilemma of client and customer engagement involves complex decision-making, with businesses constantly weighing the allocation of resources against anticipated outcomes. This section explores the intricate balance required in decision-making processes, particularly concerning financial and human resources, and operational adjustments. Through hypothetical scenarios, the multifaceted nature of these challenges is illustrated, offering insights into the strategic considerations that underpin successful engagement strategies.

Resource Allocation: Financial and Human Considerations

Effective resource allocation is pivotal in addressing the dual approach to client and customer engagement. One scenario involves a retail company deciding how to allocate its budget between enhancing its online platform (to improve customer engagement) and investing in training programs for sales staff (to enhance client relationships). A strategic investment in technology might lead to improved customer satisfaction due to a more seamless online shopping experience, potentially increasing sales. Conversely, prioritizing staff training could result in higher client retention rates through personalized service, though it may come at the expense of digital expansion.

In another example, a tech startup faces staffing model decisions—whether to hire more product developers to innovate and attract new customers or to expand its customer service team to offer superior support to existing clients. The decision hinges on assessing the long-term value of innovation versus client satisfaction, with each path leading to different financial and operational outcomes.

Operational Adjustments: Case Scenarios

Operational strategy pivots are often necessary for businesses to remain competitive and responsive to market demands. A case scenario illustrates a manufacturing company that shifted its operational strategy from mass production to a more flexible manufacturing system. This adjustment allowed the company to offer customized products, catering to specific client needs and differentiating itself in a crowded market. The transition involved significant changes in production processes and resource allocation but ultimately led to increased client satisfaction and market share.

Another scenario depicts a service-oriented business that restructured its operations to provide 24/7 customer support through a combination of in-house teams and outsourced partners. This operational change, driven by the need to enhance customer engagement, required careful planning around staffing, training, and technology investments. The result was a notable improvement in customer satisfaction ratings and loyalty, demonstrating the value of operational flexibility in meeting customer needs.

Through these hypothetical scenarios, the section underscores the complexities of strategic decision-making in the context of client and customer engagement. It highlights the importance of thoughtful resource allocation and operational adjustments, with the understanding that each decision carries implications for financial performance, customer satisfaction, and long-term business viability.

Section 1.4: Balancing Act: Catering to Both Markets

Hybrid Models: A Step-by-Step Guide

The creation of hybrid models marks a strategic evolution for businesses aiming to effectively serve both clients and customers without diluting the quality of engagement. This section outlines a step-by-step guide for developing such models, emphasizing market segmentation, service integration, and the customization of marketing messages.

Step 1: Market Segmentation

The first step involves a thorough analysis of the market to identify distinct segments within the client and customer bases. This segmentation is critical, as it allows businesses to tailor their approaches to the specific needs and preferences of each group.

Welbon Omar Salaam

Step 2: Integration of Services

Once market segments are defined, the next step is to integrate services in a manner that addresses the needs of both clients and customers. This involves designing a service delivery model that is flexible enough to offer personalized advice and solutions to clients while maintaining the efficiency and scalability required to serve a broader customer base. Diagrams in this section depict how services can be layered and interconnected, ensuring that each segment receives focused attention without compromising service quality.

Step 3: Customization of Marketing Messages

The final step is the customization of marketing messages to resonate with the identified segments. This customization ensures that communication is relevant and engaging, enhancing the effectiveness of marketing efforts. A series of diagrams demonstrate how businesses can develop and deploy targeted messages across various channels, ensuring that each message is aligned with the needs and preferences of the target segment.

Success Stories: Case Studies

The theoretical framework of hybrid models is brought to life through deep dives into case studies that illustrate their successful implementation. One such example involves a consumer electronics company that faced the challenge of catering to both technology enthusiasts (clients) looking for cutting-edge products and general consumers (customers) seeking reliable, user-friendly devices. The solution was a hybrid model that segmented its product lines and marketing strategies to address the distinct needs of each group. Quotes from the company's strategists highlight the deliberation behind this approach and the positive outcomes it yielded, including increased market share and customer satisfaction.

Another case study features a financial services firm that integrated personalized advisory services with its digital platforms, enabling it to offer customized investment advice alongside efficient, automated transaction capabilities. This hybrid approach not only expanded its client base but also deepened relationships with existing clients, as evidenced by improved retention rates and client testimonials.

These success stories, supported by quotes from business leaders, underscore the effectiveness of hybrid models in navigating the complexities of dual market engagement. They demonstrate the strategic foresight and operational flexibility required to balance the demands of diverse market segments, ultimately achieving a competitive edge in the market.

Section 1.5: Setting the Stage for Dual Engagement

Principles of Dual Engagement

The journey towards mastering dual engagement in the market begins with understanding its foundational principles. These principles guide businesses in crafting strategies that resonate with both clients seeking personalized solutions and customers pursuing products or services. Emphasizing a balance between personalization and scalability, the principles of dual engagement serve as the cornerstone for developing a strategic blueprint that businesses can adapt to their unique circumstances.

Strategic Blueprint: A Comprehensive Guide

A detailed strategic blueprint is essential for businesses aiming to navigate the complexities of dual engagement successfully. This blueprint includes a phased timeline, clearly defined key performance indicators (KPIs), and robust monitoring techniques to ensure that strategies are effective and adaptable. The section provides templates and frameworks that readers can directly apply or modify to fit their business models, offering a step-by-step approach to implementation.

Phase 1: Assessment and Planning

The first phase involves a thorough assessment of the current market position and the identification of target segments for clients and customers. This phase sets the stage for detailed planning, including setting objectives, defining KPIs such as customer acquisition costs, client retention rates, and overall satisfaction scores, and establishing a timeline for execution.

Phase 2: Execution and Communication

Execution involves rolling out targeted strategies for each segment, with a strong focus on tailored communication strategies. This phase details methodologies for creating and delivering messages that engage each segment effectively, utilizing a mix of traditional and digital marketing channels.

Phase 3: Monitoring and Adaptation

The final phase focuses on monitoring outcomes against the set KPIs and adapting strategies based on performance data. This section provides templates for tracking progress and techniques for adjusting plans to meet or exceed objectives, ensuring that businesses remain agile in their dual engagement approach.

Market Segmentation and Communication

Effective market segmentation and targeted communication strategies are pivotal in dual engagement. This part elaborates on methodologies for segmenting the market with precision, identifying the unique characteristics and preferences of each segment. It includes examples of successful campaigns that demonstrate how tailored communication can significantly impact engagement and conversion rates.

One illustrative example is a campaign by a consumer goods company that identified two key segments: environmentally conscious consumers and value-oriented shoppers. By developing distinct communication strategies for each group—highlighting sustainability for the former and cost savings for the latter—the company significantly increased its market penetration in both segments.

The strategic blueprint, coupled with insights into market segmentation and communication, equips businesses with the tools they need to engage effectively with both clients and customers. By adhering to the principles of dual engagement and employing a systematic approach to planning, execution, and monitoring, businesses can set the stage for sustained success in a competitive marketplace.

Section 1.6: Technological Enablement

Tool and Platform Reviews

Technology serves as the backbone of effective dual engagement strategies, enabling businesses to navigate the complexities of catering to both clients and customers. This section provides comprehensive reviews of various Customer Relationship Management (CRM) systems, analytics tools, and digital marketing platforms, critically assessing their utility in implementing dual engagement strategies.

CRM Systems

CRM systems are pivotal in managing interactions with clients and customers, offering a centralized repository of information that enhances communication and service delivery. For instance, Salesforce stands out for its extensive customization options and robust analytics capabilities, making it a prime choice for businesses looking to tailor their engagement strategies. However, its complexity and cost may pose challenges for smaller businesses. In contrast, HubSpot offers a more user-friendly interface and a suite of free tools suitable for small to medium-sized enterprises, though it may lack the depth of analytics and customization available in more advanced systems.

Analytics Tools

Analytics tools provide the insights necessary for informed decision-making. Google Analytics is lauded for its comprehensive tracking and reporting features, which are invaluable for understanding customer behaviors and preferences. It integrates seamlessly with digital marketing platforms, although its advanced features can be daunting for novices. Alternatively, Tableau offers powerful data visualization capabilities, making complex data more accessible, but requires a significant investment in both time and money to fully leverage its potential.

Digital Marketing Platforms

Digital marketing platforms like Google Ads and Facebook Ads play a critical role in reaching and engaging target segments. Google Ads is praised for its vast network and sophisticated targeting options, ideal for businesses aiming to reach a broad audience. However, mastering its bidding system can be challenging. Facebook Ads offers unparalleled demographic targeting, optimized for creating highly personalized campaigns, though its effectiveness can be contingent on the changing dynamics of social media usage.

Mastering the Market: A Dual Approach to Client and Customer Engagement

Case Studies with Technology

The application of technology in achieving dual engagement is further elucidated through detailed case studies. One such case involves a retail company that leveraged CRM and analytics tools to unify its online and offline customer data, creating a 360-degree view of customer interactions. This integration allowed for personalized marketing campaigns and improved customer service, significantly boosting customer satisfaction and loyalty. However, the company faced initial challenges in data integration and staff training, which were overcome through strategic planning and investment in professional development.

Another case study highlights a B2B technology service provider that used digital marketing platforms to differentiate its approach for engaging potential clients versus general customers. By using LinkedIn Ads for targeted client engagement and Google Ads for broader customer outreach, the company was able to allocate its marketing budget more effectively, resulting in increased leads and a higher conversion rate. The challenges encountered included optimizing ad spend and continuously adapting strategies to market trends, which were addressed through ongoing analysis and adjustment.

These case studies demonstrate the transformative potential of technology in facilitating dual engagement, showcasing both the challenges faced and the strategic solutions implemented. The benefits realized underscore the importance of technological enablement in contemporary business strategies, highlighting the value of investment in the right tools and platforms.

Section 1.7: Navigating the Strategic Dilemma

Key Insights and Call to Action

As we conclude the first chapter of this book, the strategic dilemma of balancing client-centric solutions with broad-based customer engagement is evident. The journey through understanding the core differences, the strategic implications, the technological enablement, and the development of hybrid models has laid a solid foundation for businesses ready to embark on this path. It's a journey that requires not only strategic foresight and operational agility but also a commitment to continuous learning and adaptation.

The call to action is clear: Businesses must boldly undertake the journey toward effective dual engagement. This is not a path for the timid but for those visionary leaders and organizations ready to challenge the status quo, innovate, and lead in their respective markets. To aid in this journey, the following checklist of action items is presented, designed to guide businesses as they strategize their dual engagement approach.

Checklist for Strategic Dual Engagement:

1. **Assessment of Current Engagement Strategies:** Evaluate your current client and customer engagement strategies. Identify areas of strength and opportunities for improvement.
2. **Market Segmentation:** Conduct detailed market segmentation to clearly define your client and customer bases. Understand their unique needs and preferences.
3. **Technology Audit:** Review your current technology stack. Identify gaps and opportunities for adopting new tools that can enhance engagement strategies.
4. **Resource Allocation:** Plan your resource allocation, balancing financial and human capital investments between client-focused and customer-focused initiatives.
5. **Operational Flexibility:** Assess your operational processes and structure for flexibility. Ensure your organization can adapt to the dynamic needs of both clients and customers.
6. **Training and Development:** Implement training programs for your team to understand and embrace the principles of dual engagement.
7. **Feedback Mechanisms:** Establish robust feedback mechanisms to continuously gather insights from both clients and customers, informing strategy adjustments.

8. **Performance Monitoring:** Set key performance indicators (KPIs) relevant to dual engagement and monitor them closely to measure success and identify areas for adjustment.
9. **Continuous Improvement:** Commit to a cycle of continuous improvement, leveraging insights from data analysis, market trends, and feedback to refine and evolve your engagement strategies.
10. **Strategic Partnerships:** Consider forming strategic partnerships that can enhance your dual engagement capabilities, providing access to new technologies, markets, or expertise.

By following this checklist, businesses can navigate the strategic dilemma with confidence, positioning themselves for success in an increasingly competitive market. The journey towards mastering dual engagement is both challenging and rewarding, offering the promise of deeper relationships, enhanced customer satisfaction, and sustained business growth.

Let this chapter serve as a blueprint and a source of inspiration as you embark on this transformative journey. The road ahead is paved with opportunities for those willing to invest in the dual engagement approach, redefining the way businesses connect with their clients and customers in the digital age.

Chapter 1: Step-By Step How to "Get... It... Done!"

Section 1.1: Decoding Market Signals
Task 1: Market Pulse Check
- **Action:** Deploy a sharp, straight-to-the-point survey to gauge what really tickles your audience's fancy. Think lean, mean, and on the screen.
- **Deadline:** 14 days to get the real talk from your market.

Task 2: Competitive Recon
- **Action:** Take a deep dive into your competitors' pool – identify their strokes of genius and where they're just treading water.
- **Deadline:** 21 days to map out your swim lanes.

Task 3: Insight Integration
- **Action:** Blend your market insights with competitive intel to sketch out where the market's heart truly lies.
- **Deadline:** 7 days to craft your market love letter.

Section 1.2: Customer Journey Optimization
Task 1: Journey Mapping
- **Action:** Lay out the red carpet for your customer journey, ensuring each step is an opportunity to dazzle and delight.
- **Deadline:** 28 days to roll out your best experience.

Task 2: Tech Touchpoints
- **Action:** Pin down tech solutions that streamline and enhance the journey. Think customer delight at the click of a button.
- **Deadline:** 42 days to tech-enable the customer path.

Section 1.3: Strategic Decision Sprints
Task 1: Resource Reallocation
- **Action:** Juggle your resources with the finesse of a startup savant. Digital dazzle or personal touch? Find your balance.
- **Deadline:** 14 days to align your assets.

Task 2: Process Pivot
- **Action:** Identify one bottleneck and give it the boot. Streamline like a pro.
- **Deadline:** 35 days to smooth sailing.

Section 1.4: Crafting the Hybrid Strategy
Task 1: Segment Savvy
- **Action:** Slice your audience finer than a startup's budget. Who are they, and what makes them tick?
- **Deadline:** 14 days to segment like a boss.

Task 2: Seamless Service Integration
- **Action:** Weave your services together so seamlessly they can't tell where one ends and another begins.
- **Deadline:** 28 days for a masterclass in integration.

Task 3: Marketing Messages that Convert
- **Action:** Custom-tailor your marketing messages like a bespoke suit. Fit each customer perfectly.
- **Deadline:** 21 days to tailor your pitch.

Section 1.5: Mastering the Art of Dual Engagement
Task 1: Strategic Blueprint Drafting

- **Action:** Map out your strategic playbook. From theories to actionable steps, make it the entrepreneur's bible.
- **Deadline:** 42 days to blueprint brilliance.

Task 2: Fine-tune Your Funnel
- **Action:** Calibrate your communication for maximum impact. Every touchpoint is a conversion opportunity.
- **Deadline:** 21 days to perfect your pitch.

Task 3: KPIs and Adaptation
- **Action:** Benchmark, measure, tweak, repeat. Set KPIs that matter and use them to steer your ship.
- **Deadline:** Continuous. Always be optimizing.

Section 1.6: Leveraging Tech for the Win

Task 1: Platform Selection
- **Action:** Choose your tech stack with the precision of a chef selecting knives. Only the best for your kitchen.
- **Deadline:** 28 days to assemble your arsenal.

Task 2: Success Story Safari
- **Action:** Venture into the wilds of case studies. Adapt the strategies of those who've thrived to your playbook.
- **Deadline:** 21 days for a tour through triumphs.

Section 1.7: Wrap-Up with Winning in Mind
Task 1: Insights to Action
- **Action:** What's the market whispering? Turn murmurs into strategy and embed these insights deep into your game plan.
- **Deadline:** Ongoing. Never stop listening.

Task 2: Elevate Feedback
- **Action:** Turn feedback into your north star. Navigate by the real reactions and desires of your market.
- **Deadline:** Continuous. Feedback is your fuel.

Task 3: Stay Agile, Stay Ahead
- **Action:** The market doesn't stand still, and neither should you. Pivot, adapt, and lead.
- **Deadline:** Forever. Innovation never sleeps.

The Bottom Line: Dive deep into the market's psyche, sharpen your strategy, embrace the tech that propels you forward, and stay ruthlessly focused on feedback and adaptation. Your entrepreneurial journey is about making waves, not just sailing them. Execute on these steps, and watch as your business not only grows but thrives in the competitive dance of sales and marketing.

Chapter 2 Pre-Breakdown: No Fluff, Just Facts

Let's get down to brass tacks. This isn't about wandering through the weeds but about getting straight to the heart of what makes your customers tick and stitching together a strategy that doesn't just sing; it soars.

Section 2.1: Fine-Tuning Your Market Radar
Mastering Market Needs with Precision

- **Task:** Initiate a deep dive into the realms of market desires. Your quest? To uncover the holy grail of what your clients and customers truly crave.
- **Direct Action:** Roll out a snappy survey. Aim for brevity to boost those response rates sky-high.
- **Sharp Insight:** Custom-fit your offerings. This is your tailor-made moment to shine by aligning closely with your audience's desires.

Decoding the Competition with Finesse

- **Task:** Embark on a reconnaissance mission into competitor territory. What secrets can you unearth about their approach and customer grievances?
- **Direct Action:** Sketch out a comparison chart of your top 3 rivals. Highlight where customers are voicing their frustrations.
- **Sharp Insight:** Opportunity knocks where competitors stumble. Identify these gaps as your golden tickets.

Gleaning Actionable Insights

- **Task:** Marry your market research findings with the intel gathered on your competitors. What emerges? A distilled essence of market yearnings.
- **Direct Action:** Draft a concise list of key customer expectations.
- **Sharp Insight:** Search for recurring themes that resonate with your brand's strengths. Here lies your path to differentiation.

Section 2.2: Sculpting Your Strategy
Crafting a Standout Value Proposition

- **Task:** With fresh insights in hand, it's time to sculpt a value proposition that clearly articulates why you're the choice of champions.
- **Direct Action:** Experiment with different pitches. Keep iterating until one resonates unmistakably with a test audience.
- **Sharp Insight:** Emphasize the wins for your customer. Benefits over features, always. What transformative outcome can they expect?

Polishing Your Strategic Gem
- **Task:** Solicit feedback on your value proposition drafts. Which one hits home?
- **Direct Action:** Choose the most compelling version and make it official.
- **Sharp Insight:** Aim for laser-like clarity and brevity. If it doesn't resonate in a heartbeat, it's back to the drawing board.

Section 2.3: Elevating Engagement with Tech
Selecting Your Digital Companions
- **Task:** Pinpoint the digital tools and platforms that will amplify your connection with customers.
- **Direct Action:** Trial run the frontrunners. Seek the perfect match for your engagement blueprint.
- **Sharp Insight:** Balance is key. Seek tools that offer both power and usability without overwhelming your team or your customers.

Sketching Out Your Engagement Blueprint
- **Task:** Armed with your chosen tech, draft a roadmap for captivating customer interactions.
- **Direct Action:** Plot a 6-month engagement strategy, starting broad before zooming in on the details.
- **Sharp Insight:** Initiate with focused efforts. Expand as you gain traction, but beware of overextension. Agility beats brute force every time.

Staying the Course: Essentials
- **Monthly Progress Pow-wows:** Establish a standing monthly rendezvous to evaluate what's flying and what's floundering.
- **Adaptation is Your Superpower:** Keep your strategy flexible. Customer feedback is your compass—let it guide your tweaks and turns.
- **Spotlight on Success:** Make time to shine a light on your achievements. Celebrating victories keeps the team energized and engaged.

Peel back the complexity, and the essence of true engagement is crystal clear: deep understanding, strategic clarity, and dynamic execution. Nail these elements, and you're not just in the game—you're playing to win.

Chapter 2
Buckle up, nerds! Time to READ. AGAIN!

Section 2.1: Common Missteps Unveiled

Misunderstanding Market Needs

A pivotal challenge in the dual approach to client and customer engagement lies in accurately identifying and understanding the distinct needs of these two groups. This section delves into the common pitfalls businesses encounter due to misunderstandings of market needs, underscored by case studies of companies that have faced setbacks or missed opportunities.

Expanded Analysis: The Cost of Misunderstanding

The misidentification of market needs can lead to significant strategic misalignments, resulting in wasted resources, lost revenue, and damaged brand reputation. One illustrative case involves a technology company that developed an advanced software platform, assuming that its high-tech features would meet the needs of all potential users. However, the company failed to recognize the significant divide between its client base—businesses seeking complex, customizable solutions—and general customers looking for user-friendly, straightforward tools. The result was a product too complex for the average customer yet not sufficiently adaptable for client-specific needs, leading to poor market reception and financial losses.

Another case study highlights a retail company that expanded its product line without adequately researching customer preferences, assuming that its existing clientele would embrace the new offerings. The expansion led to inventory surplus and markdowns, as the new products did not resonate with the intended market segments. These examples underscore the necessity of deep market understanding to avoid missteps in product and service development.

Consequences of Such Gaps

The consequences of misunderstanding market needs extend beyond immediate financial setbacks. They can lead to long-term brand damage, loss of market share, and the erosion of competitive advantage. Companies that fail to accurately assess and respond to the needs of their clients and customers risk being outpaced by more agile competitors that prioritize market understanding and alignment.

The case studies presented in this section serve as a cautionary tale for businesses striving for success in a dual engagement market. They underscore the importance of rigorous market research, continuous feedback loops, and the flexibility to adapt offerings in response to evolving market insights. Only through a deep and nuanced understanding of both client and customer needs can businesses avoid common missteps and fully capitalize on the opportunities presented by a dual engagement strategy.

Section 2.2:
Lack of Clear Strategic Focus

In-Depth Examination: The Cost of Ambiguity

Attempting to serve both markets—clients seeking tailored advice and solutions, and customers pursuing generic products or services—without a clear strategic focus can lead to significant challenges for businesses. This section explores the consequences of such ambiguity, including diluted brand value and diminished market presence. The absence of a clear strategy often results in resources being spread too thinly, messaging that fails to resonate with either audience, and ultimately, a weakened competitive position.

For example, a technology company that initially thrived by offering niche, customized solutions began to expand its product line to appeal to a broader customer base. However, without a clear strategy to manage this diversification, the company struggled to maintain its brand identity. The attempt to serve too broad a market without distinct messaging led to confusion among its core client base, resulting in a loss of trust and a decline in client retention. Similarly, a retail brand known for its premium, personalized shopping experience diluted its brand value by aggressively pursuing an online discount sales strategy to attract a wider customer base, which ultimately alienated its loyal customers and eroded its market presence.

Strategic Frameworks: Clarifying Focus

To avoid the pitfalls of a lack of strategic focus, businesses can adopt several models and frameworks designed to clarify their strategic direction and ensure alignment with core competencies and market expectations.

1. **SWOT Analysis:** This framework helps businesses identify their Strengths, Weaknesses, Opportunities, and Threats, enabling them to define a clear strategic focus that leverages their strengths and opportunities while addressing weaknesses and threats.
2. **The Ansoff Matrix:** This tool assists businesses in determining their growth strategy by evaluating opportunities for market penetration, market development, product development, and diversification, ensuring decisions align with their core competencies and market dynamics.
3. **Porter's Generic Strategies:** By adopting one of Porter's strategies—cost leadership, differentiation, or focus—a business can clarify its approach to competing in the market, whether by offering the lowest prices, unique products or services, or concentrating on a specific market segment.

4. **Blue Ocean Strategy:** This strategy encourages businesses to create new market space or "Blue Oceans," thereby making the competition irrelevant. It emphasizes the importance of innovation in products, services, and delivery methods to open up new segments of the market.

5. **Value Discipline Model:** This model suggests that companies excel by leading in one of three disciplines—operational excellence, customer intimacy, or product leadership. Choosing a discipline guides strategic focus and resource allocation to build a competitive advantage.

Implementing these strategic frameworks requires businesses to conduct thorough market research, engage in introspection to understand their true competencies, and rigorously evaluate their market environment. By doing so, they can develop a focused strategy that aligns with their strengths and market needs, enabling them to effectively serve their target audience without diluting their brand value or compromising their market presence.

A clear strategic focus is not just beneficial; it is essential for businesses navigating the complexities of serving diverse markets. By understanding the ramifications of a lack of focus and employing strategic frameworks to clarify their approach, businesses can ensure that they not only survive but thrive in competitive markets. Aligning operations, messaging, and offerings with a well-defined strategy enables businesses to maintain a strong brand identity, satisfy their core markets, and achieve sustained growth.

Section 2.3: Misconceptions About Engagement

One-Size-Fits-All Marketing

The application of a one-size-fits-all marketing strategy is not just ineffective; it's a misallocation of resources that often results in missed opportunities. This section conducts a critical analysis of why generic marketing strategies fail to resonate with specific client or customer groups and highlights how targeted marketing approaches can lead to significantly better outcomes.

Critical Analysis: The Pitfalls of Generic Strategies

Generic marketing strategies, by their nature, overlook the nuanced preferences and needs of distinct market segments. Such approaches assume a homogeneity in audience behavior and expectations that simply does not exist, leading to messages that lack relevance and personalization. This misalignment often results in diminished engagement rates, poor conversion, and a dilution of brand identity. For instance, a campaign that targets both millennials and baby boomers with the same message and medium is likely to engage neither group markets. By understanding the ramifications of a lack of focus and employing strategic frameworks to clarify their approach, businesses can ensure that they not only survive but thrive in competitive markets. Aligning operations, messaging, and offerings with a well-defined strategy enables businesses to maintain a strong brand identity, satisfy their core markets, and achieve sustained growth.

Section 2.3: Misconceptions About Engagement

One-Size-Fits-All Marketing

The application of a one-size-fits-all marketing strategy is not just ineffective; it's a misallocation of resources that often results in missed opportunities. This section conducts a critical analysis of why generic marketing strategies fail to resonate with specific client or customer groups and highlights how targeted marketing approaches can lead to significantly better outcomes.

Critical Analysis: The Pitfalls of Generic Strategies

Generic marketing strategies, by their nature, overlook the nuanced preferences and needs of distinct market segments. Such approaches assume a homogeneity in audience behavior and expectations that simply does not exist, leading to messages that lack relevance and personalization. This misalignment often results in diminished engagement rates, poor conversion, and a dilution of brand identity. For instance, a campaign that targets both millennials and baby boomers with the same message and medium is likely to engage neither group effectively, as each has unique communication preferences and values.

The inefficacy of broad-stroke strategies is compounded in digital spaces, where users are accustomed to personalized interactions. In these contexts, generic messages are not just overlooked; they're perceived as noise, contributing to a negative brand perception.

Success Stories: The Power of Targeted Marketing

Contrasting with the shortcomings of generic strategies are the success stories of businesses that have embraced targeted marketing. One notable example involves a fashion retailer that segmented its market based on lifestyle preferences and shopping behaviors, creating distinct marketing campaigns for each group. By tailoring its messages, visuals, and channel strategies to each segment, the retailer achieved a significant uplift in engagement, conversion rates, and customer loyalty. This success was underpinned by a deep understanding of each segment's characteristics, obtained through meticulous market research and data analysis.

Another success story comes from a B2B software company that used targeted content marketing to engage potential clients. By developing industry-specific content and leveraging LinkedIn for distribution, the company was able to establish thought leadership, generate quality leads, and close deals more efficiently. The focused approach not only maximized the impact of their marketing spend but also built a strong brand reputation within their target industries.

Tool and Technique Reviews: Personalizing Engagement

Several tools and techniques have proven instrumental in enabling personalized and segment-specific engagement. Marketing automation platforms, such as HubSpot and Marketo, allow businesses to automate targeted campaigns based on user behavior and preferences, ensuring relevant communications reach the right audience at the right time. Features like segmentation, lead scoring, and personalized email sequences help businesses tailor their approach to meet the specific needs of different audience segments.

Customer Relationship Management (CRM) systems play a critical role in personalizing engagement by centralizing customer data and interactions. This consolidation enables businesses to understand customer histories and preferences, facilitating targeted upselling, cross-selling, and service opportunities.

Social media analytics tools, including Sprout Social and Hootsuite Insights, offer deep dives into audience demographics, engagement patterns, and content preferences, empowering businesses to refine their social media strategies for maximum impact.

Moving beyond the misconceptions of one-size-fits-all marketing to embrace targeted strategies represents a paradigm shift in how businesses approach market engagement. By prioritizing relevance, personalization, and the strategic use of data, companies can avoid the pitfalls of generic marketing, instead forging meaningful connections with their clients and customers. The success stories and tools highlighted in this section underscore the effectiveness of a targeted approach, demonstrating its capacity to enhance brand value, improve resource efficiency, and capture market opportunities.

Section 2.4: Underestimating the Value of Feedback

The Crucial Role of Feedback in Business Evolution

In modern business, feedback from clients and customers is not just valuable; it's essential for survival and growth. Feedback loops offer critical insights into customer satisfaction, product performance, and market demand, guiding businesses in refining their strategies and offerings. This section delves into case studies of businesses that have either overlooked the importance of feedback or used it as a catalyst for significant pivots.

Case Studies: The Dual Edges of Feedback

One notable example involves a once-dominant electronics manufacturer that failed to heed customer feedback about the increasing importance of smartphone connectivity. Ignoring these signals led to a decline in market share as competitors introduced more integrated products. This case underscores the peril of overlooking customer feedback, highlighting how it can lead to missed opportunities and a loss of relevance in the market.

Conversely, a success story comes from a software company that actively sought and utilized client feedback to transform its product line. Initially focused on a single, complex software solution, the company realized through feedback that there was a strong demand for more specialized, user-friendly applications. By pivoting its product development strategy to address this feedback, the company not only retained its existing client base but also expanded its market reach, ultimately leading to increased revenue and market share.

The Importance of Feedback Loops in Refining Business Strategies

Feedback loops are vital for businesses aiming to stay aligned with market needs and expectations. They provide a mechanism for continuous improvement, allowing businesses to adapt their strategies, products, and services to meet the evolving demands of the market. Establishing effective feedback channels, actively engaging with clients and customers, and implementing a structured process for analyzing and acting on feedback are crucial steps in leveraging this valuable resource.

Moreover, the integration of advanced analytics and AI technologies in processing feedback can uncover deeper insights and trends that might not be immediately apparent, offering businesses a competitive edge in understanding and anticipating customer needs.

Underestimating the value of feedback can be a critical misstep for businesses in any industry. Case studies of both failure and success demonstrate the pivotal role feedback plays in guiding strategic decisions and fostering innovation. By embracing feedback loops and employing analytical tools to derive actionable insights, businesses can ensure their offerings remain relevant and compelling, leading to sustained growth and market leadership.

Section 2.5: Strategic Shifts and Adaptation

Pivoting to Meet Market Demands

The ability to pivot and adapt to changing market demands is a critical competency for businesses aiming to sustain growth and competitiveness. This section delves into real-world examples of companies that have successfully transitioned their focus from products to services (or vice versa), illustrating the processes, challenges, and outcomes of such strategic shifts. Additionally, it provides a guide on recognizing the need for adaptation and executing strategic shifts effectively, including risk assessment and management strategies.

Real-World Examples: Successful Pivots

One notable example is a technology company originally focused on hardware production, which pivoted to a software-as-a-service (SaaS) model in response to the growing demand for cloud-based solutions. The pivot involved significant changes in product development, sales strategies, and customer support systems. Through careful planning and execution, the company successfully transitioned to the SaaS model, resulting in increased recurring revenue, higher profit margins, and expanded market reach. This transformation was supported by strategic investments in software development capabilities and a phased approach to migrating existing customers to the new platform, ensuring minimal disruption and maintaining customer trust.

Another example comes from a traditional publishing house facing declining print sales. By shifting its focus towards digital content and online subscription services, the company tapped into new revenue streams and reached a broader audience. The transition was facilitated by leveraging existing content creation expertise, investing in digital distribution technologies, and implementing targeted marketing campaigns to attract online subscribers. The pivot not only revitalized the company's financial health but also established it as a leader in digital publishing.

Adaptation Strategies: A Guide to Effective Execution

Recognizing the need for a strategic shift often stems from market analysis, customer feedback, and competitive pressures. Once the need for adaptation is identified, the following steps can guide businesses through the execution of strategic shifts:

1. **Risk Assessment:** Evaluate the potential risks associated with the pivot, including financial implications, customer retention challenges, and operational disruptions. Develop a comprehensive risk management plan to mitigate these risks.
2. **Stakeholder Engagement:** Communicate the rationale behind the pivot to all stakeholders, including employees, investors, and customers. Transparent communication is crucial for securing buy-in and ensuring a unified approach to the transition.
3. **Resource Reallocation:** Assess the resource requirements of the new strategic focus and reallocate financial, human, and technological resources accordingly. This may involve investing in new capabilities, restructuring teams, or divesting non-core assets.
4. **Iterative Implementation:** Approach the pivot as an iterative process, starting with pilot projects or phased rollouts when possible. This allows for testing assumptions, gathering feedback, and making necessary adjustments before full-scale implementation.
5. **Performance Monitoring:** Establish key performance indicators (KPIs) relevant to the new strategic focus. Regularly monitor these KPIs to assess the pivot's

impact on business performance, making further adjustments as needed.

Strategic shifts and adaptation are essential for businesses facing evolving market conditions. The success stories of businesses that have navigated such transitions underscore the importance of strategic foresight, rigorous planning, and effective execution. By following the outlined adaptation strategies and learning from real-world examples, businesses can navigate the complexities of strategic pivots, ensuring their long-term success and relevance in the market.

Section 2.6:
Innovation as a Response to Failure

Innovation Case Studies: Transforming Challenges into Growth Opportunities

The journey of innovation is often sparked by setbacks and failures, serving as a catalyst for companies to rethink, retool, and rejuvenate their strategies and products. This section explores case studies of businesses that turned failure into a launching pad for innovation, thereby transforming challenges into significant opportunities for growth and differentiation.

One remarkable example is a leading consumer electronics company that experienced a significant setback with one of its flagship products due to safety concerns. The initial response was a swift recall, but the real turnaround came from the company's subsequent investment in research and development, leading to the introduction of advanced safety features and battery technology. This not only restored consumer trust but also set new industry standards for product safety and innovation, significantly enhancing the company's brand reputation and market position.

Another case study involves a software company that failed to gain traction with its initial product offering, a comprehensive suite perceived as overly complex and user-unfriendly. By embracing this failure as feedback, the company pivoted to develop a more intuitive, modular software solution, focusing on user experience and customization. This pivot not only salvaged the company but also propelled it to a leadership position in its sector, demonstrating the power of user-centered design and innovation.

Framework for Innovation: Cultivating a Culture of Proactive Adaptation

Fostering an innovative culture that can anticipate market shifts and proactively respond to challenges is crucial for sustained business success. This section outlines a framework for innovation that encourages creativity, resilience, and adaptability:

1. **Embrace Failure as a Learning Opportunity:** Create an organizational culture that views failure as an integral part of the innovation process. Encourage the sharing of setbacks and lessons learned to foster a supportive environment for experimentation.
2. **Encourage Cross-functional Collaboration:** Innovation thrives in environments where ideas can freely cross-pollinate. Encourage teams from different departments to collaborate on projects, bringing diverse perspectives and skills to the table.
3. **Invest in Continuous Learning:** Provide employees with resources and opportunities for professional development, ensuring they stay abreast of industry trends, technologies, and methodologies that can drive innovation.
4. **Implement Rapid Prototyping and Testing:** Adopt a lean approach to product development, where prototypes are rapidly developed and tested in the

market. This allows for quick feedback and iteration, reducing the time and cost associated with bringing new ideas to fruition.

5. **Foster an Open Innovation Ecosystem:** Engage with external innovators, startups, and academic institutions to explore new technologies and business models. This open approach to innovation can provide fresh insights and accelerate the development of groundbreaking solutions.

6. **Reward Creativity and Initiative:** Recognize and reward employees who contribute innovative ideas and take the initiative to explore new avenues for growth. This not only motivates individual contributors but also signals the organization's commitment to innovation.

Innovation as a response to failure is not merely about salvaging a dire situation; it's about reimagining the future and seizing new opportunities. The case studies and framework presented in this section underscore the importance of resilience, adaptability, and a culture that embraces experimentation. By viewing challenges as catalysts for innovation, businesses can navigate the uncertainties of the market with confidence, turning potential setbacks into strategic advantages.

Section 2.7: Turning Insights into Action

Key Takeaways and Preventative Strategies

As we conclude Chapter 2 of this book, we reflect on the journey through the multifaceted landscape of strategic business engagement. This chapter has underscored the critical importance of understanding the unique dynamics of client versus customer engagement and illuminated common pitfalls that businesses encounter along this path.

Summarization of Insights:

1. **Strategic Focus is Paramount:** A clear strategic focus enables businesses to allocate resources efficiently, tailoring their offerings to meet the specific needs of their target audience.
2. **Feedback Loops are Critical:** Active engagement with and responsiveness to feedback from clients and customers can pivot a business towards more successful outcomes.
3. **Adaptability Leads to Success:** The ability to pivot and adapt in response to market demands is a significant determinant of a business's longevity and success.

4. **Innovation Springs from Failure:** Viewing failure as a stepping stone rather than a setback can catalyze innovation and lead to breakthroughs in product and service offerings.
5. **Personalization Enhances Engagement:** Tailoring marketing strategies and product offerings to the specific needs and preferences of your audience can significantly boost engagement and loyalty.

Checklist of Preventative Measures:

For Businesses in Early Stages:

- Conduct thorough market research to understand your target audience deeply.
- Establish clear and measurable objectives for client and customer engagement.
- Invest in building robust feedback mechanisms to gather insights regularly.

For Growing Businesses:

- Regularly review and refine your strategic focus based on market trends and feedback.
- Foster a culture of innovation and adaptability within your team.
- Leverage data analytics to personalize marketing efforts and product development.

For Established Businesses:

- Continuously monitor market dynamics and be prepared to pivot your business model or offerings in response to shifts.

- Enhance your customer experience through technological integration and innovation.
- Prioritize customer and client feedback in strategic planning processes.

Call to Action:

In navigating the complex dynamics of market engagement, businesses are urged to adopt a proactive, informed, and nuanced approach to their strategic planning. Recognizing and appreciating the distinctions between client and customer engagement is not merely beneficial—it's imperative for crafting a successful strategy.

Businesses are encouraged to reflect on the insights and strategies discussed in this chapter, integrating them into a cohesive plan that aligns with their growth objectives, market positioning, and operational capabilities. By doing so, businesses can not only avoid common pitfalls but also position themselves to capitalize on opportunities, foster innovation, and build enduring relationships with their clients and customers.

Embrace these principles as you move forward, and let them guide your journey toward mastering the market through a dual approach to client and customer engagement. Your proactive and informed strategy will be your compass in the ever-evolving landscape of business success.

Chapter 2: Step-By-Step How to "Get... It... Done!"

Tackle the dual challenges of client and customer engagement head-on, avoiding classic blunders and steering your strategy towards undeniable success.

Section 2.1: Unraveling Common Missteps

Step 1: Deep-Dive into Market Needs
- **Task:** Hit the ground running with focused market research. Pinpoint exactly what ticks off your clients and customers.
- **Action Plan:** Roll out a survey pronto, aiming to wrap this baby up in a month. Use any online tool at your disposal.
- **Pro Tip:** Zero in on the pain points. Keep the survey short and sweet to actually get responses.

Step 2: Competitive Recon
- **Task:** Scope out the competition. What are they up to? More importantly, where are they dropping the ball?
- **Action Plan:** Give yourself 3 weeks to gather intel and put it all in a neat dossier.
- **Pro Tip:** Look for the chinks in their armor. Customer complaints are gold mines.

Step 3: Synthesis and Strategy
- **Task:** Marry your market research with your competitor analysis. Extract the top customer expectations.
- **Action Plan:** Dedicate 2 weeks to find the overlap and draft your game plan.
- **Pro Tip:** Hunt for patterns and align them with what you do best.

Section 2.2: Sharpening Your Strategic Edge
Step 4: Crafting a Killer Value Proposition
- **Task:** Based on your intel, forge a value proposition that'll make customers and clients sit up and take notice.
- **Action Plan:** Get creative and draft three versions within a week, then test-drive them with a focus group.
- **Pro Tip:** Benefits over features. Always. What's in it for them?

Step 5: Refinement and Rollout
- **Task:** Fine-tune your value proposition based on real feedback. Pick the winner.
- **Action Plan:** Finalize within another week.
- **Pro Tip:** Clarity is king. Make it straightforward and compelling.

Section 2.3: Tech Tactics for Engagement
Step 6: Tool Selection
- **Task:** Pin down the tech tools that will supercharge your engagement strategy.
- **Action Plan:** Spend a month experimenting with different platforms. Think CRM, social media schedulers, the works.
- **Pro Tip:** Balance is key. It needs to be user-friendly for your team and scalable as you grow.

Step 7: Engagement Blueprint
- **Task:** Develop an actionable plan using your chosen tech to personalize and elevate interactions.
- **Action Plan:** Sketch out a 6-month roadmap.
- **Pro Tip:** Start small, then scale. Don't try to boil the ocean.

Accountability and Keeping on Track

Mastering the Market: A Dual Approach to Client and Customer Engagement

- **Monthly Check-Ins:** Block a date each month to review progress. Are you hitting the mark on understanding and engaging your customers and clients?
- **Adapt Based on Real Talk:** Be ready to pivot your strategy based on what feedback is telling you.
- **Winning Moments:** Don't just move on to the next thing. Take a moment to celebrate the successes with your team.

Dive in with this roadmap to navigate the complexities of understanding and engaging your market. It's about making every move count, adjusting on the fly, and driving home the value that sets you apart. Roll up those sleeves and make it happen.

Chapter 3 Pre-Breakdown: No Fluff, Just Facts

Section 3.1: Cutting Through the Noise on Customer Expectations

Understanding what your customers want and expect is key. This isn't about guesswork; it's about diving deep into their psyche, figuring out their desires, and how these change across different folks and fields. Market research is your best friend here, helping you tailor your approach to hit right where it matters.

Section 3.2: Crafting Killer Value Propositions

Your value proposition is what sets you apart in a sea of sameness. It's that "why us" answer that should be clear, compelling, and smack dab on what makes you the better choice. Through real-deal success stories, we break down how some businesses have nailed their unique sell and share a step-by-step on how you can do the same.

Section 3.3: Digital Mastery for Engagement

The digital world is your oyster for connecting with clients and customers. From social platforms to the latest online tools, we explore how businesses can use digital goodies to up their engagement game. It's about being where your customers are, speaking their language, and making every click count.

Section 3.4: AI and Personalization Power Play

AI isn't just buzz; it's a game-changer for tailoring experiences like a boss. We dive into how smart tech can help you predict, personalize, and please, turning generic into genuine "just for you" moments. Real-world cases show the magic in action, from e-commerce upsells to bespoke banking advice.

Section 3.5: Smoothing Out the Customer Journey

This is about making every step of the customer's path with you slick and satisfying. We look at how integrating your online and offline worlds can create a seamless flow that keeps folks coming back. It's all in the mapping - understanding and connecting every touchpoint to ensure no customer feels left behind.

Section 3.6: The Feedback Loop Lifeline

Feedback isn't just nice to have; it's essential for growth, innovation, and staying on point. Through stories of businesses that have turned listening into a superpower, we outline a blueprint for setting up systems that not only gather insights but turn them into action, ensuring your offerings stay fresh and in-demand.

Section 3.7: Cementing Customer Connections

Wrapping up, we hammer home the importance of deep, meaningful customer relationships. It's about more than just transactions; it's about building bonds that last, ensuring your customers aren't just satisfied but are staunch supporters of your brand. We share actionable steps to make this dream a reality, pushing for a business model where customer closeness is not just a goal but a given.

Key Takeaways:
- Dive deep into understanding customer expectations.
- Nail your value proposition to stand out.
- Use digital tools and social media for genuine engagement.
- Leverage AI for unmatched personalization.
- Create seamless customer journeys for satisfaction and retention.
- Implement feedback loops for continuous improvement.
- Focus on building lasting relationships for sustainable growth.

Moving Forward: Make these insights the backbone of your strategy. Understand, engage, personalize, and iterate. Keep your customers at the heart of your business, and you're not just aiming for success; you're building a foundation for lasting impact.

Chapter 3
Buckle up, nerds! Time to READ.
To Victory and Beyond!

Section 3.1: Crafting a Compelling Approach

Understanding Customer Expectations

In the realm of market engagement, a nuanced understanding of customer expectations stands as a cornerstone for crafting compelling and effective business strategies. This section dives deep into the psychology of customer expectations, exploring how these anticipations vary across different markets and demographics. The role of market research in uncovering these expectations is highlighted, emphasizing its critical importance in shaping strategies that resonate with target audiences.

Expanded   Analysis:
The Psychology Behind Customer Expectations

Customer expectations are not static; they evolve with changing market dynamics, technological advancements, and shifting cultural norms. These expectations are influenced by a myriad of factors, including past experiences, perceived value, and the influence of social media and peer reviews. Understanding the psychological underpinnings of these expectations is essential for businesses aiming to engage effectively with their customers.

For instance, in the technology sector, customers might expect innovation and cutting-edge features as a baseline, while in the service industry, personalization and responsiveness might rank higher on their list of expectations. The variance in expectations across demographics is also significant. Younger consumers may prioritize speed and digital engagement, while older demographics might value reliability and high-touch customer service more highly.

The Importance of Market Research

Market research plays a pivotal role in uncovering customer expectations. Through a combination of quantitative surveys, qualitative interviews, and analysis of social media and online forums, businesses can gather valuable insights into what their customers expect from their products or services. This research not only helps in tailoring offerings to meet current expectations but also in anticipating future trends and needs.

Understanding customer expectations is a complex but critical endeavor for businesses aiming to master the market. By diving into the psychology of these expectations and leveraging market research to uncover deep insights, businesses can craft strategies that are not only compelling but also deeply aligned with the needs and desires of their target markets.

Section 3.2: Developing Strong Value Propositions

The development of a strong value proposition is fundamental to distinguishing a business in a crowded marketplace. A well-crafted value proposition communicates the unique benefits a company offers to its clients and customers, serving as a cornerstone for branding, marketing, and product development strategies. This section explores the concept through in-depth examples of businesses that have successfully differentiated themselves with compelling value propositions and provides strategic frameworks for businesses aiming to articulate their own.

Welbon Omar Salaam

In-Depth Examples: Success Stories

Several case studies illustrate how businesses have achieved market differentiation through their value propositions. One notable example is a tech startup that revolutionized the personal finance management industry. Their value proposition, "Simplify your finances with intelligent, yet easy-to-use technology," spoke directly to consumers overwhelmed by the complexity of managing their finances. The strategy behind this was to offer a seamless integration of bank accounts, investments, and savings onto one platform, making financial management accessible and straightforward. The execution involved rigorous user experience research and a marketing campaign that highlighted ease of use and peace of mind, resulting in a rapid user base growth and industry accolades.

Another example comes from the retail sector, where an online marketplace distinguished itself with the value proposition, "Empowering local artisans to reach a global audience." This marketplace curated unique, handmade items from around the world, directly connecting artisans with consumers looking for unique and meaningful products. The strategy focused on storytelling, emphasizing the impact of each purchase on individual artisans' lives. Execution included high-quality visuals, artisan profiles, and social media campaigns that showcased the people and stories behind the products, leading to a loyal customer base and significant growth.

Strategic Frameworks for Value Proposition Development

To assist businesses in crafting their value propositions, this section offers templates and exercises designed to ensure clarity, relevance, and differentiation. The strategic framework includes the following steps:

1. **Identify Customer Needs:** Start by deeply understanding the needs and challenges of your target market. This involves market research, surveys, and direct feedback mechanisms to capture the voice of the customer.
2. **Analyze Competitors:** Evaluate the value propositions of your competitors to identify gaps in the market and opportunities for differentiation. This step ensures that your value proposition is not only unique but also fills an unmet need.
3. **Articulate Benefits:** Clearly define the benefits your product or service offers, focusing on how it solves the problems identified in step one. Benefits should be

articulated in simple, compelling language that resonates with your target audience.

4. **Test and Refine:** Develop a prototype of your value proposition and test it with a segment of your target market. Use the feedback to refine your message, ensuring it accurately communicates the value you deliver.

5. **Implement and Communicate:** Once finalized, integrate your value proposition into all aspects of your business, from marketing materials and website copy to customer service scripts and product design.

Templates provided in this section include exercises for brainstorming benefits, comparing with competitors, and refining the message based on customer feedback. These tools are designed to be iterative, encouraging continuous refinement to ensure the value proposition remains relevant and compelling.

A strong value proposition is more than a statement; it's a reflection of a business's core identity and its promise to its customers. Through the examples and strategic frameworks provided, businesses can embark on the journey of developing their own unique value propositions, setting the stage for differentiation, relevance, and success in the market.

Section 3.3: Leveraging Technology for Engagement

Digital Platforms and Social Media

In the digital age, technology serves as a crucial conduit for engaging with both clients and customers. Digital platforms and social media have transformed the landscape of customer engagement, offering unprecedented opportunities for businesses to build brand loyalty and drive sales. This section critically examines the role of these digital channels in fostering customer engagement, supported by examples of businesses that have successfully navigated this domain. Furthermore, it reviews various digital marketing tools and social media strategies, offering insights into best practices and potential pitfalls.

Critical Analysis: The Role of Digital Platforms and Social Media

Digital platforms and social media are not just channels for communication; they are vibrant communities where brands can engage in meaningful interactions with their audience. The power of these platforms lies in their ability to humanize brands, facilitate direct communication, and rapidly disseminate information. Successful businesses leverage these platforms to not only promote their products or services but to listen to and learn from their audiences.

For instance, a case study of an e-commerce brand illustrates how it utilized Instagram to build a loyal community around its products. By showcasing customer stories, sharing behind-the-scenes content, and engaging in real-time conversations, the brand was able to significantly enhance its customer engagement and retention rates. Another example involves a B2B technology provider that used LinkedIn to establish thought leadership in its industry. Through regular posts, insightful articles, and active participation in industry discussions, the company strengthened its brand presence and generated valuable leads.

Tool and Technique Reviews: Digital Marketing Tools and Social Media Strategies

Navigating the plethora of digital marketing tools and social media strategies can be daunting. This section evaluates various tools and techniques, providing businesses with guidance on selecting the right mix for their objectives. From content management systems and email marketing tools to social media analytics and advertising platforms, the landscape is rich and varied.

Best practices highlighted include the importance of a content strategy that aligns with the brand's values and audience interests, the use of analytics to tailor and refine social media campaigns, and the significance of engagement over mere broadcasting.

Strategies for success emphasize authenticity, consistency in messaging, and the value of interactive content such as polls, live streams, and Q&A sessions to foster a sense of community and belonging among followers.

Common pitfalls to avoid include over-reliance on automated posting, which can detract from the personal touch critical to social media success, neglecting negative feedback or customer inquiries, and inconsistent branding across platforms, which can confuse the audience and dilute brand identity.

The integration of digital platforms and social media into customer engagement strategies represents a paradigm shift in how businesses interact with their markets. By leveraging technology to facilitate genuine connections, brands can achieve not just transactional relationships, but loyal communities of clients and customers. The critical analysis and reviews provided in this section serve as a roadmap for businesses seeking to navigate the digital landscape effectively, highlighting the importance of strategic planning, the adoption of appropriate tools, and the avoidance of common missteps. In doing so, businesses can harness the full potential of digital engagement to build lasting brand loyalty and drive sustainable growth.

Section 3.4: Personalization and AI

The advent of artificial intelligence (AI) has ushered in a new era of customer engagement, enabling businesses to offer unprecedented levels of personalization. This section delves into how companies are leveraging AI and data analytics to tailor customer interactions, from sophisticated product recommendations to customized communication strategies. Through case studies, we explore the impact of these technologies on customer satisfaction and business outcomes. Additionally, an implementation guide provides businesses with a roadmap for integrating AI-driven personalization into their operations, emphasizing technology selection, data privacy considerations, and strategies for measuring return on investment (ROI).

Case Studies: AI in Action

One compelling example involves an online retailer that implemented AI to enhance its product recommendation system. By analyzing customer browsing and purchase history, the AI algorithm predicts products that customers are likely to be interested in, leading to a significant increase in sales and customer engagement. This case study highlights the retailer's journey from the initial data collection phase to the deployment of the AI system, underscoring the challenges faced, such as data silo integration and ensuring algorithmic transparency.

Another case study features a financial services company that used AI to personalize customer communications. The company's AI system analyzes customer interactions, transaction history, and external data to generate personalized financial advice and product recommendations. This approach not only improved customer satisfaction scores but also increased cross-selling success rates. The case study details the technology selection process, the training of the AI models, and the measures taken to protect customer privacy.

Implementation Guide: Integrating AI-Driven Personalization

Integrating AI-driven personalization into business operations requires a structured approach, outlined in the following steps:

1. **Technology Selection:** Begin by evaluating AI technologies and platforms that align with your business needs and objectives. Consider factors such as scalability, integration capabilities with existing systems, and support for ongoing training and updates.
2. **Data Collection and Analysis:** Collect and analyze data from various touchpoints across the customer journey. Ensure that data quality and completeness are prioritized to feed accurate information into AI models.

3. **Data Privacy Considerations:** Implement robust data privacy measures to comply with regulations such as GDPR and CCPA. This includes securing customer consent for data collection and usage, ensuring data anonymization, and providing transparency about how AI uses customer data.
4. **AI Model Development:** Develop AI models tailored to specific personalization goals, such as product recommendation engines or personalized marketing messages. Leverage machine learning techniques to continuously improve the accuracy and relevance of these models based on customer feedback and interaction data.
5. **Integration and Deployment:** Integrate AI models into business processes and customer interaction points. This step may involve collaboration with IT departments, third-party vendors, and cross-functional teams to ensure seamless deployment.
6. **Measuring ROI:** Establish metrics to measure the impact of AI-driven personalization on customer engagement, satisfaction, and business performance. Use these insights to refine AI strategies and demonstrate the value of personalization initiatives.

By following this guide, businesses can navigate the complexities of implementing AI-driven personalization, from the initial planning stages to full-scale deployment and optimization. The transformative potential of AI and personalization offers businesses an opportunity to deepen customer relationships, enhance engagement, and drive growth in the digital age.

Section 3.5:
Enhancing the Customer Experience

Creating Seamless Customer Journeys

The essence of modern marketing and customer engagement lies in creating seamless customer journeys that integrate touchpoints across both physical and digital channels. This holistic approach ensures a consistent and satisfying experience, crucial for building loyalty and driving sales. Through real-world examples and an examination of customer journey mapping tools, this section delves into the design and implementation of comprehensive customer journey maps, highlighting strategies for achieving a cohesive customer experience.

Real-World Examples: Seamless Integration

One notable example of seamless customer journey integration comes from a leading retail chain. The company redefined its customer journey by integrating online shopping with in-store experiences. Customers can check product availability online, reserve items for in-store pickup, and receive personalized recommendations based on their shopping history upon entering the physical store. This strategy not only improved customer satisfaction but also increased sales through cross-selling opportunities. The implementation involved overhauling the IT infrastructure to ensure real-time data synchronization between online and offline channels and training staff to provide personalized customer service based on online customer profiles.

Another example features a financial services firm that enhanced its customer journey by offering a unified experience across its website, mobile app, and customer service centers. Customers can start a service request online, track its progress through the mobile app, and receive support through personalized, real-time interactions with customer service representatives. This cohesive experience was achieved by leveraging data analytics to understand customer behaviors and preferences and integrating systems to provide consistent service across all touchpoints.

Customer Journey Mapping Tools: Reviews and Tips

To aid in the creation and analysis of customer journey maps, several tools and software solutions stand out for their effectiveness and usability. This section reviews top tools such as Adobe Experience Manager, which offers comprehensive features for mapping and managing customer experiences across all touchpoints. Its analytics capabilities allow businesses to identify pain points and opportunities for enhancement within the customer journey.

Another valuable tool is Smaply, which excels in visualizing customer journeys and persona development. Smaply enables businesses to create detailed journey maps that include emotional states, touchpoints, and channels, providing insights into the customer experience at every stage.

When utilizing these tools, several tips can help businesses gain actionable insights:

1. **Start with Clear Objectives:** Define what you want to achieve with your customer journey mapping, whether it's improving customer satisfaction, increasing retention, or identifying service gaps.
2. **Incorporate Customer Feedback:** Use direct feedback from customers to validate and refine journey maps, ensuring they accurately reflect the customer experience.
3. **Focus on Pain Points:** Identify and prioritize addressing pain points in the customer journey to significantly enhance the overall experience.

4. **Iterate and Evolve:** Customer expectations and behaviors change over time. Regularly update your journey maps to reflect these changes and stay ahead of customer needs.

By detailing the design and implementation of seamless customer journey maps and reviewing essential mapping tools, businesses can enhance their approach to customer experience, ensuring satisfaction and loyalty in an increasingly competitive market.

Section 3.6: Feedback Loops and Continuous Improvement

Innovation Through Effective Feedback Loops

The dynamism of today's market necessitates not just a response to feedback but a proactive engagement with it, turning insights into continuous improvement and innovation. This section highlights how businesses across various industries have embedded effective feedback loops into their operations, harnessing customer insights to refine and enhance their product and service offerings continuously.

Innovation Case Studies

- **A Consumer Electronics Giant:** This company faced criticism for the lack of innovation in its product line. By establishing a dedicated feedback portal and engaging with users on social media, it gathered actionable insights that led to the development of a groundbreaking product feature, significantly improving user satisfaction and market share.
- **A Fast-Casual Dining Chain:** Initially struggling with customer retention, this restaurant chain implemented a feedback system across its digital ordering platform and physical locations. The insights obtained prompted menu adjustments, service improvements, and environment enhancements, leading to increased repeat business and customer loyalty.
- **A HealthTech Startup:** Leveraging AI-driven analytics, this startup refined its patient monitoring software based on continuous healthcare provider and patient feedback. The iterative improvements made the software more intuitive and effective, drastically improving patient outcomes and provider efficiencies.

Framework for Feedback

Implementing a robust framework for collecting, analyzing, and acting on feedback is crucial for businesses committed to continuous improvement. The following methodologies outline this process:

1. **Collect Diverse Feedback:** Utilize multiple channels, including social media, customer service interactions, surveys, and focus groups, to gather a broad spectrum of feedback. This diverse input ensures a well-rounded view of customer experiences and expectations.
2. **Analyze for Actionable Insights:** Employ data analytics tools to sift through feedback, identifying trends, patterns, and specific areas needing attention. Qualitative data analysis, such as sentiment analysis, can also unveil the emotional drivers behind customer feedback.
3. **Prioritize Based on Impact:** Evaluate feedback based on potential impact on customer satisfaction and business objectives. This prioritization helps focus efforts on changes that offer the most significant benefits to both the business and its customers.
4. **Implement and Monitor Changes:** Act on the insights gained by implementing targeted improvements. Use A/B testing and control groups to measure the

effectiveness of these changes, ensuring that they lead to the desired outcomes.

5. **Close the Loop with Customers:** Communicate back to customers about the changes made in response to their feedback. This transparency builds trust and reinforces the value the business places on its customer relationships.

6. **Foster a Culture of Continuous Improvement:** Encourage all levels of the organization to engage with customer feedback and participate in the continuous improvement process. This inclusive approach ensures a company-wide commitment to innovation and customer satisfaction.

The integration of effective feedback loops represents a strategic advantage in the pursuit of market leadership. By systematically collecting, analyzing, and acting on customer insights, businesses can ensure their offerings remain relevant and competitive. The case studies and framework presented illustrate the transformative potential of feedback-driven innovation, highlighting the role of continuous improvement in achieving and sustaining customer satisfaction and business success. This proactive and informed approach to strategic planning empowers businesses to navigate the complexities of client and customer engagement, turning challenges into opportunities for growth and differentiation.

Section 3.7: Building Lasting Customer Relationships

Key Takeaways and Actionable Strategies

Throughout Chapter 3, we've explored the multifaceted strategies businesses can employ to deepen their connection with customers. The chapter underscored the critical importance of understanding customer needs, the transformative potential of technology in personalizing engagement, and the ongoing commitment required to enhance the customer experience continually. Here, we summarize the chapter's main insights and offer actionable strategies to foster lasting customer relationships.

- **Deep Understanding of Customer Needs:** The foundation of any lasting relationship is understanding. Businesses must invest time and resources in comprehensively understanding their customers' needs, preferences, and pain points through direct feedback, market research, and data analytics.
- **Personalized Engagement Through Technology:** Leveraging technology to personalize customer interactions can significantly enhance engagement and satisfaction. Tools like CRM systems, AI-driven chatbots,

and personalized marketing platforms enable businesses to tailor their communications and offerings to individual customer preferences.

- **Continuous Enhancement of the Customer Experience:** The customer experience should never be static. Continuous improvement, based on feedback loops and market trends, ensures that businesses remain responsive and relevant to their customers' evolving needs.

Call to Action: Prioritizing Customer Connection

Businesses are called upon to prioritize customer connection as a fundamental pillar of their growth strategy. To implement the strategies discussed in the chapter effectively, businesses may follow this checklist:

1. **Conduct Regular Customer Needs Assessments:** Use surveys, focus groups, and social media engagement to gather insights into customer needs and expectations.
2. **Implement Personalization Technologies:** Invest in CRM and AI technologies that allow for personalized customer interactions at scale.
3. **Establish Effective Feedback Loops:** Create mechanisms for customers to provide feedback easily

and ensure this feedback is actively used to inform business decisions.

4. **Train Your Team on Customer Empathy:** Ensure your team understands the importance of empathy in customer interactions, providing them with the tools and training to respond effectively to customer needs.

5. **Monitor and Adapt to Market Trends:** Stay abreast of market trends and technological advancements that can impact customer expectations and preferences.

6. **Celebrate Successes and Learn from Failures:** Share positive customer stories across your organization and learn from instances where customer expectations were not met to foster a culture of continuous improvement.

Building lasting customer relationships is an ongoing journey that requires dedication, adaptability, and a deep commitment to understanding and meeting customer needs. By leveraging technology for personalized engagement and committing to the continuous enhancement of the customer experience, businesses can cultivate strong, enduring connections with their customers. These relationships not only drive growth and profitability but also transform customers into loyal advocates for the brand. As we move forward, let the insights and strategies outlined in this chapter guide your efforts to place customer connection at the heart of your business strategy.

Chapter 3 How To: The Action-Packed Sequel Getting Down to Business

Section 3.1: Decoding Customer Desires

Mission: Customer Espionage

- **Survey Shenanigans**:
    - **Objective**: Whip up a survey that digs deep into what tickles your customers' fancy.
    - **Deadline**: 2 weeks to launch, collect, and analyze.
- **Social Sleuthing**:
    - **Objective**: Dive into the social media abyss, unearth what your audience raves or rants about.
    - **Deadline**: 1 week of intense social media stalking (for research purposes only!).
- **The Great Synthesis**:
    - **Objective**: Merge your data into a master document of desires. Think Frankenstein, but for market research.
    - **Deadline**: 3 days to create the ultimate customer wishlist.

Section 3.2: Crafting Your Value Prop Like a Blockbuster

Mission: Unique Selling Proposition (USP) Unveiling

- **Competitor Recon**:

- o **Objective**: Scope out your rivals. What's their game? Where do they slip? Time for some undercover work.
  - o **Deadline**: 2 weeks to compile a dossier on your competitors' weaknesses.
- **Benefit Brainstorm**:
  - o **Objective**: Lock yourself in a room with snacks and figure out why your product/service is the next best thing since sliced bread.
  - o **Deadline**: 1 week to emerge with a list of undeniable benefits.
- **Pitch Perfect**:
  - o **Objective**: Craft a pitch that would make even the most cynical investor throw money at you.
  - o **Deadline**: 1 week to refine your spiel into pure gold.

Section 3.3: Digital Domination

Mission: Conquer the Digital Realm
- **Tech Toolkit**:
    - **Objective**: Assemble an arsenal of digital tools that'll make Q from James Bond jealous.
    - **Deadline**: 2 weeks to select and set up your digital marketing gadgets.
- **Content Crusade**:
    - **Objective**: Create content so engaging it stops scrollers in their tracks. Cat videos, beware.
    - **Deadline**: 1 month to launch a content campaign that goes viral (in a good way).
- **Social Media Mastery**:
    - **Objective**: Transform your social media presence into a beacon of engagement and witty banter.
    - **Deadline**: 2 weeks to overhaul your profiles and start meaningful conversations.

Section 3.4: AI and Personalization - The Future is Now

Mission: Operation Personal Touch

- **AI Ally**:
  - **Objective**: Befriend an AI tool that personalizes your customer interaction without going Skynet on you.
  - **Deadline**: 3 weeks to integrate AI without causing a robot uprising.
- **Data Dive**:
  - **Objective**: Delve into customer data like you're looking for pirate treasure. X marks the spot for insights.
  - **Deadline**: 2 weeks to map out a treasure trove of actionable data.
- **Privacy Protector**:
  - **Objective**: Fortify your data privacy measures like you're guarding the crown jewels.
  - **Deadline**: 1 week to reassure your customers their data is safer than a vault in Gringotts.

Section 3.5: The Ultimate Customer Journey

Mission: Map the Treasure Hunt

- **Journey Jigsaw**:
  - **Objective**: Piece together the ultimate customer journey map, complete with dragons to slay and treasures to find.
  - **Deadline**: 1 month to chart the epic saga of your customer's journey.

- **Seamless Experience Engineering**:
  - **Objective**: Ensure every touchpoint in the customer journey is as smooth as a baby dolphin.
  - **Deadline**: 2 weeks to streamline your processes for maximum slickness.

Section 3.6: Feedback Frenzy

Mission: Circle of Trust

- **Feedback Festival**:
  - **Objective**: Throw a feedback fiesta where every piece of customer input is celebrated like it's Cinco de Mayo.
  - **Deadline**: Ongoing party, but review the decorations every 2 weeks.
- **Innovation Incubator**:
  - **Objective**: Turn customer feedback into the next big thing before your competitors even know what hit them.
  - **Deadline**: 1 month to go from feedback to fabulous.

Section 3.7: Relationship Goals

Mission: BFFs with Your Customers

- **Empathy Exercise**:
  - **Objective**: Put yourself in your customers' shoes, even if they're clown shoes. Understand their deepest desires and darkest fears.

- o **Deadline**: Ongoing, with weekly empathy workouts.
- **Loyalty League**:
  - o **Objective**: Create a loyalty program so enticing it turns casual customers into die-hard fans.
  - o **Deadline**: 2 months to launch your customer crusade.
- **Experience Extravaganza**:
  - o **Objective**: Ensure every interaction with your brand is as memorable as the finale of your favorite TV show.
  - o **Deadline**: Ongoing, with monthly surprise elements.

Your Quest, Should You Choose to Accept: Transform your business from just another player in the market to the protagonist of an epic saga of success. Let's make it legendary, team! 🚀💥

Chapter 4 Pre-Breakdown: No Fluff, Just Facts

Section 4.1: The Client Lifecycle Unpacked

The client lifecycle is the journey your clients take with you. It's the backbone of your relationship-building strategy, from the first "hello" to them becoming your biggest cheerleaders. Here's the lowdown:

- **Awareness to Advocacy:** Starts with them noticing you, moves to considering what you've got, jumps into becoming a customer, enjoying your service, sticking by you, and finally, singing your praises.
- **Strategy for Each Stage:** Kick off with targeted marketing, give them the lowdown to pick you, make signing up a breeze, knock their socks off with your service, keep them coming back for more, and make it easy for them to tell the world about you.

Section 4.2: Tailoring Solutions like a Pro

Personalization isn't a nice-to-have; it's a must-do for addressing your clients' complex needs. It's about ditching the one-size-fits-all approach and crafting services that speak directly to each client's situation.

- **Real-World Winners:** Wealth managers who get personal with investment plans, software devs who make custom solutions a collaborative dance, and healthcare concierges who mix tech with a personal touch to keep clients healthy and happy.

- **Blueprint for Personalization:** Dig into what clients want, split them into groups with similar needs, create solutions that hit the mark, gather feedback, and use tech to keep the personal vibe going strong.

Section 4.3: Trust is Everything

Trust is the glue in your client relationships, and transparency is your trusty tool. It's about being open and honest at every turn, showing clients that they can count on you to be upfront, no matter what.

- **Trust-Building Tactics:** Speak plainly, keep promises, be upfront about problems, don't surprise them with hidden costs, update them regularly, listen to what they have to say, own up when things go sideways, and be crystal clear about how you handle their data.

Section 4.4: Tech's Role in Keeping Clients Close

Tech isn't just for streamlining operations; it's a game-changer for keeping up with your clients. CRM platforms and other digital wonders can transform how you interact, understand, and grow alongside your clients.

- **Tech That's Changing the Game:** Real-time tracking for instant strategy shifts, automated systems for smooth sailing, and AI tools for predicting the next big hit in client preferences.
- **Top Tools on the Block:** Salesforce for the serious players, HubSpot CRM for the user-friendly fans, Microsoft Dynamics 365 for the integration wizards, and Zoho CRM for the budget-savvy businesses.

Section 4.5: Holding onto Your Clients

Keeping clients in your corner is an art and a science. It's about navigating through competitive pressures, expectation gaps, and the quest for personalization, all while keeping the communication clear and your services top-notch.

- **Winning Moves:** Stay ahead of the curve, keep promises realistic, personalize like a boss, talk the talk and walk the walk, keep your services sharp, reward loyalty, tackle problems head-on, and always be ready for feedback.

Section 4.6: Feedback is Gold

Feedback isn't just noise; it's the secret ingredient for your continuous improvement recipe. It's about listening, learning, and leveling up your services to keep your clients coming back for more.

- **Feedback Mastery:** Set up easy ways for clients to chime in, encourage honest input, sift through feedback for gold, prioritize action items, make changes that count, and loop clients in on how their words sparked change.

Section 4.7: The Ties That Bind

Deepening client relationships isn't a task; it's a commitment to understanding, adapting, and growing with your clients. It's about ensuring every interaction adds value and every solution fits just right.

Final Takeaway: Mastering client relationships is about blending personalization, transparency, and technology to meet clients where they are and take them where they want to go. Dive into their needs, respect their feedback, and never stop striving for that perfect fit. Keep these principles in your toolkit, and you're set for a journey of mutual growth and lasting bonds.

Chapter 4
Buckle up, nerds! Time to READ. Elevate and Dominate!

Section 4.1:
Understanding the Client Lifecycle

The client lifecycle is a comprehensive journey that encompasses every interaction between a business and its clients, from the initial contact to the development of a long-term, loyal advocacy. This crucial framework enables businesses to strategically nurture their relationships at each stage, ensuring sustained engagement and retention. This section delves into the stages of the client lifecycle, offering insights and actionable strategies designed to enhance client engagement and foster enduring relationships.

Stages of the Client Lifecycle:

1. **Awareness:** The potential client becomes aware of your business and its offerings. This stage is critical for making a strong first impression.
2. **Consideration:** The client evaluates your offerings, comparing them with competitors. At this stage, detailed information and clear differentiation are key.
3. **Acquisition:** The client decides to engage with your business. The focus here is on making the onboarding process as smooth and welcoming as possible.
4. **Service:** The client experiences your product or service. Exceptional service delivery and support are crucial to exceeding client expectations.
5. **Loyalty:** The client develops a preference for your offerings over competitors. Consistent quality and personalized experiences help solidify this loyalty.
6. **Advocacy:** The loyal client becomes an advocate for your brand, recommending your products or services to others. Encouraging and facilitating referrals are essential at this stage.

Actionable Strategies for Enhancing Engagement and Retention:

- **Awareness:** Leverage targeted marketing campaigns and thought leadership content to introduce your brand to potential clients. Utilize SEO and social media to increase visibility.
- **Consideration:** Provide comprehensive, easily accessible information about your offerings. Use case studies, testimonials, and demos to demonstrate value and differentiate from competitors.
- **Acquisition:** Simplify the onboarding process with clear guidance and support. Personalize the experience to make new clients feel valued and understood.
- **Service:** Deliver on your promises with high-quality products and responsive customer service. Use client feedback to continually improve the service experience.
- **Loyalty:** Implement loyalty programs or exclusive offers for repeat clients. Regularly communicate to keep your brand top-of-mind and to reinforce the value of your relationship.
- **Advocacy:** Encourage satisfied clients to share their experiences through referral programs. Recognize and reward clients for their advocacy to foster a community of brand ambassadors.

Understanding and effectively managing the client lifecycle is paramount for businesses aiming to build and maintain strong client relationships. By implementing targeted strategies at each stage of the lifecycle, businesses can enhance client engagement, boost retention, and ultimately, transform satisfied clients into loyal advocates. This proactive and informed approach not only contributes to the sustained success of the business but also creates a robust foundation for growth and competitiveness in the market.

Section 4.2: Personalized Solutions for Complex Needs

In today's market, the ability to offer personalized solutions is not just an advantage; it's a necessity for businesses seeking to meet the increasingly complex needs of their clients. This section explores how businesses across various industries have mastered the art of delivering personalized client experiences, transforming generic services into tailored solutions that resonate deeply with individual client needs. Through case studies, we highlight the strategies and outcomes of these businesses, alongside a comprehensive framework for personalization that any business can adopt.

Case Studies of Personalized Client Experiences:

- **A Boutique Wealth Management Firm:** This firm stands out for its highly personalized approach to financial planning. Utilizing advanced data analytics, the firm crafts individual investment strategies that align with each client's financial goals, risk tolerance, and life stage. The result is a client base that feels understood and valued, leading to high retention rates and robust word-of-mouth referrals.
- **Custom Software Development Agency:** Specializing in bespoke software solutions, this agency involves clients in the development process from day one. Through iterative feedback loops and agile development practices, they ensure that the final product precisely meets the client's operational needs and preferences, thereby enhancing client satisfaction and loyalty.
- **Healthcare Concierge Service:** Catering to clients seeking personalized healthcare management, this service uses a combination of AI-driven insights and human expertise to offer tailored health recommendations, appointment scheduling, and treatment plans. Their success lies in the seamless integration of technology and personal touch, leading to improved health outcomes and client trust.

Framework for Personalization:

1. **Understand Client Needs:** Begin with in-depth research and direct conversations to understand the specific needs, preferences, and challenges of your clients. Utilize surveys, interviews, and data analysis to gather actionable insights.
2. **Segment Your Client Base:** Categorize clients into segments based on similar needs or characteristics. This segmentation allows for more targeted and relevant solution development.
3. **Develop Tailored Solutions:** Leverage the insights from your client understanding and segmentation to develop solutions that address the specific needs of each segment or individual client. This could involve customizing products, services, or experiences.
4. **Implement Feedback Loops:** Establish mechanisms for ongoing feedback from clients about the personalized solutions you provide. Use this feedback to refine and adjust the offerings continuously.
5. **Leverage Technology:** Employ technology such as CRM systems, AI, and analytics tools to scale personalization efforts. These technologies can help in understanding

client behaviors, predicting needs, and automating aspects of the personalized experience.
6. **Train Your Team:** Ensure your team is well-versed in the principles of personalization and equipped with the skills to execute it effectively. This includes training in client communication, empathy, and the use of relevant technological tools.
7. **Measure and Iterate:** Regularly measure the impact of your personalized solutions on client satisfaction, retention, and business growth. Use these metrics to iterate and improve your personalization strategies continuously.

Delivering personalized solutions for complex client needs is a critical strategy for businesses aiming to build strong, lasting client relationships. The case studies and framework presented in this section demonstrate the transformative power of personalization in enhancing client satisfaction and loyalty. By adopting a systematic approach to understanding and addressing individual client needs, businesses can create highly personalized experiences that not only meet but exceed client expectations, fostering a competitive edge in the market.

Section 4.3: Nurturing Trust Through Transparency

In the intricate dance of building and maintaining client relationships, trust plays the lead role, with transparency as its foundational step. This section delves into the indispensable role of transparency in cultivating trust, a critical component that strengthens the bond between businesses and their clients. Through a thorough exploration of best practices, it illuminates the path for businesses to maintain open communication and accountability, thereby fostering a trustworthy environment conducive to long-term relationships.

The Importance of Trust:

Trust, the cornerstone of any enduring client relationship, is significantly bolstered by transparency. Transparent practices demonstrate to clients that a business values honesty and openness, which in turn, builds a strong foundation of trust. This trust is crucial not only for the initial establishment of a relationship but also for its ongoing development and resilience in the face of challenges. In an era where clients are more informed and have higher expectations, the importance of trust has never been more pronounced.

Best Practices for Maintaining Open Communication and Accountability:

1. **Clear Communication:** Ensure that all communications with clients, from email updates to contract terms, are clear, concise, and devoid of jargon. This clarity helps prevent misunderstandings and sets the stage for a transparent relationship.
2. **Honesty in Service Delivery:** Be upfront about what your services can and cannot achieve. Setting realistic expectations helps prevent disappointments and builds trust over time.
3. **Prompt Disclosure of Issues:** If problems arise, communicate them to clients at the earliest opportunity, along with proposed solutions. This openness in facing challenges reinforces trust in your commitment to their best interests.
4. **Transparency in Pricing:** Provide clear, upfront information about costs, including any potential additional charges. Unexpected fees can significantly damage trust, while transparency in pricing solidifies it.
5. **Regular Updates:** Keep clients informed about the progress of their projects or the status of their services. Regular updates demonstrate your ongoing

commitment to their needs and foster a culture of openness.

6. **Feedback Mechanisms:** Implement systems for clients to easily provide feedback and ensure that this feedback is acknowledged and acted upon. This not only improves services but also shows clients that their opinions are valued and considered.

7. **Accountability in Actions:** When mistakes occur, take responsibility and outline clear steps for resolution. Demonstrating accountability and a commitment to making things right is essential for maintaining trust.

8. **Data Protection and Privacy:** Be transparent about how you collect, use, and protect client data. In today's digital age, concerns about data privacy are paramount, and transparency about data practices is a critical trust builder.

Nurturing trust through transparency is not merely a best practice but a strategic imperative for businesses aiming to thrive in the competitive marketplace. By adopting these best practices, companies can create a transparent, trustworthy environment that not only attracts clients but also retains them over the long term. This trust fosters loyalty, advocacy, and sustained business growth, proving that in the economy of relationships, transparency is indeed the best currency.

Section 4.4: The Role of Technology in Client Relationship Management

In the digital age, technology plays a pivotal role in enhancing and streamlining client relationship management (CRM). This section delves into how CRM platforms and other technological innovations have revolutionized the way businesses interact with and manage their clients. Through innovation case studies and reviews of the latest tools, we explore the transformative impact of technology on client relationship management, offering insights into leveraging these tools for maximum effectiveness.

Innovation Case Studies:

- **A Financial Services Firm:** This firm integrated an AI-powered CRM system that personalized client interactions based on historical data and predictive analytics. The system's ability to offer tailored financial advice and timely updates significantly improved client satisfaction and loyalty. This case study exemplifies how technology can transform client services into personalized experiences.

- **A Healthcare Provider:** By adopting a healthcare-specific CRM tool, this provider managed to streamline patient communications, appointment scheduling, and patient care follow-up processes. The CRM's integration with electronic health records (EHRs) allowed for a seamless flow of information, enhancing patient management efficiency and personalizing patient care.
- **An E-commerce Platform:** Utilizing a cloud-based CRM, this platform achieved remarkable success in customer retention and upselling. The CRM's advanced analytics capabilities enabled the platform to understand customer purchasing behaviors, predict future needs, and tailor marketing efforts accordingly, resulting in increased sales and customer lifetime value.

Tool Reviews:

- **Salesforce:** Often regarded as the gold standard in CRM, Salesforce offers unparalleled customization, integration capabilities, and a vast ecosystem of apps through its AppExchange. Its robust analytics, AI features, and comprehensive client management tools make it a top choice for businesses of all sizes.

- **HubSpot CRM:** Known for its user-friendly interface and no-cost entry point, HubSpot CRM provides businesses with powerful tools for client management, marketing automation, and sales tracking. Its seamless integration with the HubSpot marketing platform makes it ideal for businesses looking to combine their CRM and inbound marketing efforts.

- **Microsoft Dynamics 365:** This CRM solution stands out for its deep integration with other Microsoft products, offering businesses a cohesive platform for sales, customer service, and business operations. Dynamics 365's AI-driven insights and customizable workflows cater to businesses seeking a highly integrated client management solution.

- **Zoho CRM:** With its competitive pricing and wide range of features, Zoho CRM is particularly suited for small to medium-sized businesses. Its customization options, automation capabilities, and user-friendly interface provide a robust solution for businesses looking to enhance their CRM practices without a hefty investment.

The integration of technology into client relationship management has opened new avenues for businesses to enhance their client interactions, personalize their services, and streamline their operations. The case studies and tool reviews highlighted in this section demonstrate the significant advantages that CRM and related technologies offer in managing and nurturing client relationships. As businesses continue to navigate the complexities of the digital landscape, leveraging these technological solutions will be key to building stronger, more meaningful client connections and driving long-term success.

Section 4.5: Overcoming Challenges in Client Retention

Client retention is a critical aspect of business success, reflecting the quality of client relationships and the value delivered through products or services. However, businesses often encounter several obstacles that can hinder their ability to retain clients over the long term. This section identifies common challenges in client retention and provides strategic solutions and actionable steps to overcome these hurdles, thereby enhancing retention rates and fostering sustained client loyalty.

Common Obstacles in Client Retention:

1. **Competitive Pressure:** In highly competitive markets, clients have numerous options, making them more prone to switch providers for better offers or services.
2. **Unmet Expectations:** A gap between client expectations and the actual value or service delivered can lead to dissatisfaction and attrition.
3. **Lack of Personalization:** Failure to provide personalized experiences or recognize individual client needs can make clients feel undervalued and look elsewhere.
4. **Poor Communication:** Inadequate or ineffective communication can lead to misunderstandings, unresolved issues, and a feeling of neglect among clients.
5. **Service Complacency:** Becoming complacent with service delivery, especially for long-standing clients, can lead to a gradual decline in service quality and client engagement.

Solutions and Strategies for Improving Retention Rates:

1. **Enhancing Competitive Advantage:** Continuously innovate and improve your offerings. Utilize client

feedback to refine products or services, ensuring they remain superior to or distinct from competitors'.

2. **Setting and Managing Expectations:** Clearly communicate the value proposition and deliverables from the outset. Regularly review and manage client expectations through open dialogue to ensure alignment.

3. **Personalizing Client Experiences:** Utilize data analytics and CRM tools to understand individual client preferences and tailor experiences accordingly. Personalized attention can significantly increase client satisfaction and loyalty.

4. **Strengthening Communication Channels:** Establish robust communication protocols to ensure timely and effective interactions. Regular check-ins, newsletters, and personalized updates can keep clients informed and engaged.

5. **Recommitting to Service Excellence:** Regularly evaluate and enhance your service delivery processes. Implement quality control measures and training programs to ensure consistent, high-quality service across all client interactions.

6. **Implementing Loyalty Programs:** Develop loyalty or reward programs that offer tangible benefits to long-

term clients. Such programs can reinforce the value of staying with your service, encouraging continued patronage.

7. **Proactive Problem Resolution:** Adopt a proactive approach to identify and resolve potential issues before they escalate. Demonstrating a commitment to client satisfaction can solidify trust and loyalty.

8. **Seeking Regular Feedback:** Implement mechanisms to gather ongoing feedback from clients. Use this feedback to make informed adjustments to products, services, and processes, showing clients that their opinions are valued and acted upon.

Overcoming challenges in client retention requires a multifaceted strategy that addresses competitive dynamics, ensures the delivery of value, personalizes client experiences, and maintains open, effective communication. By implementing the solutions and strategies outlined above, businesses can enhance their client retention rates, building a foundation of loyalty and trust that supports long-term success and growth. Emphasizing continuous improvement and client engagement, companies can navigate the complexities of client retention, turning potential obstacles into opportunities for strengthening client relationships.

Section 4.6: Leveraging Feedback for Continuous Improvement

The dynamic landscape of client engagement necessitates a culture of continuous improvement, underpinned by the strategic utilization of client feedback. This section underscores the critical role of feedback loops in refining services and offerings, presenting a structured guide for effectively collecting, analyzing, and implementing client feedback to foster business growth and enhance client satisfaction.

The Importance of Client Feedback:

Client feedback serves as a crucial compass for navigating the complexities of market demands and expectations. It provides actionable insights into what businesses are doing right and areas where they may fall short, offering a direct line to understanding client needs and preferences. This feedback is invaluable for informing strategic decisions, driving product innovation, and ensuring service excellence. By actively soliciting and attentively listening to client feedback, businesses can adapt more swiftly to changing client needs, thereby maintaining relevance and competitive edge.

Mastering the Market: A Dual Approach to Client and Customer Engagement

Implementing Feedback for Continuous Improvement:

1. **Establishing Effective Feedback Channels:** Create multiple avenues for clients to provide feedback, including surveys, interviews, suggestion boxes, and digital platforms. Ensuring ease of access and convenience encourages more clients to share their insights.

2. **Encouraging Honest Feedback:** Foster an environment where clients feel comfortable providing honest and constructive feedback. This can be achieved through anonymity options, reassurances of no negative repercussions, and demonstrating how feedback leads to tangible changes.

3. **Systematic Collection and Analysis:** Collect feedback systematically and analyze it to identify patterns, trends, and specific areas needing attention. Use both quantitative and qualitative analysis methods to derive comprehensive insights from the feedback received.

4. **Prioritizing Actions Based on Feedback:** Not all feedback will warrant immediate action. Prioritize feedback based on its potential impact on client satisfaction and business objectives. Focus on changes

that offer the most significant benefits to your clients and your business.

5. **Implementing Changes:** Develop a plan for implementing the necessary changes based on client feedback. This plan should include clear timelines, responsible parties, and defined goals. Ensure that changes are manageable and scalable within the business's operational capacity.

6. **Communicating Changes to Clients:** Inform your clients about the changes made in response to their feedback. This communication demonstrates that you value their input and are committed to improving their experience. It also enhances transparency and builds trust.

7. **Monitoring and Review:** After implementing changes, monitor their impact on client satisfaction and overall business performance. Continuous monitoring allows for the review and further refinement of implemented changes, ensuring they effectively address the feedback.

8. **Fostering a Culture of Continuous Improvement:** Embed feedback-driven continuous improvement into the organizational culture. Encourage employees at all levels to embrace feedback positively and as an opportunity for growth and learning.

Leveraging client feedback for continuous improvement is not merely a reactive measure but a proactive strategy for business excellence. It allows businesses to stay aligned with client needs, anticipate market shifts, and innovate ahead of competitors. By establishing robust feedback loops and systematically implementing insights gained, businesses can enhance their service offerings, strengthen client relationships, and secure a sustainable path to growth and success. In the realm of client engagement, feedback is not just information; it's the fuel for continuous advancement and innovation.

Section 4.7: Strengthening Client Bonds

As we conclude Chapter 4 of this book, it's imperative to reflect on the strategies that forge deeper, more meaningful connections with clients. This chapter has explored the multifaceted approach to nurturing client relationships, emphasizing the significance of personalized solutions, transparency, technology in client relationship management, overcoming retention challenges, and the indispensable role of feedback for continuous improvement. Here, we summarize these strategies and issue a call to action for businesses to prioritize the cultivation of long-term client relationships as a cornerstone of their growth strategy.

Key Takeaways for Deepening Client Relationships:

1. **Personalization is Key:** Tailoring solutions to meet the specific needs and preferences of each client not only enhances satisfaction but also fosters a sense of value and partnership.
2. **Transparency Builds Trust:** Open and honest communication is the foundation of trust. By being transparent in your dealings, you solidify the trust that is essential for long-term relationships.
3. **Technology Enhances Engagement:** Leveraging CRM and other technological tools can streamline processes, offer insights, and facilitate the kind of personalized engagement that strengthens bonds.
4. **Addressing Retention Challenges:** Identifying and strategically overcoming common obstacles in client retention ensures that relationships don't just survive but thrive over time.
5. Feedback Fuels Improvement: Actively seeking and thoughtfully implementing client feedback

demonstrates a commitment to meeting their needs and continuously enhancing your offerings.

Call to Action:

In a landscape where competition is fierce and client expectations continue to evolve, prioritizing long-term client relationships is not just beneficial—it's critical for sustainable growth. The strategies outlined in this chapter provide a roadmap for businesses committed to deepening their client connections. To move forward, businesses are encouraged to:

1. **Assess and Adjust Your Approach:** Regularly evaluate your strategies for engaging with clients. Are you truly meeting their needs? Are there opportunities for more personalized engagement?
2. **Invest in the Right Tools:** Evaluate your current technological stack. Are there opportunities to implement more effective CRM tools or other technologies that could enhance client management?
3. **Cultivate a Culture of Transparency:** Ensure that your organizational culture prioritizes honesty and openness in all client communications.
4. **Embrace Feedback:** Develop a systematic approach to collecting, analyzing, and acting on client feedback. Let this feedback guide your continuous improvement efforts.

5. **Commit to Continuous Learning:** Stay informed about emerging trends and technologies that can impact client relationship management. Be willing to adapt and innovate to meet these evolving demands.

By embedding these strategies into your business model, you commit to not just meeting the immediate needs of your clients but to fostering enduring relationships that drive mutual growth and success. Let the insights and strategies shared in this chapter serve as a guide to strengthening your client bonds, setting the stage for a future where your business doesn't just grow—it flourishes through the power of strong, lasting client relationships.

Chapter 4: Step-By Step How to "Get... It... Done!"

Embark on a journey to deepen client engagement at every phase of their lifecycle, setting a foundation for lasting relationships and business growth.

Section 4.1: Kickstarting Client Awareness

Step 1: Pinpoint Discovery Channels
- **Task:** Identify where potential clients are likely to first come across your business.
- **Action:** Determine your top 3 channels within 1 week.
- **Guidance:** Analyze your audience's online behavior to prioritize channels.

Step 2: Content Creation for Consideration
- **Task:** Develop engaging content that highlights the advantages of choosing your services.
- **Action:** Draft a plan for a comparison guide or introductory webinar in 2 weeks.
- **Guidance:** Emphasize unique selling points and client benefits.

Step 3: Smoothing the Acquisition
- **Task:** Design a welcoming experience for new clients with a comprehensive onboarding package.
- **Action:** Create an onboarding guide within 2 weeks.
- **Guidance:** Focus on clarity and support to ease the client's transition into your service.

Section 4.2: Enhancing Service and Loyalty

Step 4: Establishing Ongoing Communication
- **Task:** Set up a routine for regular client check-ins to solicit feedback and reinforce your commitment.
- **Action:** Plan monthly check-ins, starting immediately.
- **Guidance:** Use this as an opportunity to adjust services and address any concerns proactively.

Step 5: Building Client Loyalty
- **Task:** Create a loyalty or rewards program that acknowledges and incentivizes repeat business.
- **Action:** Brainstorm rewards ideas and draft a loyalty program proposal in 3 weeks.
- **Guidance:** Ensure incentives are both appealing and feasible for long-term implementation.

Step 6: Encouraging Advocacy
- **Task:** Develop a referral program that motivates clients to share their positive experiences.
- **Action:** Outline the referral program structure in 2 weeks.
- **Guidance:** Keep the referral process straightforward and rewarding for both the referrer and the referee.

Section 4.3: Monitoring and Refining Strategies

Step 7: Strategy Implementation
- **Task:** Put your lifecycle engagement strategies into action, starting with the most ready.
- **Action:** Implement one strategy every month, adjusting your timeline based on capacity.
- **Guidance:** Evaluate the success of each strategy, ready to iterate based on performance.

Accountability Timeline:
- **Monthly Performance Reviews:** Dedicate the first week of each month to evaluate the effectiveness of actions taken in each lifecycle stage.
- **Quarterly Adjustments:** Every quarter, reassess and refine strategies based on cumulative feedback and results.
- **Annual Reflection:** At the end of the year, conduct a comprehensive review to celebrate successes and plan for the next cycle of improvement.

By methodically working through these steps, you're not just engaging clients; you're creating an environment where loyalty and advocacy are the natural outcomes. Remember, the client lifecycle is a continuous journey—each step you take to enhance engagement not only solidifies existing relationships but also sets the stage for new ones.

Chapter 5 Pre-Breakdown: No Fluff, Just Facts

Section 5.1: Cutting Through Affiliate Marketing

Affiliate marketing is not just a buzzword; it's a strategic powerhouse for expanding your reach. It's a win-win: your affiliates spread the word, and they get paid for their hustle. Here's the deal:

- **Performance-Based:** Pay for results, not promises. Affiliates drive traffic or sales, and they get commissions. It's marketing that pays for itself.
- **Customer Acquisition Machine:** Tap into your affiliates' networks to reach audiences you wouldn't otherwise touch. It's about getting your brand where it needs to be – in front of new eyes.
- **Strategy for Success:** Choose affiliates that mesh with your vibe, set clear rewards, and keep the lines of communication wide open. Equip them to succeed, and watch your reach grow.

Section 5.2: Forging Affiliate Alliances

Real talk: your choice of affiliates can make or break your marketing strategy. It's about aligning with those who share your target audience and can authentically vouch for your brand. Here's how to build those alliances:

- **Choose Wisely:** Partner with affiliates who get your brand and have the audience to prove it.
- **Keep It Clear:** Set expectations and rewards upfront. No one likes surprises when money's on the line.

- **Support Squad:** Give your affiliates everything they need to succeed – from swag to shout-outs.
- **Celebrate Wins:** Recognize and reward your top affiliates to keep the momentum going.

Section 5.3: Tech That Transforms Affiliate Marketing

Tech's the secret sauce in the affiliate marketing game. It's about tracking those clicks, managing the masses, and optimizing every move. Check out these tools that are changing the game:

- **AffTrack & Post Affiliate Pro:** These are not your average tracking tools. They're the whole package – fraud detection, real-time analytics, and more.
- **Impact & TUNE:** Big on automation and insights, these platforms make managing your affiliate program a breeze.
- **Awin Access:** Perfect for the up-and-comers looking to get a piece of the affiliate pie without breaking the bank.

Section 5.4: ROI or Bust

Affiliate marketing's all about that ROI. It's not just about throwing money at your affiliates and hoping for the best. Here's how to make sure you're getting bang for your buck:

- **Pick the Right Partners:** Not all affiliates are created equal. Go for quality over quantity.
- **Smart Spending:** Keep an eye on that CPA. Lower costs mean higher ROI.
- **Data-Driven Decisions:** Use those analytics to fine-tune your strategy. More data means smarter moves.

Section 5.5: Smoothing Out the Bumps

Affiliate marketing's not all smooth sailing. From iffy affiliates to tracking troubles, here's how to navigate the challenges:
- **Vet Your Crew:** Make sure your affiliates align with your brand. No square pegs in round holes.
- **Clear as Day:** Communication is key. Make sure everyone's on the same page.
- **Fraud Fighters:** Stay sharp and keep an eye out for any shady dealings.

Section 5.6: Ethical Affiliate Marketing

Keep it clean, folks. Ethical practices in affiliate marketing aren't just nice to have; they're essential. Transparency, honesty, and respect go a long way in keeping your program above board and your brand reputation solid.

Section 5.7: Expanding Your Empire

Wrapping it up, affiliate marketing's your secret weapon for growth. Choose your affiliates wisely, treat them right, and keep pushing for better, smarter strategies. The potential for reach and growth is massive – so get out there and make those connections.

Endgame: Affiliate marketing is more than just a tool; it's a growth engine. Harness it, refine it, and watch your business break new ground.

Chapter 5: Buckle up, nerds! Time to READ. ¡A la grandeza!

(To Greatness!) - Spanish for aiming at nothing less than spectacular.

Section 5.1: Understanding Affiliate Marketing

Affiliate marketing stands as a pivotal strategy in the digital era, offering businesses a dynamic avenue for customer acquisition and market expansion. This section delves into the essence of affiliate marketing, outlining its foundational principles and the crucial role it plays in driving customer acquisition. By presenting actionable strategies, businesses are equipped to harness the full potential of affiliate marketing, enhancing their reach and solidifying their market presence.

Key Insights into Affiliate Marketing:

At its core, affiliate marketing is a performance-based system where external partners (affiliates) are rewarded for directing traffic or sales to a business's website through their marketing efforts. This symbiotic relationship allows businesses to tap into the affiliates' audience, expanding their reach without the upfront costs associated with traditional advertising methods. Affiliates, in turn, earn commissions based on the conversions or sales generated from their referrals, incentivizing them to promote the business effectively.

Affiliate marketing's role in customer acquisition cannot be overstated. By leveraging the networks and credibility of various affiliates, businesses can target diverse audience segments more precisely and authentically than through direct marketing efforts alone. This strategy not only enhances visibility but also builds trust among potential customers, given the endorsements come from sources they already know and trust.

Developing an Effective Affiliate Marketing Strategy:

1. **Identify Suitable Affiliates:** The first step in crafting an effective affiliate marketing strategy involves identifying and partnering with affiliates whose audiences align with your target market. Look for affiliates with a strong online presence, credibility, and engagement within your niche.

2. **Define Clear Terms and Rewards:** Establish clear, mutually beneficial terms for your affiliate partnerships. This includes commission structures, payment schedules, and any performance incentives. Transparent and attractive terms are key to attracting and retaining top-performing affiliates.
3. **Provide High-Quality Resources:** Equip your affiliates with high-quality marketing materials and resources. This can include banners, product images, copy templates, and any relevant product information that can help them promote your offerings more effectively.
4. **Utilize Affiliate Tracking Software:** Implement reliable affiliate tracking software to monitor referrals, conversions, and commissions accurately. This technology is crucial for managing payments and assessing the performance of your affiliate program.
5. **Foster Strong Relationships:** Treat your affiliates as valuable partners. Regular communication, support, and feedback can help strengthen these relationships. Consider offering performance bonuses or additional incentives to reward top performers and encourage ongoing promotion.
6. **Monitor and Optimize:** Continuously monitor the performance of your affiliate program and individual

affiliates. Use this data to optimize your strategy, focusing on the most effective affiliates and promotional tactics to maximize ROI.

Affiliate marketing offers a powerful strategy for businesses looking to expand their reach and acquire new customers efficiently. By understanding the basics of this marketing model and implementing a well-structured affiliate program, businesses can leverage external networks to enhance their market presence significantly. The key to success lies in selecting the right affiliates, establishing clear partnership terms, and maintaining a supportive and mutually beneficial relationship with your affiliate partners. With the right approach, affiliate marketing can become a cornerstone of your business's growth and customer acquisition strategy.

Section 5.2: Building Successful Affiliate Partnerships

In the evolving landscape of digital marketing, affiliate partnerships have emerged as a strategic asset for businesses aiming to broaden their reach and deepen market penetration. This section spotlights the success stories of businesses that have harnessed the power of affiliate networks, alongside a comprehensive framework for cultivating effective affiliate relationships. Through insightful case studies and targeted guidelines, we explore the dynamics of selecting and nurturing productive affiliate partnerships, ensuring mutual growth and success.

Case Studies of Powerful Affiliate Networks:

- **A Leading Online Retailer:** This e-commerce giant's affiliate program stands as a benchmark in the industry. By offering competitive commission rates, extensive support, and access to a vast product catalog, the retailer has attracted a diverse network of affiliates ranging from individual bloggers to large-scale content sites. The key to their success lies in the seamless integration of affiliate efforts with their overarching marketing strategy, driving significant sales growth.
- **A Renowned Software Provider:** Specializing in productivity tools, this software company has leveraged affiliate marketing to target niche markets effectively. By partnering with industry influencers and professional organizations, they've tailored their affiliate program to reach specific audience segments, resulting in increased adoption rates among targeted users.

Partnership Framework for Affiliate Relationships:

1. **Strategic Selection of Affiliates:** Begin by identifying potential affiliates that align with your brand values and target audience. Look for partners with engaged followings, relevance to your product or service, and a track record of successful promotions.
2. **Transparent Communication:** Establish clear, open lines of communication from the outset. Transparent discussions regarding expectations, commission structures, and promotional guidelines are essential for a fruitful partnership.
3. **Offer Competitive Incentives:** To attract and retain top-performing affiliates, offer competitive commission rates and incentives that reward successful promotions. Consider tiered commission structures to motivate higher performance levels.
4. **Provide Marketing Support:** Equip your affiliates with a range of marketing materials and resources. High-quality content, product samples for review, and exclusive promotions can empower affiliates to create compelling content that resonates with their audience.
5. **Regular Performance Reviews:** Conduct regular reviews of affiliate performance, using data analytics to

measure the effectiveness of promotional efforts. This analysis can help identify opportunities for optimization and additional support where needed.

6. **Nurture the Relationship:** View your affiliates as long-term partners. Regular engagement, personalized communication, and recognition of their contributions can strengthen the relationship, encouraging sustained effort and loyalty.

7. **Adapt and Evolve:** The affiliate marketing landscape is continually changing. Stay abreast of industry trends and be prepared to adapt your program accordingly. Soliciting feedback from affiliates can provide valuable insights into potential improvements and innovations.

Building successful affiliate partnerships requires a strategic approach, centered on selecting the right partners, fostering open communication, and providing robust support. The case studies and framework presented in this section underscore the potential of affiliate marketing as a powerful tool for customer acquisition and business growth. By prioritizing the development of strong, mutually beneficial affiliate relationships, businesses can tap into new audiences, enhance their market presence, and achieve sustained success in the competitive digital marketplace.

Section 5.3: Affiliate Marketing Tools and Technologies

Affiliate marketing, a cornerstone of modern digital strategy, owes much of its efficiency and scalability to the advancement of specific tools and technologies. This section explores the innovations that have revolutionized affiliate marketing, providing case studies of technological advancements and reviewing the essential tools that facilitate the management and scaling of affiliate marketing efforts.

Innovation Case Studies in Affiliate Marketing:

- **Real-Time Tracking and Analytics Platform:** A breakthrough in affiliate marketing was achieved with the development of a real-time tracking platform, enabling businesses and affiliates to monitor the performance of affiliate links instantaneously. This technology allowed for immediate adjustments to strategies based on up-to-the-minute data, significantly increasing the effectiveness of affiliate campaigns.
- **Automated Affiliate Management System:** Another significant advancement was the creation of an

automated system that streamlined the entire affiliate management process, from signup to payout. This system facilitated easier recruitment, engagement, and retention of affiliates, reducing manual workload and improving program scalability.

- **AI-Powered Optimization Tools:** Leveraging artificial intelligence, these tools analyze vast amounts of data to identify the most effective affiliate marketing strategies and optimize campaign performance. By predicting which affiliate content will perform best with certain audiences, these tools help tailor marketing efforts for maximum impact.

Tool Reviews for Managing and Scaling Affiliate Marketing Efforts:

1. **AffTrack:** AffTrack offers an end-to-end solution for affiliate tracking, complete with real-time analytics, click fraud detection, and mobile tracking capabilities. It's particularly suited for businesses looking to scale their affiliate programs efficiently.
2. **Post Affiliate Pro:** Renowned for its user-friendly interface and comprehensive feature set, Post Affiliate Pro facilitates the management of affiliate programs

with tools for tracking, reporting, and commission management. Its flexibility makes it a top choice for businesses of all sizes.

3. **Impact:** Impact's partnership cloud provides a robust platform for managing all types of partnerships, including affiliates. Its ability to automate workflows, coupled with powerful analytics and optimization features, makes it invaluable for businesses aiming to grow their affiliate networks strategically.

4. **TUNE:** Offering a flexible SaaS platform for building, managing, and growing affiliate programs, TUNE specializes in performance-based marketing. Its features include customizable commission structures, detailed reporting, and fraud prevention, supporting businesses in optimizing their affiliate strategies.

5. **Awin Access:** Designed for small and medium-sized enterprises, Awin Access provides an intuitive platform for launching and managing affiliate programs. Its global reach and extensive network of affiliates make it an excellent tool for businesses looking to expand their online presence.

The evolution of affiliate marketing tools and technologies has significantly enhanced the ability of businesses to engage with and leverage affiliates for growth. From sophisticated tracking platforms to automated management systems and AI-powered optimization, these innovations have streamlined operations, improved effectiveness, and expanded the potential of affiliate marketing strategies. By selecting and utilizing the right tools, businesses can optimize their affiliate marketing efforts, ensuring scalability, efficiency, and, ultimately, a stronger return on investment.

Section 5.4: Maximizing ROI from Affiliate Marketing

Affiliate marketing, with its performance-based model, offers businesses a compelling avenue for scalable growth and customer acquisition. However, the true effectiveness of an affiliate program is measured by its return on investment (ROI). This section outlines strategies to optimize ROI in affiliate marketing, alongside a discussion on the critical performance metrics and KPIs essential for evaluating and enhancing affiliate success.

ROI Strategies in Affiliate Marketing:

1. **Selective Affiliate Recruitment:** Focus on recruiting affiliates that align closely with your target market and brand values. High-quality affiliates with engaged audiences tend to drive higher conversion rates, directly impacting your ROI.
2. **Competitive Commission Structures:** Offering competitive commissions incentivizes affiliates to prioritize your products or services. Consider tiered commissions to reward higher-performing affiliates, encouraging them to increase their promotional efforts.
3. **Effective Use of Data:** Leverage analytics to understand which affiliates, products, and marketing strategies yield the highest returns. Invest more in high-performing areas and reevaluate underperforming aspects of your affiliate program.
4. **Enhancing Affiliate Support:** Provide affiliates with high-quality marketing materials, product training, and responsive support. Well-informed and well-equipped affiliates are more effective in promoting your offerings, leading to improved ROI.
5. **Optimizing Landing Pages:** Ensure that the traffic directed by affiliates lands on optimized, conversion-focused pages. A/B testing can help identify the most

effective page elements, from headlines to call-to-action buttons.

6. **Regular Program Review and Adjustment:** Continuously monitor your affiliate program's performance and make necessary adjustments to commission rates, promotional strategies, and affiliate partnerships to maximize ROI.

Performance Metrics for Evaluating Affiliate Success:

1. **Conversion Rate:** The percentage of affiliate-referred visitors who take a desired action, such as making a purchase. High conversion rates indicate effective affiliate promotion and targeting.
2. **Average Order Value (AOV):** The average amount spent by customers referred by affiliates. Strategies to increase AOV can directly enhance ROI.
3. **Click-Through Rate (CTR):** Measures the effectiveness of affiliate links in generating interest. High CTRs suggest that affiliate content resonates well with their audience.
4. **Cost Per Acquisition (CPA):** The total cost of acquiring a customer through affiliate marketing. Lower CPAs indicate a more efficient use of marketing budgets.

5. **Lifetime Value (LTV):** The total revenue a business can expect from a single customer account. Focusing on affiliates that attract customers with high LTVs can significantly improve ROI.
6. **Return on Ad Spend (ROAS):** A specific measurement of the revenue generated for every dollar spent on affiliate marketing. A higher ROAS indicates a more profitable affiliate program.

Maximizing ROI from affiliate marketing requires a strategic approach focused on selective recruitment, competitive incentives, data-driven decisions, and continuous optimization. By closely monitoring and responding to key performance indicators, businesses can refine their affiliate marketing efforts, ensuring not only a significant return on investment but also sustainable growth and expansion. Implementing these strategies effectively enables businesses to leverage their affiliate programs as powerful engines for revenue generation and market penetration.

Section 5.5: Navigating Challenges in Affiliate Marketing

Affiliate marketing, while offering a path to expansive growth and heightened market reach, is not without its hurdles. This section delves into the common pitfalls that businesses encounter within their affiliate marketing endeavors and outlines strategic solutions and preventative measures to navigate these challenges effectively. By addressing these obstacles proactively, businesses can ensure the robustness and profitability of their affiliate marketing programs.

Common Pitfalls in Affiliate Marketing:

1. **Poor Affiliate Selection:** Partnering with affiliates who do not align with the brand's values or target audience can lead to ineffective campaigns and diluted brand messaging.
2. **Lack of Clear Communication:** Misunderstandings between the business and its affiliates regarding expectations, commission structures, or marketing strategies can hamper the effectiveness of the affiliate program.
3. **Inconsistent Brand Messaging:** Disparate and inconsistent messaging across affiliate channels can confuse potential customers and weaken brand identity.

4. **Fraudulent Activities:** Affiliate marketing is sometimes susceptible to fraudulent activities, such as fake leads or spammy tactics, which can damage the brand's reputation and result in financial losses.
5. **Inadequate Tracking and Reporting:** Without robust tracking and reporting mechanisms, it's challenging to measure the success of affiliate campaigns and make informed decisions.

Solutions and Strategies:

1. **Rigorous Affiliate Vetting:** Implement a comprehensive vetting process to ensure that potential affiliates are a good fit for your brand, with a genuine interest in your products and a relevant, engaged audience.
2. **Establish Clear Guidelines:** Develop clear, detailed guidelines covering all aspects of your affiliate program, including branding, promotion methods, and communication protocols. Regularly update affiliates on any changes to these guidelines.
3. **Maintain Brand Consistency:** Provide affiliates with up-to-date branding materials and message templates to ensure consistency across all promotional content.

Regularly review affiliate content to ensure it aligns with your brand's messaging.

4. **Implement Fraud Detection Measures:** Utilize affiliate marketing software with built-in fraud detection capabilities. Regularly monitor affiliate activities for any suspicious patterns and take immediate action to address potential fraud.

5. **Invest in Quality Tracking Software:** Adopt reliable affiliate tracking software that offers real-time data on clicks, conversions, and other key metrics. This technology is crucial for evaluating the performance of affiliates and the overall success of the program.

6. **Foster Open Communication:** Establish a culture of open communication with your affiliates. Regular check-ins, newsletters, and feedback sessions can help address any issues promptly and reinforce the partnership.

7. **Educate Your Affiliates:** Provide ongoing training and resources to help affiliates understand your products, the target market, and effective marketing strategies. Well-informed affiliates are more likely to succeed in promoting your brand.

Navigating the challenges of affiliate marketing requires a proactive, strategic approach centered on careful affiliate selection, clear communication, brand consistency, fraud prevention, and effective tracking. By implementing these solutions and strategies, businesses can mitigate common pitfalls, enhancing the effectiveness and profitability of their affiliate marketing efforts. Ultimately, overcoming these challenges paves the way for a successful affiliate program that contributes significantly to business growth and market expansion.

Section 5.6: Ethical Considerations in Affiliate Marketing

In the realm of affiliate marketing, the pursuit of success is intrinsically linked to the adherence to ethical standards. This section emphasizes the critical importance of maintaining ethical practices within affiliate marketing endeavors and outlines best practices to ensure that affiliate programs operate transparently, responsibly, and to the mutual benefit of all parties involved.

The Importance of Ethics in Affiliate Marketing:

Ethical considerations in affiliate marketing go beyond mere compliance with legal standards; they are fundamental to building trust, safeguarding brand reputation, and fostering long-term, sustainable relationships with both affiliates and customers. Ethical affiliate marketing practices ensure fairness, transparency, and respect for consumer rights, which are essential in today's increasingly informed and conscientious market.

Best Practices for Ethical Affiliate Marketing:

1. **Transparent Disclosure:** Affiliates should clearly disclose their relationship with the business in all promotional content. This transparency is crucial for building trust with consumers and adhering to regulatory requirements regarding affiliate marketing.
2. **Honest Representation:** Ensure that affiliates accurately represent products or services without making false or misleading claims. Honesty in promotion not only aligns with ethical standards but also protects consumers from potential harm.
3. **Respect for Privacy:** Adhere to privacy laws and best practices in data collection, use, and protection. Affiliates and businesses must be transparent about data practices and provide consumers with options to control their personal information.

4. **Fair Compensation:** Develop a fair and transparent commission structure that adequately compensates affiliates for their contributions. Prompt payment and clear communication about payment terms are essential for maintaining positive affiliate relationships.
5. **Quality Control:** Regularly review affiliate content and practices to ensure they meet your ethical standards and brand guidelines. Providing feedback and guidance can help affiliates align their strategies with these standards.
6. **Consumer Protection:** Commit to practices that prioritize consumer protection, including avoiding spammy promotion tactics and ensuring that the affiliate program does not contribute to consumer deception or discomfort.
7. **Continuous Education:** Educate affiliates on ethical practices, legal requirements, and the brand's values. Ongoing training and support can empower affiliates to make ethical decisions in their promotional efforts.
8. **Engagement in Ethical Networks:** Participate in affiliate networks and platforms that enforce ethical standards and practices among their members. This engagement can help elevate the overall quality and integrity of affiliate marketing efforts.

Ethical considerations form the backbone of successful and sustainable affiliate marketing strategies. By implementing the best practices outlined above, businesses can foster an ethical affiliate marketing environment that respects consumer rights, builds trust, and enhances the brand's reputation. Maintaining high ethical standards in affiliate marketing not only complies with legal obligations but also contributes to a positive brand image, customer loyalty, and long-term success. As the digital landscape evolves, the commitment to ethics in affiliate marketing remains a constant imperative, guiding businesses toward responsible growth and enduring partnerships.

Section 5.7: Expanding Reach Through Affiliates

As we conclude this exploration into the dynamic world of affiliate marketing within Chapter 5 of this book, we reflect on the pivotal insights gained and the transformative potential of affiliate marketing in expanding a business's reach. This section encapsulates the key takeaways from the chapter and issues a call to action for businesses to harness the power of affiliate marketing as a strategic lever for growth and market penetration.

Key Takeaways on Leveraging Affiliate Marketing for Growth:

1. **Strategic Affiliate Selection:** The importance of meticulously selecting affiliates that resonate with your brand ethos and have access to your target audience cannot be overstated. The right affiliates act as brand ambassadors, extending your reach to previously untapped markets.
2. **Building Robust Relationships:** Cultivating strong, mutually beneficial relationships with your affiliates is fundamental. Support, clear communication, and fair compensation are key to maintaining a motivated affiliate network.
3. **Leveraging Technology:** Advancements in affiliate marketing tools and technologies offer unprecedented opportunities for tracking, managing, and optimizing affiliate campaigns. Investing in the right tools can significantly enhance efficiency and scalability.
4. **Optimizing for ROI:** Implementing strategies to maximize the return on investment from affiliate marketing involves not only selecting the right affiliates and compensating them appropriately but also continuously analyzing performance data to refine your approach.

5. **Navigating Challenges:** Addressing and overcoming the common challenges in affiliate marketing, from ethical considerations to maintaining brand consistency, requires vigilance, commitment, and strategic planning.
6. **Ethical Practices:** Ethical considerations form the cornerstone of a successful affiliate marketing program. Transparency, honesty, and respect for consumer privacy are non-negotiable principles that safeguard your brand's reputation and ensure sustainable growth.

Call to Action:

In today's competitive digital landscape, the strategic integration of affiliate marketing into your overall customer acquisition strategy presents a valuable opportunity for business expansion. This chapter has laid out a roadmap for leveraging affiliate marketing effectively, emphasizing the need for strategic affiliate selection, ethical marketing practices, and the use of advanced tools for campaign management.

Businesses are encouraged to:

- Reevaluate their current marketing strategies to identify opportunities for incorporating or enhancing affiliate marketing efforts.

- Dedicate resources to developing a structured affiliate program that aligns with their growth objectives and market positioning.
- Embrace continuous learning and adaptation to stay ahead of the evolving trends and technologies in affiliate marketing.

By actively exploring and integrating affiliate marketing into your acquisition strategies, your business can tap into new audiences, foster brand loyalty, and achieve sustainable growth. Let the insights and strategies outlined in this chapter serve as a guide to expanding your reach through affiliates, driving forward with innovation, commitment, and a focus on mutual success.

Affiliate marketing, when executed with intention and integrity, not only amplifies your market presence but also strengthens the fabric of your business relationships, laying a solid foundation for future ventures and collaborations. Now is the time to harness the collective power of affiliates to propel your business into its next chapter of growth and market leadership.

Chapter 5: Step-By Step How to "Get... It... Done!"

Dive into the world of affiliate marketing with a strategic plan designed to elevate your business through collaborative partnerships and shared success.

Section 5.1: Launching Your Affiliate Odyssey

Step 1: Scout for Allies

- **Task:** Identify and list potential affiliate partners who resonate with your brand and can captivate your target audience.
- **Deadline:** 2 Weeks to compile a comprehensive list.

Step 2: Craft Compelling Terms

- **Task:** Design an affiliate program that's irresistible, detailing commissions, payout details, and brand guidelines.
- **Deadline:** 1 Week to finalize program details.

Step 3: Tracking Triumphs

- **Task:** Select and implement a robust affiliate tracking system that's both reliable for you and transparent for your partners.
- **Deadline:** 3 Weeks to research, choose, and set up.

Section 5.2: Fostering Fruitful Partnerships
Step 1: Engage Potential Partners
- **Task:** Reach out to your identified potential affiliates with personalized invitations to collaborate.
- **Deadline:** 2 Weeks to initiate contact and follow up.

Step 2: Empower With Resources
- **Task:** Develop and distribute a marketing toolkit to your affiliates, ensuring they have everything they need to succeed.
- **Deadline:** 1 Week to create and dispatch materials.

Step 3: Nurturing the Network
- **Task:** Establish a routine of regular check-ins and updates to maintain engagement and address any affiliate needs.
- **Deadline:** Ongoing, with monthly check-ins.

Section 5.3: Mastering Affiliate Marketing Tools
Step 1: Tool Selection
- **Task:** Investigate and decide on the affiliate marketing tools that will best serve your program's goals.
- **Deadline:** 2 Weeks to decide and implement tools.

Step 2: Training Time
- **Task:** Organize comprehensive training for both your team and affiliates on leveraging these tools effectively.

- **Deadline:** 2 Weeks post-tool selection for training completion.

Step 3: Feedback and Fine-Tuning
- **Task:** Regularly review tool performance and solicit user feedback for continuous improvement.
- **Deadline:** Ongoing, with quarterly reviews.

Section 5.4: Amplifying Returns
Step 1: Data Deep Dive
- **Task:** Analyze affiliate performance metrics to spotlight high achievers and successful strategies.
- **Deadline:** Monthly analytics review.

Step 2: Strategic Enhancements
- **Task:** Refine your affiliate program based on insights gained, focusing on boosting successful tactics and supporting affiliate stars.
- **Deadline:** Ongoing, with adjustments post-analysis.

Step 3: Cultivate Feedback Culture
- **Task:** Establish a structured feedback loop with affiliates to continually evolve and improve your program.
- **Deadline:** Ongoing, with bi-monthly feedback sessions.

Section 5.5: Steering Through Storms

Step 1: Challenge Identification

- **Task:** Preemptively pinpoint potential pitfalls within your affiliate program, from engagement to ethics.
- **Deadline:** 1 Week for comprehensive challenge mapping.

Step 2: Mitigation Strategies

- **Task:** Draft targeted solutions for each identified challenge, ready to be deployed as needed.
- **Deadline:** 2 Weeks for strategy development.

Step 3: Vigilant Monitoring

- **Task:** Keep a constant watch on your program's pulse, ready to act swiftly to navigate any turbulence.
- **Deadline:** Ongoing, with weekly check-ups.

Accountability Timeline:

- **Monthly Performance Reviews:** Dedicate time each month to analyze the health and success of your affiliate program.
- **Quarterly Strategy Assessments:** Take a step back every quarter to evaluate the effectiveness of your strategies and tools.

- **Annual Program Audit:** Commit to a thorough audit of your affiliate program each year, reassessing partnerships, technologies, and overall impact.

By breaking down your affiliate marketing strategy into these actionable steps, you're setting the stage for a program that not only expands your reach but also builds lasting partnerships and drives sustainable growth. Keep focused, stay flexible, and watch as your network becomes a significant force in your marketing arsenal.

Chapter 6 Pre-Breakdown: No Fluff, Just Facts

Section 6.1: Word-of-Mouth's Quiet Power

Forget flashy ads for a second. The oldest trick in the book, word-of-mouth, still holds the crown. It's simple: happy clients talk, and their words carry weight. Here's how to turn satisfaction into your next big marketing campaign:

- **Trust Factor:** People buy based on trust, and nothing says "trust" like a friend's recommendation.
- **Credibility & Cost-Effectiveness:** Free and credible beats paid ads any day.
- **Build Relationships:** Make your clients feel like they're part of your success story.

Section 6.2: Building a Referral Empire

Creating a culture that breathes referrals is more necessity than strategy. It's about making referrals everyone's business, not just a side task. Here's how the big players do it:

- **Tech Giants:** They've made referrals everybody's job, rewarding the matchmakers among their ranks.
- **Consultancy Firms:** By turning networking events into referral goldmines, they've shown the power of community.
- **Financial Wizards:** They've turned their client base into a referral network, offering perks that keep everyone talking.

Section 6.3: The Tech Behind Referrals

In today's game, technology is your best player in managing and boosting referrals. It's about tracking, rewarding, and enhancing every step of the referral journey. Here are some tools that change the game:

- **ReferralCandy & Ambassador:** Perfect for e-commerce, turning happy customers into brand ambassadors.
- **Talkable & Mention Me:** They take personalization to the next level, ensuring your referral program hits the mark every time.
- **Post Affiliate Pro:** Offers the control freaks everything they need to keep tabs on their referrals.

Section 6.4: Crafting Killer Referral Programs

A referral program shouldn't be rocket science. It's about rewarding your cheerleaders and making it easy for them to sing your praises. Here's the recipe for a program that gets people talking:

- **Clear Goals & Sweet Incentives:** Know what you want and make the pot sweet enough to get your clients talking.
- **Keep It Simple:** Make referring as easy as pie.
- **Talk About It:** If you're not talking about your referral program, no one else will.

Section 6.5: Smoothing Out Referral Wrinkles

Referral programs aren't without their hiccups. Participation can be low, tracking can be a headache, and sometimes people try to game the system. Here's how to iron out those kinks:

- **Boost Awareness:** Shout about your referral program from the rooftops.
- **Quality Control:** Not all referrals are created equal. Aim for quality over quantity.
- **Technology Is Your Friend:** Use it to track, reward, and keep the referral train running smoothly.

Section 6.6: The Numbers Game

If you're not measuring your referral program's success, you're flying blind. Key metrics to watch include referral rates, conversion rates, and the overall ROI of your referral efforts. Keep a pulse on:

- **Referral & Conversion Rates:** These tell you if people are talking and if those conversations are turning into cash.
- **Customer Lifetime Value:** Are referred customers sticking around longer and spending more?
- **Cost-Per-Acquisition:** Is acquiring customers through referrals actually saving you money?

Section 6.7: Community Is King

At the end of the day, your business grows in the soil of community. Referrals are just the natural fruit of a healthy, engaged community around your brand. The takeaway? Nurture your community and the referrals (and growth) will follow.

Wrap-Up: Word-of-mouth is an ancient yet unbeatable force in the marketing world. Build a culture that cherishes and rewards referrals, leverage technology to manage and enhance your program, and always, always listen to what the numbers (and your community) are telling you. That's how you turn happy clients into your most powerful marketing tool.

Chapter 6: Buckle up, nerds! Time to READ. Vers l'infini et au-delà!

(To Infinity and Beyond!)
- French, because why limit your success?

Section 6.1: The Power of Word-of-Mouth

In the digital era, where marketing channels are abundant and consumer attention is fragmented, the ancient practice of word-of-mouth remains a potent tool for business growth. This section delves into the profound impact of referrals and word-of-mouth on expanding a business's reach and enhancing its reputation. Through strategic insights and actionable strategies, businesses can harness the intrinsic value of word-of-mouth, transforming satisfied clients into vocal advocates.

Key Insights on the Impact of Referrals and Word-of-Mouth:

Word-of-mouth marketing transcends the limitations of traditional advertising by leveraging the trust and personal connections within an individual's network. This trust factor significantly amplifies the effectiveness of referrals, making them a highly coveted source of new business. Studies have shown that consumers are more likely to purchase a product or service recommended by friends or family, highlighting the intrinsic value of personal endorsements.

1. **Enhanced Credibility:** Personal recommendations carry a weight of authenticity and trust that paid advertisements cannot replicate. This credibility can significantly shorten the sales cycle and increase conversion rates.
2. **Cost-Effective Growth:** Unlike paid marketing channels, word-of-mouth generates exposure and leads without direct costs. The investment in creating exceptional client experiences pays dividends as satisfied clients naturally share their positive experiences.
3. **Strengthened Client Relationships:** Encouraging referrals can reinforce the relationship with existing clients, making them feel valued and part of the business's success story.

Actionable Strategies for Incentivizing and Facilitating Referrals:

1. **Create Exceptional Client Experiences:** The foundation of effective word-of-mouth marketing is delivering services or products that exceed expectations. Satisfied clients are naturally inclined to share their positive experiences with others.
2. **Implement a Referral Program:** Develop a structured referral program that rewards clients for bringing new business. Ensure the rewards are meaningful and align with your clients' values, whether through discounts, special services, or recognition.
3. **Make Referring Easy:** Provide clients with simple tools and processes to refer others to your business. This could include referral links, dedicated landing pages, or templated messages they can use to spread the word.
4. **Leverage Social Proof:** Encourage clients to share their experiences on social media, review sites, and other digital platforms. Social proof can amplify word-of-mouth effects, reaching a broader audience.
5. **Express Gratitude:** Show appreciation for referrals, regardless of the outcome. A simple thank you note or a

small token of gratitude can reinforce positive feelings and encourage continued advocacy.

6. **Track and Analyze Referral Sources:** Use CRM tools to track referrals and analyze the effectiveness of your word-of-mouth marketing efforts. Understanding which clients or channels generate the most referrals can help you focus your efforts and resources effectively.

The power of word-of-mouth in driving business growth is unmatched in its ability to build trust, credibility, and genuine connections with potential clients. By focusing on creating exceptional client experiences and implementing strategic referral programs, businesses can tap into the natural advocacy of their satisfied clients. The strategies outlined in this section offer a roadmap for harnessing the timeless influence of word-of-mouth, ensuring that businesses not only survive but thrive in the competitive marketplace through the endorsement of their most valuable asset: their clients.

Section 6.2: Creating a Referral-Friendly Culture

In the competitive landscape of modern business, fostering a culture of referrals within an organization is not merely a strategy but a necessity for growth and sustainability. This section highlights the successes of companies that have masterfully integrated referral practices into their corporate ethos, offering actionable insights and strategies for embedding these practices into the fabric of a company's culture.

Case Studies of Successful Referral Cultures:

- A Tech Giant: Known for its innovative products, this company has equally revolutionized referral culture by making referrals a core part of its employee responsibilities. By rewarding employees for successful client referrals and creating an environment where sharing contacts and networks is encouraged, the company has seen significant growth in its client base, fueled by high-quality leads.
- A Boutique Consultancy Firm: With a focus on personalized services, this firm attributes much of its success to a referral system deeply embedded in its culture. The firm regularly hosts networking events for clients and partners, fostering a community atmosphere that naturally encourages referrals. Their approach

demonstrates the power of relationship-building in creating a sustainable referral pipeline.

- **A Financial Services Provider:** This company has implemented a referral program that extends beyond its employees to include its clients. By offering mutual benefits for both the referrer and the referee, the company has cultivated a community of advocates, leading to increased customer loyalty and a steady stream of new business.

Culture Building: Tips for Embedding Referral Practices:

1. **Leadership Endorsement:** For a referral culture to take root, it must be actively endorsed and modeled by the company's leadership. Leaders should communicate the value of referrals and recognize individuals who contribute to the program's success.
2. **Incorporate Referrals into Core Values:** Embed the concept of referrals into the company's core values and mission statement. This integration emphasizes the importance of referrals and ensures they are a focal point of the company's strategic vision.
3. **Provide Training and Resources:** Equip employees with the training and tools they need to effectively

identify potential referral opportunities and articulate the value of the company's offerings. Regular workshops and accessible resources can enhance their confidence and effectiveness in generating referrals.

4. **Create Incentive Programs:** Develop incentive programs that reward successful referrals. These rewards can vary from financial bonuses to recognition awards, depending on what best motivates your team and aligns with company culture.

5. **Foster a Collaborative Environment:** Encourage collaboration and open communication within the team. A culture that values teamwork and mutual success is more likely to share contacts, leads, and opportunities.

6. **Celebrate Successes:** Publicly recognize and celebrate referral successes. Highlighting these achievements not only rewards the individuals involved but also reinforces the value of referrals to the entire organization.

7. **Solicit Feedback:** Regularly solicit feedback on the referral process from those involved. Understanding their experiences and challenges can provide valuable insights for refining and improving the referral culture.

Creating a referral-friendly culture is a strategic endeavor that requires commitment, clarity, and consistent effort. The companies highlighted in this section demonstrate the tangible benefits of such a culture, from accelerated growth to enhanced client loyalty. By following the outlined tips and integrating referrals into the very ethos of the company, businesses can unlock the full potential of their networks, turning every employee and client into a powerful advocate for their brand. This approach not only drives business success but also fosters a sense of community and shared purpose, reinforcing the company's values and mission.

Section 6.3: Tools for Tracking and Enhancing Referrals

In the strategic realm of referral marketing, the deployment of technology plays a crucial role in tracking, managing, and amplifying the effectiveness of referral programs. This section delves into innovative case studies where technology has significantly enhanced referral initiatives, followed by reviews of premier tools and software designed to optimize referral marketing strategies. Through technological integration, businesses can harness detailed insights, streamline processes, and ultimately, supercharge their referral programs.

Innovation Case Studies in Referral Marketing:

- **FinTech Startup Revolutionizing Referral Tracking:** A FinTech startup transformed its referral program with a bespoke analytics platform, enabling real-time tracking of referrals, conversions, and reward distributions. This technology provided granular insights into referral behaviors, allowing for targeted improvements and significantly higher conversion rates.
- **E-Commerce Giant's Referral Success:** An e-commerce leader integrated advanced machine learning algorithms to analyze referral data, identifying the most influential referrers and the types of referrals most likely to convert. This data-driven approach enabled personalized referral incentives, dramatically increasing referral program participation and sales.

Top Tools and Software for Managing Referral Programs:

1. **ReferralCandy:** A popular tool among e-commerce sites, ReferralCandy automates the referral process, offering customizable referral rewards, easy integration

with various e-commerce platforms, and detailed tracking of referral sales and activities.

2. **Ambassador:** This robust referral marketing platform is designed for businesses of all sizes, featuring a user-friendly interface, flexible reward schemes, and comprehensive campaign management capabilities. Ambassador excels in its ability to manage multiple referral programs simultaneously, making it ideal for companies with diverse product lines.

3. **Talkable:** Specializing in e-commerce and retail, Talkable offers a platform that supports custom referral campaigns, A/B testing for optimization, and advanced fraud detection. Its strength lies in creating highly tailored referral experiences that resonate with specific customer segments.

4. **Mention Me:** Mention Me integrates referral marketing with customer retention strategies, using NLP (Natural Language Processing) to analyze referral data and optimize referral messaging. Its unique approach to "Refer-a-Friend" schemes encourages not just new acquisitions but also reinforces existing customer relationships.

5. **Post Affiliate Pro:** Geared towards businesses seeking detailed control over their referral programs, Post

Affiliate Pro offers powerful tracking options, multilingual support, and a wide range of commission types. Its flexibility makes it suitable for companies with complex referral requirements.

Leveraging technology to track and enhance referral programs offers businesses a strategic advantage, providing the insights and efficiencies needed to scale their referral initiatives effectively. The case studies and tools reviewed in this section underscore the transformative impact of technology on referral marketing, from sophisticated tracking and analytics to automated management and optimization. By selecting and implementing the right tools, businesses can unlock the full potential of their referral programs, driving growth through one of the most trusted forms of marketing: the personal recommendation. As the digital landscape continues to evolve, staying abreast of technological advancements in referral marketing will be key to maintaining competitive edge and fostering sustainable business expansion.

Section 6.4: Designing Effective Referral Programs

The creation of an effective referral program is a strategic endeavor that requires thoughtful planning, compelling incentives, and clear communication. This section provides a comprehensive guide on developing referral programs that not only motivate and reward existing clients for their advocacy but also ensure the seamless acquisition of new customers. By adhering to best practices in program design and communication, businesses can unlock the full potential of referral marketing as a powerful driver of growth.

Program Design:

Creating a referral program that resonates with your client base involves several key elements, each designed to encourage participation and reward successful referrals. The foundation of an effective program lies in understanding what motivates your clients and tailoring the rewards to match these motivations.

1. **Define Clear Objectives:** Start by establishing clear goals for your referral program. Whether it's increasing overall customer base, boosting sales in a specific product line, or enhancing brand awareness, having specific objectives will shape the structure of your program.

2. **Select Appropriate Incentives:** Incentives are the cornerstone of any referral program. Choose rewards that are valuable to your clients, such as discounts, service upgrades, or exclusive access to new products. Monetary rewards or gift cards can also be effective, depending on your audience.
3. **Simplify the Referral Process:** Ensure the referral process is straightforward and easy for clients to participate in. Complicated procedures can deter potential referrers. Utilize simple forms, referral codes, or dedicated landing pages to facilitate the process.
4. **Communicate Clearly and Often:** Regular communication about the referral program is vital to keep it top of mind. Use various channels — emails, social media, account dashboards — to remind clients of the program and its benefits.

Best Practices:

To maximize the success of your referral program, consider these best practices that focus on structuring incentives and optimizing communication strategies.

1. **Tiered Rewards Structure:** Implement a tiered reward system that increases the incentives as clients refer

more new customers. This approach encourages ongoing participation and rewards the most active advocates.

2. **Personalize Communication:** Tailor your communication to the individual, acknowledging their contributions and the value they bring to your business. Personalized thank-you messages or updates on how their referrals are making an impact can enhance client engagement.

3. **Track and Measure Performance:** Utilize tracking tools to monitor the success of your referral program. Analyze which incentives are most effective, who your top referrers are, and how referral clients compare to other customer segments in terms of lifetime value and engagement.

4. **Provide Social Proof:** Share success stories and testimonials from clients who have benefited from the referral program. This not only serves as social proof but also illustrates the tangible rewards of participation.

5. **Ensure Transparency:** Be transparent about how the referral program works, including the terms and conditions, how rewards are calculated, and when they will be distributed. Clarity builds trust and encourages more active involvement.

An effective referral program is a strategic asset that can significantly contribute to business growth and client satisfaction. By designing a program that is easy to understand and participate in, offering meaningful incentives, and communicating effectively with clients, businesses can encourage a culture of advocacy. Implementing these guidelines will help ensure that your referral program not only attracts new customers but also deepens engagement with existing clients, fostering a community of loyal brand ambassadors.

Section 6.5: Overcoming Referral Program Challenges

Referral programs are a powerful tool for growth, leveraging the trust and networks of existing clients to attract new ones. However, managing these programs comes with its set of challenges, from ensuring engagement to tracking success accurately. This section outlines common pitfalls encountered in referral program management and provides strategic solutions for overcoming these hurdles, ensuring the program's longevity and effectiveness.

Common Pitfalls in Managing Referral Programs:

1. **Low Participation Rates:** A common challenge is the lack of active participation from existing clients, often due to unawareness or perceived complexity of the referral process.
2. **Quality of Referrals:** Not all referrals are equal. Some may not fit the target customer profile, leading to low conversion rates and inefficient use of resources.
3. **Tracking and Attribution Difficulties:** Accurately tracking referrals and attributing them to the correct source can be complex, especially without the right tools, leading to potential disputes and dissatisfaction.
4. **Maintaining Program Momentum:** Initial enthusiasm for referral programs can wane over time, making it challenging to keep clients engaged and actively referring.
5. **Fraudulent Referrals:** There's a risk of fraudulent activity, where individuals attempt to game the system to earn rewards without bringing in genuine new business.

Solutions and Strategies for Implementation:

1. **Enhance Awareness and Simplify Participation:** Use multiple communication channels to promote your

referral program and ensure the process is as simple as possible. Clear instructions and streamlined mechanisms can significantly boost participation rates.

2. **Define and Communicate Ideal Referral Profiles:** Help your clients understand what constitutes an ideal referral by clearly communicating the traits and characteristics of your target customers. This can improve the quality of referrals received.

3. **Leverage Technology for Tracking:** Invest in referral program software that offers robust tracking and attribution features. Such tools can automate the process, reduce disputes, and provide valuable insights into program performance.

4. **Refresh and Incentivize Regularly:** Keep the program exciting by regularly updating incentives and introducing limited-time offers or contests. Continuous communication about program benefits and success stories can also maintain momentum.

5. **Implement Fraud Detection Measures:** Use software with fraud detection capabilities and set clear terms and conditions for participation. Regular audits and checks can help identify and mitigate fraudulent activities.

6. **Offer Training and Support:** Provide resources and training to help participants understand how to make

referrals effectively. Support can range from how-to guides to personalized assistance for top referrers.

7. **Foster a Culture of Referral:** Embed the value of referrals into your company culture. Recognize and celebrate successful referrals internally to reinforce their importance and encourage ongoing participation.

8. **Collect Feedback and Iterate:** Regularly solicit feedback from program participants to identify areas for improvement. Be prepared to adapt and refine your program based on this feedback to meet evolving needs and expectations.

While referral programs present unique management challenges, the right strategies and tools can overcome these obstacles, enhancing the program's effectiveness and contributing significantly to business growth. By fostering active participation, ensuring quality referrals, leveraging technology for tracking, and maintaining program momentum, businesses can turn their referral programs into a vital source of new customer acquisition. The key lies in continuous evaluation, adaptation, and commitment to creating a mutually beneficial ecosystem for both the referrer and the referee, thereby driving sustainable growth through the power of word-of-mouth.

Section 6.6: Measuring Referral Program Success

The efficacy of a referral program is pivotal to its continuation and growth. Understanding how to measure this success is critical for businesses looking to optimize their referral initiatives. This section delves into the key metrics and indicators essential for evaluating the effectiveness of a referral program and discusses how leveraging client feedback can serve as a powerful tool for continuous improvement.

Metrics for Success in Referral Programs:

1. **Referral Rate:** This metric measures the percentage of existing clients who are making referrals. A high referral rate indicates strong client engagement and satisfaction with your products or services.
2. **Conversion Rate:** The conversion rate of referred prospects into paying customers is a direct indicator of the quality of referrals and the effectiveness of your referral process.
3. **Customer Lifetime Value (CLTV) of Referred Clients:** Comparing the CLTV of referred clients to that of non-

referred clients can provide insights into the long-term value referrals bring to your business.

4. **Cost Per Acquisition (CPA):** Evaluating the cost of acquiring a new customer through referrals versus other marketing channels helps in understanding the cost-effectiveness of the referral program.
5. **Referral Program ROI:** Calculating the return on investment for your referral program, considering all costs involved against the revenue generated from referred customers, is essential for evaluating its financial impact.
6. **Time to Conversion:** The time it takes for a referral to convert into a customer can help assess the efficiency of the referral process and the readiness of referred leads.
7. **Participant Satisfaction:** Gauging the satisfaction of both the referrer and referee provides insights into the program's reception and areas for improvement.

Feedback Loops for Continuous Improvement:

- **Regular Surveys:** Conducting regular surveys with participants of the referral program can uncover valuable insights into their experiences, perceptions, and suggestions for enhancement.

- **Feedback Channels:** Establishing clear channels for feedback, such as dedicated email addresses or feedback forms, encourages participants to share their thoughts and experiences.
- **Analyzing Feedback Trends:** Systematically analyzing feedback to identify common themes or issues can highlight areas of the referral program that require adjustment or improvement.
- **Actionable Insights:** Translating feedback into actionable insights is crucial. Whether it involves simplifying the referral process, adjusting rewards, or enhancing communication, making informed changes based on client feedback can significantly enhance the program's effectiveness.
- **Communicating Changes:** Inform participants about changes made based on their feedback. This transparency not only demonstrates your commitment to continuous improvement but also fosters a sense of ownership and value among your clients.
- **Iterative Process:** Treat the refinement of your referral program as an iterative process. Continuous evaluation and adjustment, driven by both quantitative metrics and qualitative feedback, ensure the program remains

effective and aligned with participants' needs and expectations.

Measuring the success of a referral program extends beyond quantitative metrics to encompass the qualitative insights gleaned from participant feedback. By closely monitoring key indicators of program effectiveness and establishing robust feedback loops, businesses can continuously refine their referral initiatives, enhancing both their reach and impact. This dual approach ensures that referral programs not only contribute to immediate business growth but also align with long-term strategic objectives, fostering an ecosystem of sustained client engagement and advocacy.

Section 6.7: Leveraging the Community for Growth

As we culminate our exploration into the transformative power of referral marketing within "Mastering the Market" it is evident that the heart of sustained business growth lies in nurturing a robust referral ecosystem. This final section encapsulates the myriad benefits of such an ecosystem and extends a compelling call to action for businesses to strategically harness the power of referrals and community advocacy for enduring expansion and success.

Key Takeaways on the Benefits of a Strong Referral Ecosystem:

1. **Enhanced Trust and Credibility:** Referrals inherently carry a high level of trust, as they often come from within one's own network. This trust translates into a higher likelihood of engagement and conversion, thereby boosting credibility and brand reputation.
2. **Cost-Effective Customer Acquisition:** Referral programs, rooted in the principle of word-of-mouth marketing, present a cost-effective alternative to traditional advertising methods, significantly lowering customer acquisition costs.
3. **Higher Quality Leads:** Referred customers often exhibit better fit and higher engagement levels, as they have been pre-vetted by existing customers who understand both the needs of their peers and the capabilities of your offerings.
4. **Increased Customer Lifetime Value:** Customers acquired through referrals tend to have a higher lifetime value, showing greater loyalty and engagement over

time compared to those acquired through other channels.
5. **Community Building:** A well-executed referral program fosters a sense of community among customers, encouraging a culture of mutual support and shared success that extends beyond mere transactions.

Call to Action:

The journey through the nuances of referral marketing underscores a pivotal truth: at the intersection of community and commerce lies untapped potential for exponential growth. **Businesses poised on the brink of expansion are called upon to:**

- **Embrace the Referral Mindset:** Integrate referral marketing as a core strategy within your business model. Recognize the power of referrals not just as a marketing tool but as a foundational element of your growth strategy.
- **Cultivate Your Community:** Invest in building and nurturing a community around your brand. Engage with your customers, listen to their feedback, and encourage them to share their positive experiences with others.

- **Innovate and Iterate:** Continuously refine your referral program based on data-driven insights and customer feedback. Stay adaptable, embracing innovation to keep your referral initiatives fresh and relevant.
- **Recognize and Reward:** Acknowledge the contributions of your community in driving growth. Implement meaningful reward mechanisms that resonate with your referrers and reinforce their importance to your business.
- **Lead with Authenticity:** In all referral marketing efforts, prioritize authenticity and transparency. Genuine relationships are the cornerstone of a successful referral ecosystem and sustainable growth.

Harnessing the power of referrals unlocks a pathway to sustainable growth, characterized by deeper customer relationships, enhanced brand loyalty, and an expansive community of advocates. By actively leveraging this community for growth, businesses can transcend traditional marketing limitations, forging a future where success is shared and amplified within a vibrant ecosystem of support. Let the insights and strategies unveiled in this chapter serve as a beacon, guiding your business towards leveraging the community for unparalleled growth and lasting success.

Chapter 6: Step-By Step How to "Get... It... Done!"

Unlock the potential of referral marketing and transform satisfied clients into your most powerful advocates. Here's your blueprint for building a referral empire.

Section 6.1: Kickstarting Word-of-Mouth Wonders
Step 1: Service Supercharge

- **Task:** Amp up your game to leave clients not just satisfied, but thrilled.
- **Deadline:** Ongoing, with quarterly service enhancement reviews.

Step 2: Referral Program Rollout

- **Task:** Craft a referral program that's too good to ignore. Make sure it's a win-win for everyone.
- **Deadline:** 1 Month to launch.

Step 3: Referral Ease

- **Task:** Eliminate every possible hiccup in the referral process. Think easy-peasy.
- **Deadline:** 2 Weeks to streamline.

Section 6.2: Cultivating a Referral-Rich Environment
Step 1: Internal Buzz Building

- **Task:** Get your team pumped about referrals. Their enthusiasm is contagious.
- **Deadline:** 2 Weeks to integrate into team goals.

Step 2: Referral Savvy Squad
- **Task:** Transform your team into referral wizards with top-notch training.
- **Deadline:** 1 Month for initial training sessions.

Step 3: High-Fives All Around
- **Task:** Celebrate referral victories big and small. Let everyone know it's a big deal.
- **Deadline:** Ongoing, with monthly recognition moments.

Section 6.3: Mastering Referral Metrics
Step 1: Tech Tool Triumph
- **Task:** Pick a referral tracking champion that makes tracking as easy as pie.
- **Deadline:** 1 Month to select and implement.

Step 2: Tech Whizzes
- **Task:** Make sure everyone's on board and comfy with your shiny new tool.
- **Deadline:** 2 Weeks post-implementation for training.

Step 3: Data Detective Work
- **Task:** Keep a keen eye on what the numbers are whispering about your referral program.

- **Deadline:** Monthly analytics deep dive.

Section 6.4: Crafting a Killer Referral Program
Step 1: Goal Getter
- **Task:** Pin down what you're really after with your referral program. Get specific.
- **Deadline:** 1 Week to define goals.

Step 2: Incentive Innovation
- **Task:** Brainstorm incentives that light up your clients' eyes. Remember, it's about them.
- **Deadline:** 2 Weeks to finalize and set up.

Step 3: Program Promotion
- **Task:** Shout from the digital rooftops about your awesome new program.
- **Deadline:** Launch campaign over 1 Month, then ongoing promotion.

Section 6.5: Smoothing Out Referral Roadblocks
Step 1: Problem Patrol
- **Task:** List potential snags in your referral paradise and strategize fixes.
- **Deadline:** 1 Week to strategize post-launch.

Step 2: Awareness Avalanche

- **Task:** Don't let your referral program be the best-kept secret. Blast awareness.
- **Deadline:** Ongoing, with bi-weekly check-ins on new strategies.

Step 3: Program Polish
- **Task:** Fine-tune your referral machine based on real-world running.
- **Deadline:** Continuous, with quarterly review and adjustments.

Section 6.6: Success Story Sculpting
Step 1: KPI Kingdom
- **Task:** Decide what success looks like in hard numbers. Set those KPIs in stone.
- **Deadline:** 2 Weeks to establish KPIs.

Step 2: Report Rituals
- **Task:** Make data review and reporting a sacred part of your routine.
- **Deadline:** Monthly reporting cycle.

Step 3: Feedback Loop
- **Task:** Chase down feedback like it's gold. Because it is.
- **Deadline:** Ongoing, with bi-monthly surveys or feedback sessions.

Section 6.7: Community Growth Gladiators

Step 1: Community Cultivation

- **Task:** Turn your client base into a thriving, talking, sharing community.
- **Deadline:** 3 Months to launch community initiatives.

Step 2: Success Showcase

- **Task:** Make heroes out of your referral stars. Share their stories far and wide.
- **Deadline:** Ongoing, with at least one success story shared monthly.

Step 3: Never-Ending Innovation

- **Task:** Keep your referral program from going stale. Always be on the lookout for fresh ideas.
- **Deadline:** Bi-annual program innovation review.

Dive deep, take these steps seriously, and watch your referral program become a cornerstone of your marketing strategy. It's about making every client a beacon for new business. Get it done, and the rewards will follow.

Chapter 7 Pre-Breakdown: No Fluff, Just Facts

Section 7.1: The Balancing Act

Get this straight: client and customer engagement aren't separate beasts. You've got to walk the tightrope, keeping both sides happy without tripping over. Here's the deal:

- **Mix It Up:** Your strategies for clients and customers should vibe off each other.
- **Different Strokes:** Tailor your game plan to fit each group's wants, but keep your eye on the prize.
- **Stay Loose:** Be ready to switch gears based on what's happening around you.

Section 7.2: Two Faces, One Coin

Ditch the one-size-fits-all approach. Hybrid models are where it's at, blending client handling with customer care to hit the sweet spot. Here's how some big names pulled it off:

- **Tech Titans:** They're killing it by marrying high-touch client management with a killer online community vibe.
- **Retail Giants:** These folks have cracked the code by treating sellers like gold while keeping buyers happy as clams.

- **Wellness Wonders:** Personalized plans meet user-friendly apps, showing the health crowd they really care.

Section 7.3: Data: The Great Equalizer

If you're not using data to tweak your engagement strategies, you're flying blind. It's all about striking that perfect balance, and here's how the smart ones do it:

- **Retail Rulers:** They're personalizing shopping like nobody's business, thanks to a deep dive into the data pool.
- **Finance Whizzes:** These guys are playing matchmaker between their big-shot clients and everyday customers, all thanks to some savvy number crunching.
- **Healthcare Heroes:** Patient data isn't just for records; it's gold for crafting experiences that hit home.

Section 7.4: Speak Their Language

You can't chat up clients and customers the same way. It's about knowing who's on the other end and tweaking your pitch to match. Here's the playbook:

- **Break Them Down:** Segment your audience to get a clear picture of who you're talking to.
- **Pick Your Channel:** Not everyone hangs out in the same spots. Choose your platforms wisely.

- **Tweak the Tone:** Professional for LinkedIn, casual for Instagram. It's all about context.

Section 7.5: Products That Pop

Your products and how you talk about them should be in lockstep with your engagement game. It's a dance, and you need to be in rhythm. Innovate, adapt, and keep your ear to the ground.

Section 7.6: When Worlds Collide

Clients want one thing; customers another. Welcome to the tug-of-war. The trick is finding common ground without selling anyone short. It's tough, but it's doable with some clever maneuvering.

Section 7.7: Singing from the Same Song Sheet

Bringing it all home: if you're not aligning your client and customer strategies, you're missing out on a killer harmony. It's about blending the best of both worlds to create a chorus that resonates with everyone.

Wrap-Up: Mastering engagement is no walk in the park. It takes smarts, flexibility, and a willingness to listen and adapt. But get it right, and you're golden. Keep your clients close, your customers closer, and always be ready to switch up your strategy on the fly. That's how you win in the engagement game.

Welbon Omar Salaam

Chapter 7: Buckle up, nerds! Time to READ. Auf zum Sieg! (On to Victory!)

- German, sounding serious about winning.

Section 7.1:

Understanding the Balance

In the intricate dance of business growth and sustainability, mastering the balance between client and customer engagement strategies emerges as a pivotal challenge. This section delves into the significance of this balance, offering key insights and actionable strategies to harmonize these efforts in alignment with overarching business goals. Achieving an effective equilibrium not only enhances the customer experience but also fosters long-term loyalty and advocacy, driving sustainable growth.

Key Insights on Balancing Client and Customer Engagement:

1. **Complementary Strategies:** Client and customer engagement, while distinct, should not be siloed

strategies. Instead, they should complement each other, with each approach informed by insights gained from the other. This synergy enhances the overall effectiveness of engagement efforts.

2. **Diverse Needs, Unified Goal:** Recognizing the diverse needs and preferences of clients and customers is crucial. Tailoring engagement strategies to meet these varied requirements, while steering towards a unified business goal, is key to maintaining balance.

3. **Flexibility and Adaptability:** The balance between client and customer engagement is dynamic, not static. Businesses must remain flexible and adaptable, ready to adjust strategies in response to evolving market trends, customer feedback, and business objectives.

Actionable Strategies for Achieving Effective Balance:

1. **Conduct Thorough Segmentation:** Start by clearly defining and understanding the segments within your client and customer bases. Detailed segmentation allows for the customization of engagement strategies that resonate with each group's specific needs and preferences.

2. **Develop Integrated Communication Plans:** Create communication plans that align client and customer messaging, ensuring consistency in brand voice and values across all touchpoints. This integration fosters a cohesive brand experience.

3. **Leverage Cross-Functional Insights:** Encourage collaboration between teams responsible for client and customer engagement. Cross-functional insights can unveil opportunities for synergy and innovation in engagement tactics.

4. **Implement Feedback Loops:** Establish robust feedback mechanisms for both clients and customers. Regularly review feedback to refine and balance engagement strategies, ensuring they remain aligned with the expectations and needs of both groups.

5. **Monitor Engagement Metrics Closely:** Utilize engagement metrics (such as NPS scores, retention rates, and conversion rates) to gauge the effectiveness of your strategies. This data-driven approach facilitates informed adjustments to maintain the right balance.

6. **Prioritize Relationship Building:** Regardless of whether the focus is on clients or customers, prioritize genuine relationship building. Personalized interactions

and understanding individual needs are universal strategies that enhance engagement across the board.

7. **Embrace Technological Advancements:** Utilize technology to streamline engagement processes, personalize communications, and gather actionable insights. The right technology stack can support a balanced approach to client and customer engagement.

Balancing client and customer engagement strategies is not just about juggling two sets of expectations; it's about creating a harmonious strategy that amplifies the strengths of each approach. By understanding the unique dynamics of client and customer relationships and employing tailored, flexible strategies, businesses can achieve a balance that not only meets diverse needs but also drives unified business growth. In the pursuit of sustainable success, the ability to maintain this balance is both an art and a strategic imperative.

Section 7.2: Hybrid Models of Engagement

In today's dynamic market landscape, businesses are increasingly adopting hybrid models of engagement that seamlessly integrate client and customer strategies. This innovative approach allows for a more holistic and effective method of building relationships, enhancing loyalty, and driving growth. Through the lens of successful case studies, this section explores how businesses have achieved synergy between client and customer engagement, alongside presenting adaptable hybrid strategies for businesses aiming to cultivate a dual approach.

Case Studies of Successful Hybrid Engagement Models:

- **A Leading Software Company:** This company has mastered the art of hybrid engagement by offering personalized software solutions to its clients while maintaining an active community forum for end-users. The integration of high-touch client management with community-driven customer support has not only increased client retention rates but also fostered a loyal customer base.
- **Global E-commerce Platform:** By combining a dedicated account management team for sellers (clients) with a robust customer service framework for buyers,

this e-commerce giant has created a seamless experience that caters to the needs of both parties. This dual approach has contributed to its marketplace's exponential growth and high satisfaction rates.

- **Innovative Health and Wellness Start-Up:** This start-up has adopted a hybrid model by providing personalized health plans and consultations for its clients, coupled with a user-friendly app that offers ongoing support and engagement for customers. This strategy has effectively bridged the gap between personalized service and scalable customer engagement.

Hybrid Strategies for Effective Dual Approach:

1. **Integrated Communication Channels:** Develop communication strategies that address both client and customer needs, leveraging platforms that facilitate both personalized outreach and broader community engagement.
2. **Customized and Scalable Solutions:** Offer solutions that can be customized for individual client needs while also being scalable to meet the wider customer base's requirements. This might involve tiered service options or modular product offerings.

3. **Unified Brand Experience:** Ensure that both clients and customers encounter a consistent brand experience, regardless of their interaction level. This consistency reinforces brand identity and fosters trust across all engagement points.
4. **Cross-functional Teams:** Create cross-functional teams that understand the nuances of both client and customer engagement, promoting a culture of knowledge sharing and innovation that benefits all stakeholders.
5. **Data-driven Insights:** Utilize data analytics to gather insights on both client and customer behaviors, preferences, and feedback. These insights can inform a more cohesive and responsive engagement strategy.
6. **Feedback Loops and Continuous Improvement:** Implement mechanisms for collecting and acting on feedback from both clients and customers. This continuous loop of feedback and improvement keeps the hybrid model responsive and effective.
7. **Technology as an Enabler:** Leverage technology to facilitate the hybrid model, using CRM systems, engagement platforms, and analytics tools to manage relationships, personalize experiences, and track performance across both client and customer spectrums.

The hybrid models of engagement showcased through these case studies and strategies reveal a powerful approach for businesses to simultaneously cater to the nuanced needs of clients and customers. By adopting such a model, businesses can ensure a more integrated, consistent, and effective engagement strategy that drives mutual growth and satisfaction. The key to success lies in understanding the distinct yet interconnected needs of clients and customers, fostering a culture of flexibility, and leveraging technology to create a cohesive ecosystem of engagement.

Section 7.3: Leveraging Data for Balanced Engagement

In the age of information, data analytics has become the cornerstone of developing effective and balanced engagement strategies for both clients and customers. This section explores the transformative role of data analytics in supporting businesses to achieve an equilibrium in engagement efforts, ensuring both segments receive optimal attention without compromising the quality of interactions. Through innovation case studies and methodologies for data utilization, we delve into how businesses can harness data to refine, target, and balance their engagement initiatives effectively.

Innovation Case Studies in Data-Driven Engagement:

- **Retail Giant's Personalized Shopping Experience:** A leading retail chain implemented advanced data analytics to track customer purchase patterns, preferences, and feedback. By analyzing this data, they were able to offer personalized shopping experiences, recommendations, and promotions to customers, while also providing valuable insights to their clients (suppliers) about product performance and consumer trends.

- **Financial Services Firm's Client-Customer Synergy:** Utilizing data analytics, a financial services firm developed a model that identifies cross-sell opportunities between their institutional clients and retail customers. This approach not only increased product uptake but also balanced the firm's focus on both client services and customer satisfaction.

- **Healthcare Provider's Dual Engagement Platform:** By leveraging patient data, a healthcare provider was able to customize patient care plans (client engagement) while also using aggregated data to improve patient portal services (customer engagement). This dual approach enhanced patient outcomes and satisfaction rates.

Methodologies for Leveraging Data to Balance Engagement Efforts:

1. **Segmentation Analysis:** Use data analytics to segment your audience based on behaviors, preferences, and needs. Tailored engagement strategies can then be developed for different segments, ensuring that both clients and customers receive personalized and relevant interactions.
2. **Predictive Analytics:** Implement predictive analytics to forecast future engagement trends and preferences of both clients and customers. This foresight allows businesses to proactively adjust their engagement strategies, maintaining a balance between nurturing existing client relationships and attracting new customers.
3. **Engagement Scoring:** Develop scoring systems to quantify engagement levels of clients and customers. This data-driven approach helps identify areas where

engagement may be lagging, allowing for targeted strategies to reinvigorate interest and interaction.

4. **Feedback Loop Integration:** Utilize customer and client feedback data to continually refine engagement strategies. By analyzing feedback in real-time, businesses can quickly identify and address imbalances in engagement efforts.

5. **Cross-Channel Data Synthesis:** Aggregate data from various channels to gain a holistic view of engagement across all touchpoints. This comprehensive understanding ensures that efforts are evenly distributed, enhancing the overall experience for both clients and customers.

6. **Data Privacy and Ethics:** While leveraging data, prioritize privacy and ethical considerations to maintain trust. Transparent data practices and adherence to regulations are paramount in sustaining long-term relationships.

The strategic utilization of data analytics empowers businesses to navigate the complex terrain of balancing engagement between clients and customers. The case studies and methodologies outlined here underscore the pivotal role of data in informing, optimizing, and equalizing engagement strategies.

By embracing a data-driven approach, businesses can ensure that their engagement efforts are not only effective but also equitably distributed, fostering growth, loyalty, and satisfaction among both clients and customers. In the journey towards balanced engagement, data analytics emerges as both the map and the compass, guiding businesses to a harmonious and dynamic interaction landscape.

Section 7.4: Customizing Communication for Diverse Audiences

In the multifaceted world of business engagement, the ability to customize communication for diverse audiences — specifically, clients and customers — is paramount. This nuanced approach not only ensures that messages resonate more deeply but also strengthens relationships and fosters loyalty. This section outlines strategic communication methods and best practices for effectively tailoring messages to meet the unique needs and preferences of each group, enhancing the overall impact of engagement efforts.

Communication Strategies for Diverse Audiences:

1. **Segmentation:** Begin by segmenting your audiences based on relevant criteria such as demographics, behavior, and preferences. This segmentation allows for more targeted and meaningful communication that addresses the specific interests and needs of each group.
2. **Channel Preferences:** Identify and utilize the preferred communication channels for each segment. While clients may prefer direct emails or professional networking platforms, customers might be more engaged through social media or newsletters.
3. **Tone and Language:** Adjust the tone and language of your communications to suit the audience. Professional and technical language may be appropriate for B2B clients, whereas a more conversational and relatable tone might better engage B2C customers.
4. **Personalization:** Leverage data analytics to personalize communication at an individual level. Personalized messages, addressing recipients by name and referencing their past interactions or preferences, significantly enhance engagement.
5. **Feedback Mechanisms:** Incorporate opportunities for feedback into your communications. This not only

demonstrates that you value their input but also provides valuable insights for further customization.

Best Practices for Crafting Resonant Messages:

1. **Clarity and Conciseness:** Ensure your messages are clear and to the point. Avoid jargon or overly complex language that might obscure your message, especially when communicating with a broad customer base.
2. **Value Proposition:** Highlight the unique value proposition for each audience segment within your communication. Emphasize how your product or service addresses their specific challenges or goals.
3. **Consistent Branding:** While customizing messages, maintain consistent branding across all communications. This consistency reinforces brand recognition and trust among both clients and customers.
4. **Engaging Content:** Incorporate engaging elements such as stories, testimonials, or compelling visuals that relate to the audience's interests and experiences. This approach can significantly increase the impact and memorability of your messages.
5. **Timing and Frequency:** Optimize the timing and frequency of your communications based on audience

preferences and behaviors. Over-communicating can lead to disengagement, whereas too little contact may cause your message to be forgotten.

6. **Legal Compliance:** Always ensure that your communication strategies comply with relevant laws and regulations, such as GDPR for email communications. This is critical for maintaining trust and avoiding potential legal issues.

Customizing communication for diverse audiences is a critical component of successful engagement strategies. By understanding and addressing the distinct needs, preferences, and behaviors of clients and customers, businesses can craft messages that not only resonate more deeply but also drive meaningful engagement. Implementing the outlined strategies and best practices will enable organizations to communicate more effectively, fostering stronger relationships and driving sustainable growth in a competitive market landscape.

Section 7.5: Aligning Product Offerings with Engagement Strategies

The integration of product offerings with engagement strategies is a nuanced art that requires a deep understanding of both client and customer needs. This alignment ensures that products and services not only meet the expectations of diverse market segments but also resonate with them on a deeper level, enhancing satisfaction and loyalty. This section explores the importance of product alignment and provides strategies for adapting offerings based on feedback, fostering a culture of innovation that keeps pace with evolving demands.

Product Alignment:

Aligning product offerings with engagement strategies involves a deliberate and informed approach to product development and marketing. It requires businesses to:

1. **Understand Client and Customer Needs:** Deep dive into the specific needs, preferences, and pain points of

both clients and customers through market research, surveys, and direct feedback mechanisms.

2. **Segmentation:** Use segmentation to categorize your audience into distinct groups with similar needs and tailor your products and engagement strategies to each segment.

3. **Value Proposition:** Clearly articulate how your products or services address the unique needs of each segment, ensuring that your value proposition is communicated effectively across all engagement channels.

4. **Consistency Across Touchpoints:** Ensure that the messaging about your products or services is consistent across all customer touchpoints, from social media to customer service, reinforcing your value proposition.

Adaptation and Innovation:

Adapting and innovating product offerings based on feedback is crucial for maintaining relevance and competitiveness in the market.

1. **Feedback Loops:** Establish robust feedback loops that capture insights from both clients and customers. Use

this feedback to identify areas for product improvement or opportunities for new offerings.
2. **Agile Product Development:** Adopt an agile approach to product development, allowing for quick adaptation based on market feedback. This flexibility ensures that your offerings remain aligned with client and customer needs.
3. **Innovation Based on Insights:** Leverage the insights gained from engagement efforts to drive product innovation. Understanding emerging trends and changing preferences can inspire new features, services, or entirely new products.
4. **Cross-functional Collaboration:** Encourage collaboration between product development, marketing, sales, and customer service teams. This cross-functional approach ensures a holistic view of client and customer needs, informing better product alignment.
5. **Pilot Programs and Beta Testing:** Before a full-scale launch, test new products or features with a select group of clients and customers. This testing phase can provide valuable feedback and help fine-tune offerings.
6. **Communicate Changes and Enhancements:** When adaptations are made, communicate these changes back to your clients and customers. Highlighting how

feedback has been incorporated into product improvements reinforces the value you place on their input.

Aligning product offerings with engagement strategies is not a one-time effort but a continuous process of adaptation and innovation. By staying attuned to the needs and feedback of both clients and customers, businesses can ensure that their products not only meet but exceed expectations, driving deeper engagement and fostering long-term loyalty. In today's rapidly changing market landscape, the ability to adapt and innovate based on direct feedback is a powerful differentiator, positioning businesses for sustainable growth and success.

Section 7.6: Navigating Conflicts Between Client and Customer Needs

Balancing the needs and expectations of clients and customers is a delicate endeavor, fraught with potential conflicts that can challenge even the most customer-centric organizations. This section addresses common conflicts that arise between client and customer needs and provides strategic approaches for resolution, alongside frameworks to prioritize actions when interests diverge.

Conflict Resolution:

Identifying Common Conflicts:
- **Product Customization vs. Standardization:** Clients may demand customized solutions that conflict with the broader needs of the customer base seeking standardized products.
- **Pricing Strategies:** Conflicts can arise when clients seek preferential pricing that might undermine the perceived value among the wider customer base.
- **Resource Allocation:** Balancing the allocation of resources between servicing high-value clients and meeting the expectations of the larger customer pool can lead to conflicts.

Strategies for Resolution:
- **Transparent Communication:** Establish open lines of communication with both clients and customers. Transparency about the decision-making process can mitigate feelings of neglect or unfair treatment.

- **Compromise and Flexibility:** Seek compromise solutions that address the core needs of both parties. Flexibility in approach and offerings can often bridge the gap between conflicting needs.
- **Value-driven Decision Making:** Make decisions based on the long-term value to the business, considering both immediate financial impacts and the long-term relationships with clients and customers.
- **Feedback Loops:** Utilize feedback from both groups to inform adjustments and improvements. This input can provide a basis for understanding and resolving conflicts.

Prioritization Frameworks:

1. **Impact Analysis:** Evaluate the potential impact of each need on the business, including financial implications, brand reputation, and future growth opportunities. Prioritize actions that offer the most significant overall benefit.
2. **Stakeholder Mapping:** Identify and map the interests of all stakeholders, including both clients and customers.

Understanding the influence and interest of each group can guide prioritization and conflict resolution efforts.

3. **Cost-Benefit Analysis:** Conduct a cost-benefit analysis to assess the trade-offs of meeting specific needs. This analysis can help identify the most cost-effective path that maximizes benefits across the board.
4. **Scenario Planning:** Develop scenarios to explore the outcomes of different decision paths. Scenario planning can aid in visualizing the potential consequences and guiding more informed decisions.
5. **Decision Matrix:** Create a decision matrix that weighs the importance of various factors, including customer satisfaction, revenue potential, and alignment with strategic goals. This tool can help clarify which actions will best serve the organization's interests.

Navigating conflicts between client and customer needs requires a nuanced understanding of the value each group brings to the organization, coupled with strategic thinking and empathetic communication. By employing conflict resolution strategies and prioritization frameworks, businesses can make informed decisions that respect and address the diverse needs of their clientele while steering the organization towards sustainable growth. Ultimately, the goal is to foster an environment where both clients and customers feel valued, understood, and satisfied, thereby strengthening their loyalty and support for the business.

Section 7.7:

Achieving Strategic Harmony

As we conclude Chapter 7 of this book, it's paramount to underscore the significance of seamlessly integrating client and customer engagement strategies. This holistic approach is not merely a tactic but a strategic imperative that underpins the sustained growth and resilience of businesses in today's competitive landscape. This section encapsulates the core insights on achieving strategic harmony and extends a compelling call to action for businesses to embrace and cultivate this balance, ensuring enhanced engagement, satisfaction, and loyalty among both clients and customers.

Key Takeaways on Integrating Client and Customer Strategies:

1. **Unified Approach:** The integration of client and customer strategies fosters a unified approach to engagement, ensuring that all interactions are aligned with the overarching business goals and brand values.
2. **Enhanced Engagement:** By addressing the distinct needs and preferences of both clients and customers within a cohesive strategy, businesses can enhance the quality of engagement, driving deeper connections and loyalty.
3. **Increased Efficiency:** Strategic harmony allows for the optimization of resources, eliminating redundant efforts and focusing on initiatives that offer the highest return on investment across both segments.
4. **Agility and Responsiveness:** A balanced approach equips businesses with the agility to respond to market changes, client expectations, and customer feedback swiftly, maintaining relevance and competitive edge.
5. **Sustainable Growth:** Ultimately, the integration of client and customer engagement strategies supports sustainable growth, building a solid foundation of satisfied clients and customers who are more likely to advocate for the brand.

Call to Action:

Mastering the Market: A Dual Approach to Client and Customer Engagement

In the quest for sustainable business success, the harmonization of client and customer engagement strategies emerges as a cornerstone. Businesses are urged to:

- **Embrace a Holistic View:** Look beyond the traditional silos of client and customer management. Understand that the synergy between these strategies can unlock new opportunities for growth and innovation.
- **Invest in Understanding:** Commit to ongoing research and analysis to deepen your understanding of both client and customer needs. This insight is crucial for tailoring engagement strategies that resonate on a personal level.
- **Foster Flexibility:** Cultivate an organizational culture that values flexibility and adaptability. The ability to adjust strategies in response to feedback and market dynamics is key to maintaining strategic harmony.
- **Leverage Technology:** Utilize technology not just as a tool for efficiency, but as a means to gain insights, personalize engagement, and streamline communication across all touchpoints.
- **Measure and Refine:** Continuously measure the impact of your integrated strategies on business outcomes. Use these insights to refine and enhance your approach,

always with an eye toward greater alignment and efficiency.
- **Seek Feedback:** Encourage and prioritize feedback from both clients and customers. This feedback is a valuable resource for adjusting strategies and ensuring that your efforts are effectively meeting the needs of all stakeholders.

Achieving strategic harmony between client and customer engagement strategies is an ongoing journey, marked by continuous learning, adaptation, and innovation. By embracing this integrated approach, businesses can ensure not only the satisfaction and loyalty of their current clientele but also pave the way for future growth and success. The balance between client and customer needs is not a static goal but a dynamic equilibrium, constantly shifting in response to changes in the market, technology, and consumer behavior. In this ever-evolving landscape, the commitment to strategic harmony stands as a beacon for businesses aiming to thrive in the complex world of modern commerce.

Chapter 7: Step-By Step How to "Get... It... Done!"

Dive into the heart of your business's engagement strategy—balancing the scales between client and customer needs. Here's how you thread that needle without breaking a sweat.

Section 7.1: Balancing Act Blueprint

Step 1: Segment Smackdown

- **Task:** Slice and dice your audience. Know who's who in the zoo—clients vs. customers.
- **Deadline:** 1 Week.

Step 2: Unified Messaging Strategy

- **Task:** Whip up a communication plan that sings the same tune across all fronts but hits the right notes for each segment.
- **Deadline:** 2 Weeks.

Step 3: Feedback Loop Lockdown

- **Task:** Install a feedback collection beast mode—make it easy, make it actionable.
- **Deadline:** Continuous with monthly check-ins.

Section 7.2: Hybrid Engagement Hustle
Step 1: Opportunity Overhaul
- **Task:** Hunt down chances to merge client and customer engagement without stepping on toes.
- **Deadline:** 2 Weeks.

Step 2: Team Takedown
- **Task:** Assemble an Avengers-level squad from across departments to brainstorm and implement hybrid tactics.
- **Deadline:** 1 Week for formation, ongoing for operations.

Step 3: Strategy Scrutiny
- **Task:** Keep a hawk-eye on those hybrid models—what's working, what's not, and why.
- **Deadline:** Bi-monthly review cycle.

Section 7.3: Data-Driven Dance
Step 1: Analytics Arsenal
- **Task:** Gear up with the best analytics tools money can buy—or at least the best you can afford.
- **Deadline:** 1 Month for setup and integration.

Step 2: Customized Combat
- **Task:** Tailor your engagement weapons based on intel from the data frontlines.

- **Deadline:** Ongoing, with quarterly strategy adjustments.

Step 3: Privacy and Ethics Patrol
- **Task:** Guard your data like Fort Knox. Transparency, consent, security—no exceptions.
- **Deadline:** Yesterday, today, tomorrow—always.

Section 7.4: Communication Command Center
Step 1: Audience Deep Dive
- **Task:** Get to know your segments like the back of your hand—channel preferences, content cravings, all of it.
- **Deadline:** 2 Weeks.

Step 2: Content Cannon
- **Task:** Fire off engaging, tailored content across all channels. Make every shot count.
- **Deadline:** Monthly content calendar with weekly executions.

Step 3: Time and Frequency Fine-Tuning
- **Task:** Dial in the when and how often. Keep tabs on what rhythm gets your audience grooving.
- **Deadline:** Ongoing, with monthly adjustments.

Section 7.5: Product Alignment Assault
Step 1: Needs Matchup

- **Task:** Ensure your products/services fit like a glove with client and customer needs.
- **Deadline:** 1 Month for initial review, then ongoing tweaks.

Step 2: Feedback Fusion
- **Task:** Turn customer and client feedback into your product development fuel.
- **Deadline:** Ongoing, with bi-monthly review sessions.

Step 3: Alignment Announcement
- **Task:** Shout from the rooftops how feedback has shaped your offerings.
- **Deadline:** After every significant product update or release.

Section 7.6: Conflict Conquer
Step 1: Conflict Identification
- **Task:** Sniff out potential clashes between client and customer needs like a bloodhound.
- **Deadline:** Ongoing vigilance.

Step 2: Resolution Roadmap
- **Task:** Map out a peace plan for every potential skirmish.
- **Deadline:** 2 Weeks to develop, then adapt as needed.

Step 3: Prioritization Protocol

- **Task:** When push comes to shove, know who and what gets saved first.
- **Deadline:** 1 Week to establish, with quarterly reviews.

Section 7.7: Harmony Hero

Step 1: Strategy Symphony
- **Task:** Tune your engagement strategies to play in perfect harmony.
- **Deadline:** 1 Month for comprehensive strategy overhaul.

Step 2: Innovation Incubator
- **Task:** Make flexibility and innovation your team's modus operandi.
- **Deadline:** Kick-off within 2 Weeks, then build into your DNA.

Step 3: Success Showcase
- **Task:** Measure, monitor, and magnify your wins in balancing client and customer engagement.
- **Deadline:** Set baseline metrics within 1 Month, then celebrate quarterly.

Lock in on these actions to master the art of engagement in a way that resonates across the board. It's about striking the right chord with every message, every product, and every interaction. Get it done, and watch your business sing.

Welbon Omar Salaam

Chapter 8 Pre-Breakdown: No Fluff, Just Facts

Section 8.1: Cut the BS: Communication Musts

Let's get real about talking to your audience. It's not rocket science, but you've got to hit these marks if you want anyone to listen up.

- **Be Clear and Quick:** Don't beat around the bush. Get to the point before they scroll away.
- **Stay Relevant:** Talk about what matters to them, not just what you want to push.
- **Keep It Consistent:** Your brand voice shouldn't have an identity crisis across platforms.
- **Show You Get Them:** Throw in a dash of empathy to show you understand their pains and joys.
- **Invite the Talkback:** Make it a two-way street. Encourage reactions, responses, and feedback.
- **Be Ready to Pivot:** Locked and loaded plans are great until they're not. Adapt based on what the crowd tells you.

Section 8.2: Messaging That Fits the Platform

Your message needs to shape-shift to fit where you're posting it. Here's the lowdown on not sounding like a square peg in a round hole on different digital platforms.

Real Talk on Platform Mastery:

- **Twitter:** Keep it snappy. Hashtags are your friends but don't go #Overboard.
- **Instagram:** It's all about the visuals. Make it pretty or go home.
- **LinkedIn:** Suit up. Keep it professional and insightful.
- **Facebook:** It's the all-rounder. Mix up your content but keep it engaging.

Section 8.3: Breaking Down the Walls: Overcoming Communication Barriers

Stuff gets in the way of your message getting through. Here's how to bulldoze those barriers down.

- **Cultural Clashes:** Know your audience's backgrounds to avoid faux pas.
- **Language Barriers:** Keep it simple or get a translator.
- **Info Overload:** Don't be the needle in the haystack. Make your message stand out.
- **Tech Troubles:** Use tech that works for your audience, not against them.

- **Bias:** Check your and their biases at the door.

Section 8.4: Storytelling: Your Secret Weapon

People love a good story. Use that to your advantage to make your brand stick in their minds.

Epic Wins with Storytelling:

- **Find Your Saga:** What's your brand's story? Drill down to the core.
- **Keep It Real:** Authenticity wins. No one likes a try-hard.
- **Make Them the Hero:** Show how your brand plays a part in their journey.
- **Conflict is Good:** Show the problem, be the solution.
- **Visuals + Emotions = Gold:** Make them feel and see your story.

Section 8.5: Listen Up: Fine-Tuning Your Message with Feedback

Feedback isn't just noise—it's gold. Here's how to mine it for all it's worth to sharpen your message.

Feedback Finesse:

- **Survey the Scene:** Regular check-ins with your crowd keep you in tune.
- **Social Listening:** What's the word on the virtual street about you?

- **Focus Groups:** Get the dirt straight from the horse's mouth.
- **Customer Service Chats:** Complaints and praises are the real deal. Listen up.
- **A/B Testing:** What works better? There's only one way to find out.

Section 8.6: Staying on the Right Side: Ethical Messaging

Don't be that guy. Keep your messaging above board and out of the shady zones.

Keeping It Clean:

- **Know the Rules:** Ignorance ain't bliss. Stay updated on laws and regulations.
- **Full Disclosure:** Sponsored post? Say so.
- **Respect Privacy:** Don't be creepy with data.
- **Truth in Advertising:** If your product can't do it, don't say it can.
- **Cultural Sensitivity:** Don't step on toes; understand where your audience is coming from.

Section 8.7: Mastering the Message

Bottom line: Your message is everything. Nail it, and you're golden. Miss the mark, and you're just another voice in the chaos.

Essentials for Messaging Mastery:

- **Elevate Communication:** Make it part of your strategy, not an afterthought.
- **Ethics Aren't Optional:** Do the right thing, always.
- **Customize and Personalize:** Speak directly to their soul (well, almost).
- **Stay Educated:** Keep up with the digital Joneses.
- **Tech is Your Friend:** Use it to make your message clearer, louder, and more personal.
- **Feedback is a Gift:** Use it to make your next message even better.

Get these right, and you're not just talking; you're communicating. And in today's world, that's the key to everything.

Chapter 8: Buckle up, nerds! Time to READ. Al successo! (To Success!)

- Italian, with a side of pasta and achievements.

Section 8.1: Principles of Effective Communication

In the complex tapestry of modern business, effective communication stands as the cornerstone of successful engagement with diverse audiences. This section delves into the foundational principles for crafting messages that not only engage but also resonate deeply with every segment of your audience. By understanding and applying these key insights, businesses can develop a communication strategy that bridges the gap between company objectives and audience needs, fostering a connection that transcends mere transactions.

Key Insights on Foundational Principles of Communication:

1. **Clarity and Conciseness:** The essence of your message should be clear and straightforward, avoiding ambiguity that could lead to misinterpretation. Conciseness ensures that the message is digestible, respecting the audience's time and attention span.
2. **Relevance:** Tailor your messages to align with the interests, needs, and challenges of your audience. Relevance is the magnet that draws attention and fosters engagement.
3. **Consistency:** Maintaining a consistent tone, style, and message across all communication channels reinforces your brand identity and builds trust with your audience.
4. **Empathy:** Demonstrating understanding and consideration for the audience's perspective creates an emotional connection, making your messages more impactful.
5. **Engagement:** Encourage two-way communication by inviting feedback, questions, or interactions. Engagement transforms passive receivers into active participants in the conversation.
6. **Adaptability:** Be prepared to adjust your communication strategy based on feedback, audience analytics, and changing market dynamics. Flexibility ensures continued relevance and effectiveness.

Actionable Strategies for Effective Communication:

1. **Segment Your Audience:** Identify and segment your audience based on demographics, psychographics, and behavior. This segmentation allows for more targeted and relevant messaging.
2. **Develop Key Messages:** Craft key messages that encapsulate your value proposition and differentiators. Ensure these messages are adaptable to suit various audience segments while maintaining a core consistent theme.
3. **Choose the Right Channels:** Select communication channels based on where your audience segments are most active and receptive. The choice of channel can significantly impact the effectiveness of your message.
4. **Create a Content Calendar:** Plan your communication efforts using a content calendar. This tool helps ensure regular and timely interactions with your audience, keeping your brand top of mind.
5. **Leverage Storytelling:** Incorporate storytelling into your communication strategy. Stories are powerful vehicles for conveying complex ideas in an engaging and memorable way.

6. **Measure and Iterate:** Continuously measure the impact of your communication efforts through analytics and feedback. Use these insights to refine and improve your strategy over time.
7. **Train Your Team:** Ensure that everyone involved in communication efforts understands these principles and is equipped to apply them. Consistency in execution across the team amplifies the effectiveness of your strategy.

The principles of effective communication are universal, yet their application must be tailored to the unique contours of your audience. By embedding clarity, relevance, consistency, empathy, engagement, and adaptability into your communication strategy, you can speak effectively to all segments of your audience, driving engagement and building lasting relationships. In the rapidly evolving landscape of customer and client engagement, mastering the art of communication is not just an advantage—it's a necessity.

Section 8.2: Tailoring Messages Across Platforms

In the digital age, the capacity to tailor messages across various platforms is crucial for engaging diverse audiences effectively. This section highlights exemplary businesses that have mastered platform-specific messaging and offers strategic guidelines for adapting content to meet the unique context and audience of each digital platform. Through understanding these nuances, businesses can maximize their engagement and resonance with target demographics.

Case Studies of Platform-Specific Messaging Excellence:

- **Technology Giant on Twitter:** A leading technology company uses Twitter to provide quick updates, tech support, and engage in real-time conversations with its audience. Their strategy includes using hashtags for trending topics, which amplifies their reach and engagement.
- **Fashion Retailer on Instagram:** A high-end fashion retailer leverages Instagram to showcase their latest collections through visually captivating posts and stories. They use Instagram's shopping feature to directly link products, making it easy for customers to purchase items they see.

- **Financial Services on LinkedIn:** A financial services firm excels in using LinkedIn for sharing industry insights, reports, and thought leadership articles. Their content is tailored to professionals seeking to enhance their industry knowledge, positioning the firm as an authoritative source.

Platform Strategies: Guidelines for Adapting Messages:

1. **Understand Platform Dynamics:** Each social media platform has its own set of unwritten rules and audience expectations. Understanding these can guide the tone, format, and type of content that will be most effective.
2. **Visuals for Instagram and Pinterest:** Use high-quality, visually appealing images or videos that capture attention and tell a story. These platforms are highly visual and content should be designed to stand out in a crowded feed.
3. **Conciseness for Twitter:** Twitter's character limit requires messages to be concise and impactful. Use clear language and incorporate trending hashtags to increase visibility and engagement.
4. **Professionalism for LinkedIn:** Content on LinkedIn should be more professional and informative, focusing

on industry insights, company achievements, and professional development topics.

5. **Interactivity on Facebook:** Utilize Facebook's features such as polls, live videos, and events to foster community and encourage interaction. Tailor messages to be conversational and community-oriented.

6. **Adapt Tone and Language:** Adjust the tone and language of your messages to fit the platform and its predominant audience. A casual, playful tone may work well on Instagram but not on LinkedIn.

7. **Optimize for Search and Discovery:** Use keywords, hashtags, and tagging on platforms like YouTube and Instagram to enhance discoverability. Understanding SEO principles for each platform can significantly increase your content's reach.

8. **Engagement Monitoring:** Pay close attention to how your audience interacts with your content across platforms. Use these insights to continually refine and tailor your messaging strategy.

9. **Platform-Specific Calls to Action:** Customize your calls to action based on the platform and the desired audience action. Whether it's encouraging comments, shares, or clicks to your website, make sure your CTA is clear and compelling.

Tailoring messages across platforms is not just about altering content; it's about embracing and reflecting the unique culture and audience of each digital space. By studying successful case studies and adhering to platform-specific guidelines, businesses can craft messages that not only reach but deeply resonate with their intended audiences. This strategic approach to communication ensures that every interaction is meaningful, enhancing overall engagement and bolstering the brand's presence across the digital landscape.

Section 8.3: Overcoming Communication Barriers

Effective communication is the keystone of successful client and customer engagement, yet various barriers can impede this process, diluting messages and reducing their impact. Identifying these common barriers and implementing strategies to overcome them is crucial for businesses aiming to ensure their messaging is clear, impactful, and resonant. This section explores the challenges inherent in messaging across diverse platforms and audiences, alongside offering actionable solutions to navigate and dismantle these obstacles.

Challenges in Messaging: Common Communication Barriers

1. **Cultural Differences:** Variations in cultural backgrounds can lead to misunderstandings or misinterpretations of messages, especially in global markets.
2. **Language Barriers:** Even subtle differences in language use, idioms, or jargon can alienate parts of the audience or obscure the intended meaning.
3. **Overload of Information:** In an era of information overload, capturing and retaining the audience's attention becomes increasingly challenging.
4. **Technological Hurdles:** Inadequate or incompatible technology can hinder the delivery and reception of messages, especially in digital communications.
5. **Perceptual Biases:** Preexisting perceptions or biases can color the reception of messages, leading to resistance or disengagement.

Overcoming Barriers: Strategies for Clear, Impactful Messaging

1. **Embrace Cultural Sensitivity:** Research and understand the cultural nuances of your audience. Tailor

your messages to be culturally relevant and respectful, avoiding generalizations or stereotypes.

2. **Simplify Language:** Use clear, concise language and avoid industry jargon when communicating with a broader audience. For multilingual communications, consider professional translations to ensure accuracy.

3. **Prioritize and Streamline Information:** Focus on delivering value-packed messages that are direct and to the point. Use bullet points, headings, and visual aids to break down information and facilitate easier comprehension.

4. **Leverage Appropriate Technology:** Choose communication platforms and technologies that are accessible and familiar to your audience. Ensure content is optimized for different devices, particularly mobile.

5. **Address Perceptual Biases:** Acknowledge and directly address potential biases that may influence how your messages are received. Use testimonials, endorsements, or data to build credibility and trust.

6. **Feedback Loops:** Incorporate mechanisms for receiving and analyzing feedback on your communications. This direct insight can help identify and address barriers in real-time.

7. **Personalization:** Tailor messages to meet the specific interests and needs of your audience segments. Personalization enhances relevance and engagement, breaking through the noise of generic messaging.
8. **Continuous Education:** Educate your audience about your products, services, and industry trends. Knowledge helps to break down barriers of misunderstanding and builds a foundation for clearer communication.
9. **Empathy in Messaging:** Craft your messages with empathy, considering the audience's perspective, challenges, and needs. Empathetic messaging fosters a stronger connection and opens the door to more effective communication.

Overcoming communication barriers requires a multifaceted approach that combines cultural sensitivity, linguistic clarity, technological savvy, and perceptual awareness. By identifying and strategically addressing these challenges, businesses can ensure their messages not only reach their intended audiences but also resonate deeply, prompting engagement and action. As the landscape of client and customer interaction continues to evolve, so too must the strategies to ensure clear, impactful, and effective communication.

Section 8.4: The Role of Storytelling in Engagement

Storytelling, an ancient art form, has found its place at the heart of modern business strategies, acting as a powerful tool for building deeper connections with clients and customers. This section explores how businesses have successfully leveraged storytelling to enhance their engagement efforts and offers practical techniques for weaving compelling narratives into your communication strategy.

Storytelling Case Studies:

- **Outdoor Apparel Brand:** An outdoor apparel company shared stories of adventurers and conservationists who use their products, emphasizing the brand's commitment to sustainability and adventure. This storytelling approach not only showcased their apparel in action but also aligned the brand with the values and aspirations of their audience.
- **Tech Startup:** A tech startup utilized storytelling to demystify their complex product for a non-technical audience. By narrating the journey of their product

development and the real-life challenges it solves, they made their technology relatable and accessible.
- **Non-Profit Organization:** A non-profit leveraged storytelling to highlight the impact of donations, sharing personal stories of individuals and communities transformed by their work. These narratives fostered emotional connections and motivated action among supporters.

Crafting Your Story: Techniques for Incorporating Storytelling into Your Communication Strategy:

1. **Identify Your Core Narrative:** Every brand has a unique story. Identify yours by reflecting on your company's history, mission, and the challenges you've overcome. This narrative should be the foundation of your storytelling strategy.
2. **Emphasize Authenticity:** Authentic stories resonate more deeply with audiences. Share genuine experiences and lessons learned, showing vulnerability where appropriate. Authenticity builds trust and fosters a genuine connection.
3. **Use Characters Your Audience Can Relate To:** Incorporate characters or personas in your stories that

reflect your audience's demographics, challenges, and aspirations. Relatable characters make your story more engaging and memorable.

4. **Incorporate Conflict and Resolution:** Good stories involve a conflict or challenge and a resolution. Highlighting how your products or services have helped overcome a particular problem can illustrate their value in a compelling way.

5. **Employ Visuals and Emotions:** Enhance your stories with visuals, such as images, videos, or infographics. Emotional appeals can significantly increase engagement, making your message stick.

6. **Adapt Stories for Different Platforms:** Tailor your stories to fit the format and audience of each platform. A detailed story might work well on your blog, while a succinct version could be more appropriate for social media.

7. **Encourage User-Generated Stories:** Invite your clients and customers to share their own stories related to your brand. User-generated content not only provides authentic narratives but also deepens community engagement.

8. **Measure and Refine:** Track the impact of your storytelling efforts through engagement metrics,

feedback, and conversion rates. Use these insights to refine your approach and narratives.

The role of storytelling in engagement cannot be overstated. By turning to storytelling, businesses can transcend traditional marketing tactics, creating emotional resonance and fostering a deeper connection with their audience. The case studies and techniques presented here offer a blueprint for integrating storytelling into your communication strategy, enabling your brand to captivate, engage, and inspire action across all customer and client interactions. In the dynamic landscape of market engagement, storytelling emerges as a timeless tool, weaving the fabric of human experience into the heart of brand narratives.

Section 8.5:
Feedback Mechanisms for Message Refinement

In the realm of client and customer engagement, the ability to listen and adapt based on feedback is as crucial as the initial message itself. Establishing effective feedback loops allows businesses to refine and adjust their messaging, ensuring it resonates more deeply and effectively with their audience. This section explores the strategic utilization of customer feedback for message refinement and outlines practical implementation strategies for collecting and acting on this invaluable input.

Feedback Loops: Utilizing Customer Feedback to Refine and Adjust Messaging

Feedback loops create a dynamic process where businesses can continuously learn from and respond to their audience's reactions and preferences. This iterative approach not only enhances the relevance and impact of communication efforts but also fosters a sense of being heard and valued among clients and customers, strengthening relationships and loyalty.

Implementation Strategies:

1. **Surveys and Questionnaires:** Regularly distribute surveys and questionnaires to gather direct feedback on your communication efforts. Tailor questions to uncover insights on message clarity, relevance, and emotional impact.
2. **Social Media Listening:** Employ social media listening tools to monitor mentions of your brand, products, and

services. Analyzing comments, shares, and engagement can provide a wealth of feedback on public perception and the effectiveness of your messaging.

3. **Focus Groups:** Conduct focus groups with segments of your target audience to dive deeper into their perceptions and reactions to your messaging. This qualitative approach can uncover nuanced insights that surveys may miss.

4. **Customer Service Interactions:** Leverage customer service interactions as a feedback channel. Train customer service representatives to document comments related to messaging and communication effectiveness.

5. **Analytics and Metrics:** Utilize analytics tools to measure engagement, conversion rates, and other key metrics tied to your communication efforts. Data trends can indicate areas where message refinement is needed.

6. **Feedback Widgets:** Incorporate feedback widgets on your website and in your emails. These tools allow for easy, on-the-spot feedback from clients and customers engaging with your content.

7. **A/B Testing:** Conduct A/B testing on various elements of your messaging, including headlines, calls to action,

and content formats. Comparing performance between versions can guide more effective messaging strategies.

8. **Community Forums:** Encourage discussion and feedback within community forums or on your social media platforms. Active engagement with your audience in these spaces can provide direct insights into their preferences and perceptions.

9. **Acting on Feedback:** Establish a system for regularly reviewing feedback and implementing changes based on insights gathered. Prioritize adjustments that align with your strategic goals and have the potential for the greatest impact on engagement.

10. **Communicate Changes:** Once refinements are made, communicate back to your audience about the changes implemented based on their feedback. This transparency reinforces the value you place on their input and encourages continued engagement and feedback sharing.

Feedback mechanisms are integral to refining messaging and enhancing communication effectiveness. By actively listening to and acting on customer and client feedback, businesses can ensure their messaging remains dynamic, relevant, and impactful. Implementing the strategies outlined above not only improves the quality of communication but also deepens the relationship between businesses and their audiences, fostering a collaborative environment where feedback is valued and utilized for mutual benefit. In the ever-evolving landscape of market engagement, the ability to adapt based on direct feedback is a powerful tool for sustained success and growth.

Section 8.6: Ethical Messaging: Navigating Legal and Ethical Aspects of Marketing Communication

Navigating the legal and ethical aspects of marketing communication is a critical responsibility for any business striving to maintain trust and credibility with its audience. As digital platforms evolve and consumer awareness increases, the importance of ethical messaging and compliance with relevant laws cannot be overstated. This section delves into the strategies businesses can employ to ensure their messaging is both legally compliant and ethically sound, fostering a culture of integrity and respect in all communications.

Ethical messaging goes beyond mere legal compliance; it involves communicating with honesty, transparency, and respect for the audience's rights and dignity. It means avoiding misleading claims, respecting privacy, and acknowledging the impact of your messages on the broader social and environmental context.

Compliance Strategies: Ensuring Adherence to Laws and Ethical Standards

1. **Familiarize with Regulations:** Stay informed about the latest in marketing and advertising laws, including regulations related to privacy (such as GDPR in Europe and CCPA in California), anti-spam laws (like CAN-SPAM Act), and industry-specific guidelines.
2. **Transparent Disclosure:** Ensure that any partnerships, sponsorships, or affiliate relationships are clearly disclosed in your messaging. Transparency is crucial in maintaining trust and avoiding accusations of misleading your audience.
3. **Respect for Privacy:** Implement robust data protection measures to safeguard your audience's personal

information. Obtain consent before collecting data, and provide clear options for opting out of communication.
4. **Avoid Misleading Claims:** Ensure all claims made in your messaging are verifiable and supported by evidence. Misleading claims can damage your brand reputation and lead to legal consequences.
5. **Cultural Sensitivity:** Be mindful of cultural differences and strive for inclusivity in your messaging. Avoid stereotypes and ensure your communication is respectful and considerate of diverse audiences.
6. **Ethical Use of Data:** Use audience data responsibly to personalize and target your messaging. Avoid invasive or manipulative tactics that could erode trust or infringe on personal boundaries.
7. **Continuous Education:** Keep your team informed about ethical and legal standards in communication. Regular training sessions can help prevent inadvertent violations and foster a culture of ethical awareness.
8. **Legal Consultation:** When in doubt, consult with legal professionals specializing in marketing and advertising law. This can help avoid potential legal pitfalls and ensure your messaging strategy is fully compliant.
9. **Feedback Mechanisms:** Implement mechanisms for receiving and addressing concerns or complaints related

to your messaging. Being responsive to feedback demonstrates your commitment to ethical practices.

10. **Review and Audit:** Regularly review your communication materials and practices to ensure they align with legal requirements and ethical standards. Audits can help identify areas for improvement and prevent potential issues.

Legal and ethical considerations in communication are not just regulatory hurdles; they are opportunities to demonstrate your business's values and commitment to doing what's right. By adopting comprehensive compliance strategies and prioritizing ethical messaging, businesses can build deeper trust and loyalty with their audience, setting a foundation for long-term success. In the dynamic landscape of marketing communication, a commitment to legal compliance and ethical integrity is a powerful differentiator that can elevate your brand above the competition.

Section 8.7:
Mastering the Art of Messaging

As we conclude Chapter 8 of this book, it's paramount to underscore the transformative power of effective communication. The art of messaging extends far beyond the mere transmission of information; it's about building connections, inspiring action, and fostering deep, lasting relationships with diverse audiences. This final section recaps the essential role that strategic, clear, and ethical communication plays in the realm of business and issues a call to action for businesses to place messaging at the heart of their strategic endeavors.

Key Takeaways on the Critical Role of Effective Communication:

1. **Foundation for Engagement:** Effective communication is the foundation upon which meaningful engagement with clients and customers is built, enabling businesses to resonate with diverse audiences on a profound level.
2. **Driver of Connection:** Through tailored and compelling messaging, businesses can transcend traditional barriers, creating emotional connections that drive loyalty and advocacy.

3. **Enhancer of Brand Perception:** Clear, consistent, and authentic communication enhances brand perception, establishing trust and credibility in the market.
4. **Facilitator of Adaptation:** Strategic communication enables businesses to adapt swiftly to changing market dynamics, audience needs, and feedback, ensuring relevance and competitiveness.
5. **Guardian of Ethical Standards:** Commitment to ethical messaging underscores a business's dedication to integrity, fostering a culture of transparency and respect that appeals to both clients and customers.

Call to Action: Prioritizing Clear, Compelling, and Ethical Communication

In the journey toward mastering the market, the strategic integration of clear, compelling, and ethical communication is not optional—it's imperative. Businesses are called upon to:

- **Elevate Messaging Strategy:** Recognize communication as a strategic asset. Invest in developing messaging that is not only clear and compelling but also deeply aligned with your brand values and audience expectations.

- **Embrace Ethical Practices:** Commit to the highest standards of ethical communication. Ensure that your messaging is honest, transparent, and respectful, reflecting your brand's integrity.
- **Adapt and Personalize:** Leverage insights and feedback to continually adapt and personalize your messaging. The ability to speak directly to the individual needs and preferences of your audience sets your brand apart.
- **Foster Inclusivity:** Craft messages that embrace and reflect the diversity of your audience. Inclusivity in communication not only broadens your reach but also enriches your brand's relationship with its community.
- **Leverage Technology:** Utilize the latest technological tools to enhance the effectiveness and reach of your messaging. From analytics to automation, technology offers unparalleled opportunities to refine and amplify your communication efforts.
- **Educate and Train:** Ensure your team understands the importance of strategic communication. Regular training on best practices and ethical standards will empower them to contribute effectively to your messaging goals.

Mastering the art of messaging is a journey marked by continuous learning, adaptation, and commitment to excellence. By prioritizing strategic, clear, and ethical communication, businesses can navigate the complexities of engaging diverse audiences, turning challenges into opportunities for connection and growth. In the ever-evolving landscape of client and customer engagement, the mastery of messaging emerges as a cornerstone of success, driving meaningful interactions, deepening loyalty, and paving the way for a future where every voice is heard, and every message matters.

Chapter 8: Step-By Step How to "Get... It... Done!"

Let's cut through the noise. In the digital age, your voice needs to not just be heard; it needs to resonate, connect, and inspire action. Here's how you turn your communication from background static into a clear, compelling broadcast.

Section 8.1: Communication Command Center
Step 1: Communication Clean-Up
- **Task:** Rip through your current channels. What's muddy? Clarify. What's inconsistent? Align.
- **Timeline:** 1 Week.

Step 2: Feedback Frontline
- **Task:** Open the floodgates for feedback. Surveys, social listening—get the good, the bad, and the ugly.
- **Timeline:** 2 Weeks.

Step 3: Team Training Tactics
- **Task:** Get your team on the same page—clear, concise, and empathetic communication.
- **Timeline:** 3 Weeks.

Section 8.2: Message Mastery
Step 1: Platform Recon
- **Task:** Scout out each digital platform. What works where? Instagram loves visuals; LinkedIn loves insights.
- **Timeline:** 1 Week.

Step 2: Content Crafting
- **Task:** Tailor your tales. Each platform gets its flavor of your brand story.

- **Timeline:** Ongoing, with weekly schedules.

Step 3: Engagement Evaluation
- **Task:** Watch what they do, not what they say. Track likes, shares, comments—adjust fire accordingly.
- **Timeline:** Monthly analytics dive.

Section 8.3: Barrier Breakdown

Step 1: Barrier Identification
- **Task:** List out the communication walls. Language barriers? Technical jargon?
- **Timeline:** 1 Week.

Step 2: Strategy Siege
- **Task:** Each barrier gets a breach plan. Simplify, translate, elucidate.
- **Timeline:** 2 Weeks.

Step 3: Implementation and Intel
- **Task:** Roll out changes, keep ears to the ground. Is the message getting through?
- **Timeline:** Continuous monitoring.

Section 8.4: Storytelling Squadron

Step 1: Narrative Nexus
- **Task:** What's your saga? Sharpen it—make it relatable, authentic, irresistible.
- **Timeline:** 2 Weeks.

Step 2: Cross-Platform Chronicle
- **Task:** Weave your narrative thread through every digital tapestry you've got.
- **Timeline:** Ongoing, integrated into content calendar.

Step 3: User-Generated Galvanization

- **Task:** Get them telling their stories. Hashtags, contests—make it a movement.
- **Timeline:** Quarterly campaigns.

Section 8.5: Feedback Loop Front

Step 1: Feedback Channels
- **Task:** Make it easy for them to talk back. Comment sections, feedback forms—open the gates.
- **Timeline:** Setup in 1 Week.

Step 2: Feedback Frenzy
- **Task:** Dive into the feedback. Find patterns, insights, gold.
- **Timeline:** Bi-weekly reviews.

Step 3: Actionable Adjustments
- **Task:** Take that gold, make changes. Show them you're listening.
- **Timeline:** Implement changes within 1 Month of insight.

Section 8.6: Ethical Engagement

Step 1: Legal and Ethical Lighthouse
- **Task:** Know the rules. Privacy laws, transparency requirements—make sure you're above board.
- **Timeline:** Review every 6 Months.

Step 2: Compliance Compass
- **Task:** Regular checks and balances. Keep your communication clean and compliant.
- **Timeline:** Quarterly audits.

Step 3: Ethical Elevation
- **Task:** Build a team that values integrity in every message.

- **Timeline:** Ongoing training and discussion.

Section 8.7: Communication Conquest

Step 1: Strategic Synthesis
- **Task:** Your communication game is now lethal. Make sure every message hits with impact.
- **Timeline:** Immediate implementation, with ongoing optimization.

Step 2: Tech-Enhanced Transmission
- **Task:** Deploy the digital arsenal. Analytics, automation, AI—make your messages smarter, faster, more personal.
- **Timeline:** Start integrating new tools within 3 Months.

Step 3: Never-Ending Narrative
- **Task:** The digital world spins fast. Keep pace with continuous learning, adapting, and evolving.
- **Timeline:** Forever. This is your new normal.

By slicing through the complexity and getting straight to the heart of effective communication, you'll not only capture attention but also cultivate genuine connections and drive action. Ready, set, communicate.

Chapter 9 Pre-Breakdown: No Fluff, Just Facts

Section 9.1: The Real Deal on Digital Platforms

Digital platforms are your golden ticket to scaling up, reaching out, and locking in your audience. Here's cutting straight to the chase on using these platforms to fuel your growth.

Straight Talk on Growth:

- **Customer Grabbing:** Use social media and online ads to pull in your crowd.
- **Engagement:** Keep them hooked with killer content on social media.
- **Loyalty:** Emails aren't dead. Use them to keep your customers close.
- **Global Selling:** E-commerce platforms are your ticket to worldwide sales.
- **Smart Decisions:** Use data analytics to sharpen your game.

Section 9.2: Website Magic for User Engagement

Your website is your digital storefront. Make it count. Here's how to ensure it grabs attention, engages visitors, and keeps them coming back for more.

Real-World Wins:
- **Simplify Navigation:** If they can't find it, they won't buy it.
- **Speed It Up:** Slow load times kill sales.
- **Content is King:** Make it valuable and make it count.
- **Mobile-Friendly:** Everyone's on their phones. Make sure your site works there too.
- **SEO:** Get on Google's good side. It's how people find you.

Section 9.3: Social Media - Your Engagement Powerhouse

Social media is where your brand comes to life. It's not just about posting; it's about connecting. Here's how to use it to its full potential.

Winning Strategies:

- **Know Your Audience:** Who are they? What do they want? Be there.
- **Content Calendar:** Plan your attack. Consistency is key.
- **Engage:** Talk to them, not at them. Social media is a two-way street.
- **Leverage Influencers:** Their voice can amplify yours.
- **Analyze & Adapt:** Keep what works, ditch what doesn't.

Section 9.4: Email Marketing - Don't Underestimate Its Power

Think email's dead? Think again. It's personal, direct, and effective. Here's how to make it work for you.

Campaigns That Convert:
- **Segmentation:** Tailor your messages. Personal touches go a long way.
- **Catchy Subject Lines:** Get them to actually open those emails.
- **Value:** Always offer something useful. No one likes spam.
- **Mobile Optimization:** Yep, they're reading on their phones here too.
- **Test Everything:** What works today might not tomorrow. Stay sharp.

Section 9.5: SEO - Be Seen or Be Invisible

Visibility is the name of the game, and SEO is how you play. Here's how to climb to the top of those search results and stay there.

Success Stories:

- **Keywords:** Know what your customers are searching for.
- **Quality Content:** Help your customers, and Google will help you.
- **User Experience:** Make your site a joy to visit.
- **Mobile Optimization:** Again, because everyone's on their phones.
- **Backlinks:** Get reputable sites to link to you. It's like a vote of confidence.

Section 9.6: Data - Your Blueprint for Improvement

If you're not analyzing your digital performance, you're flying blind. Here's how to use data to make informed decisions and keep your strategies sharp.

Insights to Action:
- **Set Benchmarks:** Know where you're starting from.
- **Implement Changes:** Use data to guide your tweaks and transformations.
- **Monitor Results:** See what's working and what's not.
- **Learn & Repeat:** It's an ongoing cycle. Embrace it.

Section 9.7: Embracing Digital for Evolution

Digital isn't just part of the game; it is the game. To thrive, businesses must embrace digital strategies head-on, continuously adapting to stay ahead.

Key Moves:
- **Commit to Digital:** Make it central, not optional.
- **Continuous Learning:** The digital landscape is always changing. Keep up.

- **Foster Innovation:** Try new things. Some will stick, some won't.
- **Data-Driven Decisions:** Let insights guide your path.
- **Customer Experience First:** Happy customers are returning customers.
- **Think Holistically:** Your digital strategy should be unified across all channels.

Embracing digital fully is your only option if you want to stay relevant and competitive. It's about leveraging every tool in your digital arsenal to connect, engage, and convert. Ready to level up?

Chapter 9: Buckle up, nerds! Time to READ. 成功へ!

(Seikō e!) - Japanese, slicing through obstacles like a samurai.

Section 9.1: Digital Platforms as Growth Levers

In the contemporary landscape of business, digital platforms emerge not merely as tools but as pivotal levers for growth, offering unparalleled opportunities for customer acquisition, engagement, and retention. This section delves into the strategic importance of these platforms and outlines actionable strategies for leveraging their potential to drive business growth.

Key Insights: Embracing Digital Platforms for Business Expansion

Digital platforms, ranging from social media to e-commerce websites, have become integral to modern business strategies. Their role transcends conventional boundaries, enabling businesses to reach global audiences, gather insightful data, and deliver personalized customer experiences. The strategic deployment of these platforms can significantly enhance visibility, drive sales, and foster long-term customer loyalty.

Actionable Strategies: Maximizing the Potential of Digital Platforms

> **Customer Acquisition through Targeted Advertising:**
> - Utilize the sophisticated targeting capabilities of digital platforms like Facebook, Instagram, and Google Ads to reach potential customers based on demographics, interests, and behaviors.
> - Develop compelling content and offers that resonate with the target audience, optimizing campaigns through A/B testing to ensure maximum conversion rates.
>
> Engagement and Brand Building on Social Media:
> - Establish a strong presence on relevant social media platforms to engage with audiences

through quality content, interactive posts, and real-time communication.
- Use storytelling and brand narratives to connect emotionally with users, turning followers into brand advocates.

Retention via Personalized Email Marketing:
- Implement advanced segmentation and personalization techniques in email marketing to deliver tailored messages that address individual customer preferences and behaviors.
- Automate email campaigns for cart abandonment, product recommendations, and loyalty rewards to keep customers engaged and encourage repeat purchases.

Utilizing E-commerce Platforms for Global Reach:
- Expand market presence by listing products on major e-commerce platforms such as Amazon, eBay, and Alibaba, leveraging their vast customer bases and distribution networks.
- Optimize product listings with high-quality images, detailed descriptions, and SEO-friendly content to enhance visibility and attractiveness to potential buyers.

Data-Driven Decision Making with Analytics Tools:

- Leverage analytics tools provided by digital platforms to gain insights into customer behavior, campaign performance, and market trends.
- Use data to refine marketing strategies, product offerings, and customer service practices, ensuring a continuous cycle of improvement and growth.

Innovative Use of Technology for Enhanced Customer Experiences:

- Adopt the latest technologies such as AI, VR, and AR to create unique and immersive experiences on digital platforms, setting the brand apart from competitors.
- Implement chatbots for 24/7 customer service and personalized shopping assistance, improving customer satisfaction and operational efficiency.

Digital platforms hold the key to unlocking new avenues for business growth, offering scalable, cost-effective, and highly targeted methods for reaching and engaging customers. By understanding and strategically leveraging these platforms, businesses can achieve significant gains in customer acquisition, engagement, and retention. Success in the digital age requires a proactive and innovative approach, utilizing the full spectrum of digital platforms to create a comprehensive and dynamic online presence that drives growth and fosters lasting customer relationships.

Section 9.2: Website Optimization for Enhanced Engagement

In the digital era, a business's online presence is often the first point of interaction with potential clients and customers. The optimization of a website not only improves this first impression but also enhances user engagement, drives conversions, and solidifies a brand's market position. This section delves into transformative case studies of businesses that have successfully optimized their websites and outlines best practices for creating user-friendly, engaging, and conversion-optimized online platforms.

Case Studies of Transformative Website Optimization:

- **E-commerce Retailer:** An e-commerce platform specializing in sustainable goods overhauled its website design, focusing on user experience (UX) improvements.

Enhanced product filters, faster loading times, and a streamlined checkout process led to a significant increase in sales and customer satisfaction.

- **B2B Service Provider:** A B2B company offering digital marketing services revamped its website with a focus on content optimization and lead generation. By implementing targeted landing pages, a resource hub with valuable industry insights, and clear call-to-action (CTA) buttons, they saw a marked increase in lead quality and engagement.

- **Non-Profit Organization:** By redesigning its website to highlight impactful stories, integrate social proof, and improve donation processes, a non-profit significantly increased its online donations. The optimization emphasized emotional engagement and ease of use, driving both traffic and conversions.

Optimization Techniques: Best Practices for Website Enhancement:

1. **User Experience (UX) Design:** Prioritize the user's journey through your website, ensuring navigation is intuitive, information is easily accessible, and the overall experience is seamless across devices.

2. **Loading Speed:** Optimize website loading times by compressing images, leveraging browser caching, and minimizing the use of heavy scripts. Faster websites reduce bounce rates and improve user satisfaction.
3. **Content Strategy:** Develop a content strategy that aligns with your audience's interests and search intent. High-quality, valuable content boosts SEO, engages readers, and positions your brand as an industry leader.
4. **Mobile Optimization:** Ensure your website is fully responsive and optimized for mobile devices. With the increasing prevalence of mobile browsing, mobile-friendliness is a crucial factor for engagement and SEO.
5. **Conversion Rate Optimization (CRO):** Implement CRO best practices by using compelling CTAs, simplifying forms, and creating clear paths to conversion. A/B testing can help identify the most effective elements.
6. **Visual Elements:** Use high-quality images, videos, and infographics to break up text and convey information in an engaging way. Visuals can significantly enhance the user's experience and facilitate information retention.
7. **Accessibility:** Design your website with accessibility in mind, ensuring that all users, including those with disabilities, can navigate and interact with your content effectively.

8. **SEO Best Practices:** Apply SEO best practices, including keyword optimization, meta tags, and structured data, to improve your website's visibility in search engine results pages (SERPs).

9. **Feedback and Analytics:** Utilize website analytics and user feedback to continuously monitor performance and identify areas for improvement. Data-driven insights are invaluable for ongoing optimization efforts.

10. **Security Measures:** Implement robust security measures, including SSL encryption, to protect user data and build trust with your website visitors.

Website optimization is a multifaceted endeavor that requires a strategic approach to improve user engagement, conversion rates, and brand perception. By studying successful case studies and adhering to established best practices, businesses can transform their online presence into a powerful engagement tool. In the competitive digital landscape, a well-optimized website is not just an asset; it's a necessity for businesses aiming to thrive and connect meaningfully with their audiences.

Section 9.3: Maximizing Social Media Impact

In the ever-evolving landscape of digital marketing, social media stands out as a pivotal arena for businesses seeking to enhance their market presence, engage with diverse audiences, and achieve strategic business goals. This section outlines effective strategies and tactics for leveraging social media platforms to maximize impact, foster engagement, and drive results that align with overarching business objectives.

Social Media Strategies: Aligning with Business Goals and Audience Preferences

1. **Define Clear Objectives:** Start by establishing clear, measurable goals for your social media activities, such as increasing brand awareness, driving website traffic, or boosting sales. These objectives should align with your broader business goals.
2. **Understand Your Audience:** Conduct thorough research to understand the demographics, interests, and behaviors of your target audience. This insight will inform which platforms to focus on and the type of content that will resonate.
3. **Choose the Right Platforms:** Not all social media platforms are suitable for every business. Select platforms where your target audience is most active and

where your content can shine. This may include Facebook, Instagram, LinkedIn, Twitter, or newer platforms like TikTok.

4. **Develop a Content Calendar:** Plan your content in advance with a calendar that outlines what to post, when to post, and which platforms to use. This ensures a consistent and strategic approach to content creation.

5. **Emphasize Quality and Value:** Create high-quality, engaging content that provides value to your audience. This could be educational articles, entertaining videos, insightful infographics, or interactive polls and quizzes.

Engagement Tactics: Engaging Effectively with Audiences Across Various Social Media Platforms

1. **Personalize Your Interactions:** Respond to comments, messages, and mentions in a personalized manner. Acknowledging individuals by name and addressing their specific comments or questions can significantly enhance engagement.

2. **Leverage User-Generated Content:** Encourage your followers to share their own content related to your brand, products, or services. User-generated content not

only fosters community engagement but also serves as authentic endorsements for your brand.

3. **Utilize Social Media Stories:** Make use of the Stories feature available on platforms like Instagram, Facebook, and Snapchat. Stories are a great way to share behind-the-scenes content, limited-time offers, or quick updates in a more informal and engaging manner.

4. **Run Contests and Giveaways:** Contests and giveaways can generate excitement and engagement on your social media channels. Ensure that the entry requirements align with your engagement goals, such as tagging friends, sharing content, or using a specific hashtag.

5. **Incorporate Live Streaming:** Live streaming events, Q&A sessions, or product launches can create a sense of immediacy and exclusivity, encouraging real-time interaction with your audience.

6. **Analyze and Adapt:** Utilize social media analytics tools to track the performance of your content and engagement strategies. Analyze the data to understand what works best and adapt your approach accordingly for continuous improvement.

7. **Stay Updated on Trends:** Social media trends evolve rapidly. Stay informed about the latest trends and features within each platform and consider how these

can be integrated into your strategy to keep your content fresh and relevant.

Maximizing social media impact requires a strategic approach that aligns with your business goals and resonates with your target audience. By developing a thoughtful social media strategy and employing effective engagement tactics, businesses can harness the power of these platforms to expand their reach, engage with audiences more deeply, and drive meaningful results. In the dynamic world of social media, the ability to adapt, innovate, and connect authentically with your audience is key to achieving sustained success and impact.

Section 9.4: The Power of Email Marketing

Email marketing remains a cornerstone of digital marketing strategy, offering unparalleled directness and personalization in reaching out to clients and customers. This section examines the efficacy of impactful email marketing campaigns and lays down strategic blueprints for crafting email initiatives that not only engage audiences but also drive significant conversions.

Email Marketing Excellence: Examples of Impactful Campaigns

- **Subscription Service Launch:** A subscription-based meal kit service sent out an email series to potential customers, highlighting the convenience, quality, and variety of their offerings. The campaign utilized personalized content based on recipients' dietary preferences, resulting in a substantial increase in subscriptions.
- **Customer Loyalty Program:** A retail brand launched a loyalty program with an email campaign that included personalized discounts, early access to new products, and exclusive content. The emails were segmented based on past purchase behavior, leading to high engagement rates and increased repeat purchases.
- **Awareness Campaign for Non-Profit:** A non-profit organization aiming to raise awareness about a global issue utilized a storytelling approach in their email campaign, sharing real stories of individuals impacted by the issue. The campaign included clear calls to action, encouraging donations and sharing within networks, significantly boosting their fundraising efforts.

Building Effective Campaigns: Strategies for Crafting Email Campaigns

1. **Segment Your Audience:** Divide your email list into segments based on demographics, behavior, or past interactions with your brand. Tailored content to specific segments increases relevance and engagement.
2. **Personalize Your Messages:** Go beyond using the recipient's name. Incorporate personalized content recommendations, reminders based on past purchases, or updates relevant to the recipient's interests.
3. **Craft Compelling Subject Lines:** Your subject line is the first impression. Make it catchy, clear, and concise to increase open rates. A/B testing subject lines can help identify what resonates best with your audience.
4. **Design for Mobile:** Ensure your emails are mobile-friendly, with responsive design and easily clickable links. A significant portion of emails is first opened on mobile devices.
5. **Utilize Automation:** Automated email sequences, triggered by specific actions like signing up for a newsletter or abandoning a cart, can provide timely and relevant content to guide the customer journey.

6. **Include Clear Calls to Action (CTAs):** Every email should have a clear purpose, whether it's to inform, engage, or convert. Make your CTAs prominent and persuasive to drive the desired action.
7. **Test and Optimize:** Continuously test different elements of your emails, including layout, content, and timing. Use analytics to measure performance and refine your strategy based on insights.
8. **Respect Privacy and Consent:** Adhere strictly to regulations like GDPR and CAN-SPAM. Ensure recipients have opted in to receive emails and make it easy for them to unsubscribe if they choose.
9. **Integrate with Other Channels:** Use email as part of a multi-channel strategy. Encourage recipients to connect with your brand on social media, visit your website, or attend events.
10. **Deliver Value:** Above all, your emails should provide value to the recipient. Whether educational, entertaining, or promotional, ensure that each communication enriches the recipient's interaction with your brand.

Email marketing's power lies in its directness and capacity for personalization, making it an essential tool for engaging with clients and customers in a meaningful way. By implementing the strategies outlined above, businesses can harness the full potential of email marketing to enhance their digital presence, foster lasting relationships, and drive measurable results. In the digital marketing mix, a well-executed email campaign stands as a testament to the enduring relevance and effectiveness of email as a communication channel.

Section 9.5: Leveraging SEO for Visibility and Growth

Search Engine Optimization (SEO) is a critical component of any digital marketing strategy, serving as the backbone for enhancing visibility, driving organic traffic, and fostering sustainable growth. This section delves into the transformative power of SEO through success stories and outlines strategic techniques businesses can employ to climb search engine rankings and capture the attention of their target audience.

SEO Success Stories:

- **Local Bakery's National Recognition:** A small-town bakery leveraged local SEO strategies, including optimizing their Google My Business listing and gathering positive online reviews. This focus not only dominated local search results but also caught the attention of a national food magazine, significantly boosting their online orders.

- **E-commerce Platform's Revenue Surge:** An e-commerce site specializing in eco-friendly products implemented a comprehensive SEO strategy, focusing on long-tail keywords, user experience optimization, and high-quality content creation. The result was a 200% increase in organic traffic and a significant uptick in conversion rates.

- **Tech Startup's Global Reach:** A tech startup utilized SEO to target specific international markets, optimizing their website for different languages and regional search engines. This strategic approach led to a marked increase in global visibility and user engagement, paving the way for international partnerships.

SEO Strategies: Techniques for Enhancing Search Engine Rankings

1. **Keyword Research and Optimization:** Identify and incorporate relevant keywords and phrases that your

target audience uses to search for your products or services. Use these keywords strategically in your website's content, titles, meta descriptions, and URLs.

2. **Content Quality and Relevance:** Produce high-quality, informative content that addresses the needs and interests of your audience. Regularly updating your website with fresh content can also signal to search engines that your site is a valuable resource.

3. **Site Structure and Navigation:** Ensure your website has a clear, logical structure that's easy for both users and search engine crawlers to navigate. Use internal linking wisely to guide visitors through your site and to distribute page authority throughout.

4. **Mobile Optimization:** With the increasing prevalence of mobile searches, having a mobile-friendly website is essential. Google's mobile-first indexing means that your site's mobile version will primarily determine your search engine rankings.

5. **Page Load Speed:** Optimize your website's loading speed by compressing images, minimizing code, and leveraging browser caching. Fast-loading pages improve user experience and contribute positively to your SEO rankings.

6. **Secure and Accessible Website:** Implement HTTPS to secure your site and protect user data. Additionally, ensure your website is accessible to search engine bots by using a robots.txt file and an XML sitemap.
7. **Local SEO:** For businesses targeting local markets, optimize for local search by claiming your Google My Business listing, securing local citations, and incorporating location-specific keywords into your content.
8. **Link Building:** Acquire high-quality backlinks from reputable sites within your industry. Backlinks serve as endorsements for your site, boosting your credibility and rankings.
9. **Social Signals:** While not a direct ranking factor, social media activity related to your website can enhance your SEO efforts by driving traffic and increasing brand visibility.
10. **Analytics and Monitoring:** Regularly monitor your SEO performance using tools like Google Analytics and Google Search Console. Use the insights gained to refine and adjust your strategy for continuous improvement.

Leveraging SEO effectively can transform a business's digital presence, turning a website into a powerful tool for visibility, engagement, and growth. The success stories and strategies highlighted in this section underscore the importance of a well-executed SEO strategy. By focusing on optimizing for both search engines and user experience, businesses can achieve higher rankings, drive organic traffic, and ultimately, catalyze growth in an increasingly competitive digital landscape.

Section 9.6: Analyzing Digital Performance for Continuous Improvement

The digital landscape is dynamic, with continuously shifting algorithms, consumer behaviors, and technological advancements. To stay competitive and effective, businesses must adopt an iterative approach to their digital strategies, grounded in robust analysis and insights. This section explores the critical role of digital analytics in guiding strategic decisions and outlines the process of iterative optimization for enhancing digital platform performance.

Analytics and Insights: Utilizing Digital Analytics to Drive Strategy

Digital analytics provides a wealth of data on user interactions, engagement patterns, and conversion metrics. By harnessing this information, businesses can:

1. **Understand User Behavior:** Track how users interact with your website or digital platform, identifying paths they take, pages they linger on, and points where they drop off. This insight helps in refining user experience and content strategy.
2. **Measure Performance:** Evaluate the effectiveness of marketing campaigns, content, and features against set KPIs and objectives. Analytics allow for a granular understanding of what drives success and areas that require improvement.
3. **Segment Audience:** Identify different user segments based on behavior, demographics, and preferences. Tailored strategies can then be developed to address the specific needs and interests of each segment.
4. **Optimize Conversion Rates:** Analyze conversion paths to identify bottlenecks or friction points. Insights gathered can inform adjustments to streamline the user journey and enhance conversion rates.
5. **Inform Content Strategy:** Content performance analytics highlight topics, formats, and channels that

resonate most with your audience, guiding content creation and distribution efforts.

Iterative Optimization: The Cycle of Analysis, Learning, and Optimization

Iterative optimization is a continuous cycle that involves:

1. **Setting Benchmarks:** Establish baseline performance metrics for all digital activities. These benchmarks are crucial for measuring progress and the impact of optimization efforts.
2. **Implementing Changes:** Based on insights derived from analytics, implement targeted changes to your digital platforms, marketing strategies, or content. These changes should be informed by data and aligned with your overall business objectives.
3. **Monitoring Impact:** After implementing changes, closely monitor analytics to assess their impact. Look for shifts in user behavior, engagement rates, and conversion metrics.
4. **Learning from Data:** Analyze the outcomes of your changes. Did performance improve? What unexpected outcomes occurred? Learning from each iteration is key to refining strategies and tactics.

5. **Repeating the Cycle:** Iterative optimization is an ongoing process. With each cycle, refine your approach based on the latest data, testing new ideas and continuously seeking to enhance performance.
6. **Experimentation:** Embrace experimentation within the optimization cycle. A/B testing different approaches can reveal valuable insights and uncover innovative strategies for engagement and conversion.
7. **Feedback Integration:** Incorporate feedback from users and stakeholders into the optimization process. Direct input can provide context to the data and highlight areas that analytics alone might not reveal.
8. **Adapting to Trends:** Stay informed about digital trends and emerging technologies. Integrating new tools and approaches into your optimization cycle can keep your strategies ahead of the curve.

In the fast-paced world of digital marketing, success hinges on the ability to adapt and improve continuously. Leveraging digital analytics for insights and adopting an iterative approach to optimization enables businesses to refine their digital presence actively. This cycle of analysis, learning, and optimization is not just about reacting to past performance but proactively shaping strategies to meet future challenges and opportunities. Through diligent application of these principles, businesses can enhance their digital performance, drive growth, and maintain a competitive edge in the digital marketplace.

Section 9.7: Embracing Digital for Business Evolution

As we conclude Chapter 9 of "Mastering the Market," it's essential to reflect on the journey through the digital landscape and its undeniable impact on modern business strategies. This chapter has navigated through various facets of digital marketing and platform optimization, underscoring the transformative potential these elements hold for businesses aiming to thrive in a digitally driven market. This closing section synthesizes key takeaways from the chapter and issues a call to action for businesses to wholeheartedly embrace digital strategies as integral components of their growth and evolution.

Key Takeaways: The Transformative Potential of Digital Platforms

1. **Digital Presence as a Catalyst for Growth:** An optimized, engaging digital presence—from websites to

social media—serves not just as a business card but as a dynamic engine for growth, visibility, and engagement.

2. **SEO as a Visibility Multiplier:** Effective SEO strategies are crucial for enhancing online visibility, driving organic traffic, and establishing a brand as an authoritative source in its niche.

3. **The Power of Content:** High-quality, relevant content is the cornerstone of digital engagement, capable of attracting, educating, and converting audiences across various stages of the customer journey.

4. **Social Media's Engagement Lever:** Social media platforms offer unparalleled opportunities for direct engagement, community building, and brand advocacy, amplifying a brand's voice in crowded marketplaces.

5. **Email Marketing's Personal Touch:** Tailored email marketing campaigns foster personal connections, nurture leads, and drive conversions with measurable results.

6. **Data-Driven Decision Making:** Leveraging digital analytics empowers businesses to make informed, strategic decisions, optimizing digital performance and ROI continuously.

7. **Adaptability and Innovation:** The digital domain demands adaptability and ongoing innovation, as

emerging technologies and shifting user behaviors necessitate constant evolution of strategies.

Call to Action: Integrating Digital Strategies into Business Growth Plans

The journey through digital transformation is not a mere option but a necessity for businesses seeking to capture the opportunities of the digital age. To this end, businesses are called upon to:

- **Commit to Digital Excellence:** View digital marketing and platform optimization not as ancillary efforts but as central pillars of your business strategy.
- **Invest in Continuous Learning:** The digital landscape is ever-evolving. Dedicate resources to staying abreast of trends, technologies, and best practices to keep your strategies ahead of the curve.
- **Foster a Culture of Innovation:** Encourage experimentation and innovation within your organization. The willingness to try new approaches and learn from outcomes can distinguish leaders in the digital arena.

- **Leverage Data for Insights:** Embrace analytics as a tool for continuous improvement, allowing data-driven insights to guide your digital marketing efforts.
- **Prioritize User Experience:** In all digital initiatives, prioritize the needs and preferences of your target audience, crafting experiences that are engaging, accessible, and rewarding.
- **Integrate Across Channels:** Develop a cohesive digital strategy that seamlessly integrates various platforms and channels, ensuring a unified brand experience for your audience.

Embracing digital strategies is not just about leveraging new technologies but about reimagining how businesses connect with clients and customers, deliver value, and achieve growth. As the digital realm continues to expand and evolve, so too must the strategies businesses employ to navigate it. By integrating digital approaches comprehensively into their growth plans, businesses can ensure they not only survive but thrive, turning the challenges of the digital age into opportunities for innovation, engagement, and sustained success.

Chapter 9: Step-By Step How to "Get... It... Done!"

Alright, let's strip it down to brass tacks. You're here to not just play in the digital sandbox but to dominate. Here's your no-BS guide to cranking up your digital game to 11.

Section 9.1: Digital Platform Domination

Step 1: Digital Deep Dive
- **Task:** Rip apart your digital presence. What's working? What's as effective as a chocolate teapot? Fix it.
- **Deadline:** 1 week.

Step 2: Goal-Setting Grenade
- **Task:** Throw down your digital goals like a challenge to the universe. More followers? Higher sales? Speak it into existence.
- **Deadline:** 2 days.

Step 3: Strategy Strike
- **Task:** Launch calculated strikes on each platform. Facebook ads, keyword-rich blogs, TikTok dances—if it gets you seen, do it.
- **Deadline:** Ongoing, with monthly reviews.

Section 9.2: Website Warfare

Step 1: UX Blitz
- **Task:** March through your website. If it's slow, confusing, or looks like it's from 1998, overhaul it.
- **Deadline:** 3 weeks.

Step 2: Content and SEO Slaughter

- **Task:** Overhaul your content. Make Google love you. If it doesn't rank, it stanks.
- **Deadline:** 1 month.

Step 3: CRO Crusade
- **Task:** Make every click count. Test. Optimize. Repeat.
- **Deadline:** 2 months, then ongoing.

Section 9.3: Social Media Siege

Step 1: Platform Pillage
- **Task:** Pick your battlefields. Where are your customers? Be there or be square.
- **Deadline:** 1 week.

Step 2: Content Cannon
- **Task:** Fire off content that hits the mark—educate, entertain, engage.
- **Deadline:** Ongoing, with weekly planning.

Step 3: Engagement and Espionage
- **Task:** Talk back. Spy on analytics. Adjust. The more you engage, the more you win.
- **Deadline:** Daily engagement, monthly analytics review.

Section 9.4: Email Marketing Missile

Step 1: Segmentation Sniper
- **Task:** Divide and conquer. Segment your list like a pro.
- **Deadline:** 2 weeks.

Step 2: Personalization and Automation Attack
- **Task:** Get personal. Automate. Make them feel seen.
- **Deadline:** 1 month for setup, then review quarterly.

Step 3: Campaign Commando

- **Task:** Launch, learn, tweak, repeat. Every email is a potential gold mine.
- **Deadline:** Ongoing, with monthly performance reviews.

Section 9.5: SEO Skirmish

Step 1: SEO Scouting
- **Task:** Know your territory. Keywords are your map.
- **Deadline:** 2 weeks for initial research, then ongoing.

Step 2: On-page and Off-page Onslaught
- **Task:** Make every page a fortress. Build alliances with backlinks.
- **Deadline:** 1 month for overhaul, then maintenance.

Step 3: Local SEO Lunge
- **Task:** Dominate the local scene. Make sure Google My Business knows you're the boss.
- **Deadline:** 2 weeks for setup, then regular updates.

Section 9.6: Digital Performance Drill

Step 1: Analytics Arsenal
- **Task:** Arm yourself with data. If you're not measuring, you're guessing.
- **Deadline:** 1 week for full setup.

Step 2: Review and Reconnaissance
- **Task:** Regularly recon your data. Adjust your strategies like a digital ninja.
- **Deadline:** Monthly deep dives.

Step 3: Optimization Offensive
- **Task:** Test. Learn. Implement. This is the circle of digital life.
- **Deadline:** Continuous cycle of improvement.

Section 9.7: Full Digital Fusion

Step 1: Strategy Synthesis
- **Task:** Your digital strategy shouldn't be an island. Integrate or die.
- **Deadline:** 1 month for initial integration, then review quarterly.

Step 2: Innovation Incursion
- **Task:** Keep your edge sharp. New tools, platforms, tactics—stay hungry.
- **Deadline:** Constant vigilance.

Step 3: Digital Transformation Triumph
- **Task:** Overhaul your processes, your mindset, your coffee machine—whatever it takes to stay relevant.
- **Deadline:** It's a marathon, not a sprint. Commit to continuous evolution.

There you have it. Your digital dominion awaits. Follow these steps, stay ruthless, and watch your business evolve from a digital dweller to a digital dynamo. Let's get... it... done!

Chapter 10 Pre-Breakdown: No Fluff, Just Facts

Section 10.1: Sales Funnel Decoded

Cut the buzzwords. The sales funnel is your blueprint from "Who are you?" to "Take my money!" Here's how you stop potential customers from bailing out before checkout.

Funnel 101:
- **Awareness:** Get on their radar. If they don't know you, they can't buy from you.
- **Interest:** Spark curiosity. Make them think, "Hmm, tell me more."
- **Consideration:** They're checking you out, so strut your stuff. Why you over the other guy?
- **Conversion:** The make-or-break moment. Get that "Yes!"
- **Loyalty:** Keep them coming back for more. A one-time buyer is a missed opportunity.

Tactics That Work:
- **Awareness:** SEO, social media buzz, and some well-placed ads. Be seen.
- **Interest:** Value-packed content. Blog posts, videos, webinars. Educate them.
- **Consideration:** Show off your happy customers. Reviews, case studies, free trials. Prove your worth.
- **Conversion:** Make buying as easy as breathing. Clear CTAs, streamlined checkout.
- **Loyalty:** Reward them. Special offers, loyalty programs, and stellar support.

Section 10.2: Top of the Funnel Tactics

You want a crowd at the top so you can filter down to the die-hards at the bottom. Here's how you draw the masses.

Real Talk on Attraction:
- **Content Marketing & SEO:** Be the answer they find on Google.
- **Social Media & Influencers:** Get talked about. Leverage buzz.
- **Email Lead Magnets:** Offer something irresistible in exchange for their email.
- **Interactive Campaigns:** Quizzes, contests, and challenges. Engage them.
- **Referral Programs:** Turn your customers into your sales force.

Section 10.3: Lead Nurturing - Keep Them Hooked

Got their attention? Great. Now keep them interested. It's like dating; you gotta put in the effort to get to "I do."

Strategies That Stick:
- **Segment & Personalize:** Tailor your messages. Nobody likes feeling like just another email address.
- **Educate & Offer Value:** Keep feeding them info they care about.
- **Score & Prioritize:** Not all leads are created equal. Focus where it counts.
- **Exclusive Offers:** Make them feel special. VIP treatment leads to loyalty.

Section 10.4: Conversion - Seal the Deal

Getting them to the checkout is a marathon, not a sprint. Here's how you cross the finish line together.

Conversion Commandments:
- **Simplify the Process:** Don't lose them at the last hurdle. Make buying easy.
- **Strong CTAs:** Tell them exactly what to do next. Click here. Buy now.
- **Social Proof:** Nothing says "buy me" like a bunch of happy customers.
- **Test & Optimize:** Always be tweaking. What works today might not tomorrow.

Section 10.5: After the Sale - Turning Buyers into Believers

The sale is just the beginning. Now, make them love you so much they can't help but come back for more.

Loyalty Loop:
- **Personalized Thank-Yous:** A little gratitude goes a long way.
- **Onboarding & Education:** Help them get the most out of their purchase.
- **Exclusive Perks:** Special deals for returning customers.
- **Engagement & Feedback:** Keep the conversation going. Listen and adapt.

Section 10.6: Feedback - Your Funnel's Best Friend

Your sales funnel isn't set in stone. Listen, learn, and tweak. Rinse and repeat.

Feedback Fundamentals:

- **Surveys & Interviews:** Ask and you shall receive... invaluable insights.
- **Analytics:** Numbers don't lie. Dive deep into your data.
- **A/B Testing:** What works better? There's only one way to find out.
- **Adapt & Evolve:** Use what you learn to constantly refine and improve your funnel.

Section 10.7: Mastering the Funnel - Never Stop Improving

Owning your sales funnel is about understanding every twist and turn. It's a constant game of optimization.

Final Wisdom:
- **Know Your Funnel Inside Out:** Each stage is an opportunity.
- **Stay Agile:** What worked yesterday won't necessarily work tomorrow.
- **Leverage Tech:** Tools and analytics are your eyes and ears.
- **Customer Is King:** Their experience dictates your strategy. Keep them happy, keep them buying.

Mastering your sales funnel is about strategy, persistence, and a whole lot of customer love. Get it right, and you're not just making sales; you're building a brand that lasts.

Chapter 10: Buckle up, nerds! Time to READ.

К успеху! (K uspekhu!) - Russian, with the determination of a Siberian tiger.

Section 10.1:

Understanding the Sales Funnel

The sales funnel is a conceptual framework that illustrates the journey potential customers go through from first becoming aware of a product or service to the final decision of purchase and beyond, towards loyalty. This section breaks down the stages of the sales funnel and provides actionable strategies tailored to each stage to maximize conversions, guiding businesses through the nuances of effectively moving potential clients and customers through this funnel.

Key Insights: Stages of the Sales Funnel

1. **Awareness:** The top of the funnel, where potential customers first learn about your product or service. At

this stage, the focus is on capturing attention and sparking interest.
2. **Interest:** Once awareness is established, potential customers start showing interest in learning more about what you offer. This stage is about educating and providing value.
3. **Consideration:** At this point, potential customers evaluate your offerings against competitors. They are considering whether your product or service meets their needs.
4. **Conversion:** The critical point where a decision is made, and the customer takes action, such as making a purchase or signing up for a service.
5. **Loyalty:** Post-purchase, the focus shifts to retaining customers through excellent service, support, and engagement, turning them into loyal advocates for your brand.

Actionable Strategies: Tailored to Each Stage of the Sales Funnel

Awareness Strategies:

- Utilize SEO and content marketing to increase visibility.

- Engage in social media campaigns and influencer partnerships to broaden reach.
- Implement targeted advertising to attract potential customers.

Interest Strategies:

- Offer valuable content, such as ebooks, webinars, and blogs, that addresses common questions and challenges.
- Use email marketing to nurture leads by providing insights and solutions related to their interests.

Consideration Strategies:

- Showcase testimonials, case studies, and reviews to build credibility and trust.
- Provide detailed product information, demos, or free trials to help potential customers evaluate your offering.

Conversion Strategies:

- Optimize the checkout process to be as straightforward and seamless as possible.
- Offer time-limited promotions or discounts to encourage immediate action.
- Implement a strong call-to-action (CTA) that guides users towards making a purchase or signing up.

Loyalty Strategies:

- Develop a loyalty program that rewards repeat business and encourages referrals.
- Engage with customers post-purchase through follow-up emails, support, and community building.
- Solicit feedback and act on it to improve products and services continually.

Understanding and optimizing each stage of the sales funnel is essential for effectively guiding potential customers from initial awareness to loyal advocacy. By tailoring strategies to the unique needs and behaviors at each funnel stage, businesses can enhance the customer journey, increase conversions, and build a loyal customer base. In the competitive marketplace, a well-structured sales funnel is not just a tool for driving sales;

it's a strategic asset for building lasting relationships and fostering growth.

Section 10.2: Attracting the Top of the Funnel

Attracting a wide audience to the top of the sales funnel is the critical first step in a customer's journey towards making a purchase. This section explores how successful businesses have excelled in drawing potential customers into their sales funnel, highlighting innovative case studies and discussing effective engagement techniques that can be applied across industries.

Case Studies: Successful Audience Attraction

- **Tech Startup's Viral Campaign:** A tech startup launched a viral marketing campaign for its new app, leveraging social media challenges to generate buzz. The campaign's interactive nature not only increased awareness but also encouraged massive participation, effectively funneling a broad audience into their ecosystem.
- **E-commerce Platform's SEO Mastery:** An e-commerce platform specializing in handmade goods optimized its

website for search engines through strategic keyword targeting, content marketing, and user experience enhancements. This approach significantly increased organic traffic, attracting a diverse audience interested in unique, artisanal products.

- **Non-Profit's Storytelling Approach:** A non-profit organization utilized storytelling through video content to highlight the impact of their work. These emotionally compelling stories were shared across social media and email marketing, resonating with a wide audience and drawing them into the organization's mission and message.

Engagement Techniques: Drawing Potential Customers into the Sales Funnel

1. **Content Marketing:** Develop and distribute valuable, relevant content that addresses the interests and needs of your target audience. Blog posts, infographics, podcasts, and videos can attract attention and spark interest in your brand.
2. **SEO Strategies:** Optimize your online content with targeted keywords and phrases to improve visibility in search engine results. A strong SEO strategy ensures that

your website attracts visitors actively searching for solutions you offer.

3. **Social Media Engagement:** Use social media platforms to connect with potential customers by sharing engaging content, participating in conversations, and leveraging hashtags to increase reach. Social media ads can also target specific demographics to attract a broader audience.

4. **Influencer Partnerships:** Collaborate with influencers who align with your brand values to tap into their followers. Influencers can introduce your brand to a wider audience in a trusted and authentic way.

5. **Email Marketing Lead Magnets:** Offer valuable resources, such as ebooks, webinars, or discount codes, in exchange for email sign-ups. This technique not only attracts potential customers but also begins the process of nurturing leads through your funnel.

6. **Interactive Campaigns:** Launch interactive campaigns, such as contests, quizzes, or user-generated content initiatives, to engage and attract a wide audience. These campaigns can create excitement and encourage participation, leading to increased brand awareness.

7. **Customer Referral Programs:** Encourage existing customers to refer friends and family to your brand. A

referral program can effectively expand your reach by leveraging the networks of your satisfied customers.
8. **Targeted Advertising:** Utilize targeted advertising on platforms like Google AdWords and Facebook to reach potential customers based on specific demographics, interests, and behaviors. This precision targeting helps draw a relevant audience into your funnel.

Attracting a wide audience to the top of the sales funnel requires a multifaceted approach, leveraging content marketing, SEO, social media, influencer partnerships, and more. By studying successful case studies and applying proven engagement techniques, businesses can effectively draw potential customers into their sales funnel, setting the stage for nurturing leads and ultimately driving conversions. In today's competitive market, the ability to attract and engage a broad audience is essential for funneling potential customers towards making a purchase and fostering long-term loyalty.

Section 10.3: Nurturing Leads Through the Funnel

Nurturing leads through the sales funnel is a critical process that transforms initial interest into loyal customer relationships. It involves strategic engagement, personalized communication, and providing value at each stage of the buyer's journey. This section explores effective strategies for maintaining interest and guiding leads toward making a purchase, along with tailored communication tactics to facilitate their decision-making process.

Effective Nurturing: Strategies for Moving Leads Towards Purchase

1. **Segmentation for Personalization:** Segment your leads based on their behavior, interests, and stage in the sales funnel. Tailored content that addresses specific needs or questions at each stage significantly increases the chance of conversion.
2. **Educational Content:** Provide valuable information and resources that help leads solve problems or make informed decisions. Blogs, whitepapers, webinars, and tutorials can establish your brand as a trusted authority.
3. **Email Drip Campaigns:** Utilize automated email sequences that deliver the right message at the right

time. Drip campaigns can educate, inspire, and gently push leads closer to a purchase decision.

4. **Engagement Scoring:** Implement lead scoring to identify the most engaged and sales-ready leads. Focus intensified nurturing efforts on these high-potential contacts.

5. **Feedback Loops:** Encourage and monitor feedback from your leads. Understanding their concerns or objections can provide valuable insights for refining your nurturing strategies.

6. **Social Proof:** Leverage testimonials, case studies, and user reviews in your communications. Social proof can alleviate concerns and validate the decision to choose your product or service.

7. **Exclusive Offers:** Provide special offers or incentives to leads in the funnel, such as free trials, discounts, or exclusive access to new products. These can accelerate the decision-making process.

Communication Tactics: Tailoring Communication Through the Decision-Making Process

1. **Awareness Stage:** In this initial stage, focus on broad, educational content that addresses common questions

or introduces your industry. Use storytelling and visual content to spark interest and build brand awareness.

2. **Consideration Stage:** As leads show interest, offer more detailed information specific to your products or services. Comparison guides, product demos, and case studies can help differentiate your offerings from competitors.

3. **Decision Stage:** For leads ready to make a purchase, personalized communication becomes key. Direct email outreach, personalized consultations, or tailored proposals can address final concerns and facilitate the buying decision.

4. **Retention Stage:** Post-purchase, continue engaging with customers through thank-you messages, onboarding content, and regular check-ins. This stage is crucial for building loyalty and encouraging repeat business.

5. **Re-engagement:** For leads that have stalled or gone cold, develop re-engagement campaigns that reignite interest. Highlight new features, offerings, or share significant industry news to bring them back into the funnel.

6. **Utilize Multi-Channel Communication:** Engage leads across multiple platforms, including email, social media,

SMS, and retargeting ads. Consistent, cross-channel messaging reinforces your presence and keeps your brand top of mind.

7. **Monitor and Adapt:** Regularly review the performance of your nurturing strategies and communications. Analytics and lead feedback can guide adjustments to improve effectiveness over time.

Nurturing leads through the sales funnel is an art that combines strategic communication, personalization, and patience. By implementing targeted nurturing strategies and tailoring communication to guide leads through their decision-making process, businesses can effectively convert initial interest into lasting customer relationships. This nuanced approach ensures that leads receive the right information and engagement at each stage, building trust and paving the way for successful conversions.

Section 10.4: Conversion Optimization Strategies

The ultimate goal of navigating through the sales funnel is conversion: turning potential leads into loyal customers. This intricate process requires a strategic approach, leveraging data-driven insights and user-centric designs to enhance the conversion pathway. In this section, we'll explore case studies of businesses that have significantly improved their conversion rates and delve into actionable optimization tips that can be applied across various digital platforms to maximize the likelihood of conversion.

Conversion Case Studies:

- **E-Commerce Retailer's Checkout Revamp:** An e-commerce site overhauled its checkout process, simplifying steps, adding multiple payment options, and introducing a guest checkout feature. These changes led to a 50% decrease in cart abandonment and a significant uplift in conversion rates.
- **SaaS Company's Free Trial Strategy:** A Software as a Service (SaaS) company redesigned its free trial sign-up page, emphasizing clarity and value proposition, and reducing form fields. The result was a 40% increase in sign-up conversions, with more users upgrading to paid plans.
- **Content Platform's A/B Testing:** A digital content platform implemented A/B testing for its subscription

models, experimenting with different pricing tiers, benefits, and presentation styles. Through continuous testing, they identified an optimal structure that doubled subscription rates.

Optimization Tips for Increasing Conversion Rates:

1. **Simplify the User Journey:** Analyze the path to conversion and remove any unnecessary steps or friction points. Ensure that navigating your website or platform is intuitive, with a clear and direct path to conversion actions.
2. **Enhance Page Load Speed:** Optimize your website's load time, as delays can significantly impact bounce rates and conversions. Compress images, leverage browser caching, and minimize the use of heavy scripts.
3. **Leverage Social Proof:** Incorporate reviews, testimonials, and case studies prominently on your site. Social proof builds trust and can greatly influence decision-making in your favor.
4. **Optimize Call-to-Action (CTA) Elements:** Ensure your CTAs are clearly visible and compelling. Use action-oriented language, and test different colors, positions,

and sizes to determine what works best for your audience.

5. **Employ A/B Testing:** Regularly test different elements of your web pages and marketing materials (e.g., headlines, images, button colors) to understand what variations perform the best and why.

6. **Focus on Value Proposition:** Clearly articulate the value and benefits of your product or service. Highlight what sets you apart from competitors and address potential objections your leads might have.

7. **Personalize User Experience:** Use data analytics to offer personalized experiences, recommendations, and content. Personalization can significantly increase engagement and the likelihood of conversion.

8. **Streamline Forms:** Reduce the number of fields in your forms to the essentials. Each additional field can decrease the likelihood of form completion. Consider using progressive profiling to collect more information over time.

9. **Implement Live Chat Support:** Offering immediate assistance or answering questions through live chat can remove barriers to conversion, providing users with the information they need to make a decision.

10. **Create Urgency and Scarcity:** Use limited-time offers, countdown timers, or limited stock notifications to create a sense of urgency or scarcity, encouraging leads to act quickly.

Conversion optimization is a continuous process of testing, learning, and refining. By understanding and implementing these actionable strategies, businesses can significantly improve their conversion rates, turning more leads into customers. Each of the case studies and tips provided underscores the importance of a user-centric approach, where understanding the needs, behaviors, and preferences of your potential customers can lead to meaningful improvements in your conversion pathway. In the competitive landscape of digital marketing, those who master the art of conversion optimization will find themselves well-positioned to achieve sustained growth and success.

Section 10.5: Fostering Post-Purchase Loyalty

In the competitive marketplace, fostering post-purchase loyalty is as crucial as attracting new customers. This section delves into strategies and techniques aimed at engaging customers after a purchase, building long-term loyalty, and encouraging repeat business. By focusing on customer satisfaction and value beyond the initial sale, businesses can cultivate a loyal customer base that not only continues to purchase but also becomes a powerful advocate for the brand.

Loyalty Building: Strategies for Engaging Customers Post-Purchase

1. **Personalized Thank You Communications:** Send personalized thank-you emails or notes after a purchase, acknowledging your customer's choice to choose your brand. This simple gesture can make customers feel valued and appreciated.
2. **Customer Onboarding:** For products or services that require it, offer an onboarding process that helps customers get the most out of their purchase. Educational resources, tutorials, and support can enhance customer satisfaction and reduce buyer's remorse.

3. **Exclusive Offers for Repeat Customers:** Reward repeat customers with exclusive offers, discounts, or early access to new products. This not only incentivizes further purchases but also makes customers feel recognized and valued.
4. **Loyalty Programs:** Implement a loyalty program that rewards customers for their ongoing business. Points systems, VIP tiers, or rewards for referrals can motivate continued engagement and purchases.
5. **Engagement Through Content:** Continue to provide valuable content that resonates with your customer base. Newsletters, blogs, and social media can keep your brand top-of-mind and maintain interest.

Retention Techniques: Keeping Your Brand Top-of-Mind

1. **Regular Check-Ins:** Implement a strategy for regular check-ins with customers through email or social media, asking for feedback on their purchase or offering help and support. This shows you care about their experience beyond the sale.
2. **Remarketing Campaigns:** Use remarketing campaigns to re-engage customers who have already made a purchase. Tailored messaging based on past purchases

can remind customers of your brand and encourage repeat visits to your site.

3. **Community Building:** Foster a sense of community among your customers through online forums, social media groups, or customer events. A strong community can increase loyalty and turn customers into brand advocates.

4. **Customer Feedback Loop:** Actively seek and respond to customer feedback. Implementing changes based on customer suggestions can significantly enhance loyalty and show that you value their input.

5. **Surprise and Delight:** Employ surprise and delight tactics, such as unexpected upgrades, gifts, or personalized recommendations. Small surprises can have a big impact on customer perception and loyalty.

6. **Responsive Customer Service:** Provide exceptional, responsive customer service post-purchase. Quick and helpful responses to questions or issues can turn a potentially negative experience into a positive one, reinforcing loyalty.

Fostering post-purchase loyalty is an ongoing effort that requires attention to detail, personalization, and a genuine interest in the customer's satisfaction and success with your product or service. By implementing the strategies and techniques outlined above, businesses can build a loyal customer base that not only continues to engage and purchase but also serves as a valuable source of referrals and advocacy. In the long run, the efforts put into building and maintaining customer loyalty can significantly contribute to a brand's reputation, sustainability, and growth.

Section 10.6: Utilizing Feedback to Refine the Funnel

The sales funnel is a dynamic model, not set in stone. Its effectiveness hinges on continuous refinement and optimization, driven by feedback from customers and leads at every stage. This section delves into the critical role of feedback loops in refining the sales funnel, ensuring it remains efficient, customer-centric, and aligned with evolving market demands.

Feedback Loops: Implementing Feedback Mechanisms

Feedback mechanisms are integral to understanding how leads and customers interact with your funnel. They provide insights into user behavior, preferences, and pain points, offering a roadmap for targeted improvements. Implementing these mechanisms involves several strategies:

1. **Surveys and Questionnaires:** Post-interaction surveys or questionnaires can gather specific insights about each stage of the funnel. Questions should be tailored to uncover why leads move forward, stall, or exit the funnel.
2. **Customer Interviews:** Direct conversations with customers offer in-depth insights into their experiences. Such interviews can reveal nuances that surveys might miss, providing a richer context for optimization.
3. **Analytics and Tracking:** Digital analytics tools track how users navigate through your funnel, identifying drop-off points and behaviors that indicate interest or hesitation.
4. **Social Media and Online Reviews:** Feedback from social media and review platforms can offer unfiltered insights into customer satisfaction and areas needing improvement.
5. **A/B Testing:** Regularly testing different elements of your funnel (e.g., landing pages, email campaigns, CTAs) can provide direct feedback on what resonates with your audience and what doesn't.

Iterative Improvement: Ongoing Feedback Leads to Perpetual Optimization

The process of iterative improvement, fueled by continuous feedback, involves several key steps:

1. **Analyze Feedback:** Start by thoroughly analyzing the feedback collected through various mechanisms. Look for patterns or recurring themes that point to specific areas of the funnel needing attention.
2. **Prioritize Changes:** Not all feedback will have equal impact on your funnel's performance. Prioritize changes based on potential impact on conversion rates and customer satisfaction.
3. **Implement Adjustments:** Make targeted adjustments to address the feedback. This could involve redesigning landing pages, tweaking email sequences, or altering your value proposition.
4. **Monitor Results:** After implementing changes, closely monitor your funnel's performance to see the impact of those adjustments. Use analytics to track conversions, engagement, and other relevant metrics.
5. **Repeat the Cycle:** The optimization of your sales funnel is an ongoing process. Continually collect and analyze

feedback, implement changes, and monitor results to ensure your funnel evolves with your audience's needs and expectations.

Utilizing feedback to refine the sales funnel is an essential practice for businesses aiming to enhance their market presence and customer engagement. By establishing robust feedback loops and committing to iterative improvement, businesses can ensure their sales funnel remains a powerful tool for conversion and growth. This approach not only optimizes the funnel's effectiveness but also aligns business strategies with real customer needs, fostering a customer-centric model that drives loyalty and long-term success.

Section 10.7: Mastering Funnel Dynamics

As we conclude Chapter 10 of this book, it's imperative to reflect on the intricate journey through the sales funnel—a pivotal structure that guides potential customers from initial awareness to loyal advocacy. This section encapsulates the core elements of a robust sales funnel strategy, emphasizing the importance of a scientific and methodical approach to optimizing each stage for enhanced conversion rates and customer loyalty.

Key Takeaways: Essential Components of a Successful Sales Funnel Strategy

1. **Segmentation and Personalization:** Tailoring the journey for different audience segments ensures relevance and increases engagement at each funnel stage.
2. **Content Strategy:** Valuable and targeted content is crucial for attracting leads at the top of the funnel and nurturing them through to conversion.
3. **User Experience:** A seamless, intuitive user experience across all digital touchpoints facilitates smooth progression through the funnel stages.
4. **Data-Driven Insights:** Leveraging analytics and feedback to understand behavior and preferences enables continuous refinement of the funnel.
5. **Engagement and Follow-Up:** Consistent engagement and strategic follow-up communications keep leads warm and move them toward purchase decisions.
6. **Conversion Optimization:** Regular testing and optimization of landing pages, CTAs, and other

conversion elements are vital for turning interest into action.

7. **Loyalty Programs:** Post-purchase engagement strategies, including loyalty programs, ensure customers feel valued and encourage repeat business.
8. **Feedback Loops:** Implementing systematic feedback mechanisms allows for the funnel's perpetual refinement based on actual customer experiences.

Call to Action: Applying a Scientific Approach to Sales Funnel Optimization

The journey through the sales funnel is not a one-size-fits-all process but a dynamic and ongoing cycle of attraction, engagement, conversion, and retention. To truly master funnel dynamics, businesses are encouraged to:

- **Adopt a Holistic View:** Understand the sales funnel as a comprehensive journey that requires attention at every stage, from initial awareness to post-purchase loyalty.
- **Embrace Experimentation:** Employ a scientific approach by hypothesizing, testing, analyzing, and iterating on different strategies to find what works best for your audience.

- **Leverage Technology:** Utilize advanced analytics, automation tools, and CRM systems to gain insights, streamline processes, and personalize interactions.
- **Foster a Culture of Continuous Improvement:** Encourage teams to seek out feedback, learn from data, and be agile in implementing changes to adapt to evolving market conditions and consumer expectations.
- **Prioritize Customer Experience:** Always place the customer's needs and experiences at the forefront of funnel optimization efforts. A satisfied customer is the most valuable asset in achieving long-term success.

Mastering the dynamics of the sales funnel is an essential endeavor for any business aiming to thrive in today's competitive landscape. By understanding the critical components of a successful funnel strategy and adopting a scientific approach to its optimization, businesses can significantly improve conversion rates and foster enduring customer loyalty. This journey of continuous learning, adaptation, and customer-centric innovation is what ultimately defines the path to market mastery and sustained growth.

Chapter 10: Step-By-Step How to "Get... It... Done!"

Alright, let's cut through the fluff. You're here to make your sales funnel not just good, but legendary. Here's the no-nonsense, straight-to-the-point guide to revamping your sales funnel. Roll up your sleeves; it's game time.

Section 10.1: Sales Funnel Bootcamp

Step 1: Map It Out
- **Task:** Break down your funnel into crystal-clear stages: Awareness, Interest, Consideration, Conversion, Loyalty.
- **Deadline:** 1 week.

Step 2: KPI Crusade
- **Task:** Nail down your KPIs for each stage. Traffic, leads, conversion rates, retention—get those numbers ready.
- **Deadline:** 2 days.

Step 3: Funnel Forensics
- **Task:** Dive deep into your current funnel. Find where prospects drop off and why they ghost you.
- **Deadline:** 3 days.

Section 10.2: Top of the Funnel Tactics

Step 1: Visibility Victory
- **Task:** Amp up your SEO and social media game. It's time to get seen.
- **Deadline:** 1 week.

Step 2: Lead Magnet Mastery
- **Task:** Craft irresistible lead magnets. Ebooks, webinars—whatever makes your audience tick.

- **Deadline:** 2 weeks.

Step 3: Channel Check
- **Task:** Evaluate and optimize your lead-gen platforms. If it's not working, fix it or ditch it.
- **Deadline:** 1 week.

Section 10.3: Lead Nurturing Ninja Moves

Step 1: Segment Like a Boss
- **Task:** Slice and dice your audience. Personalize like their next purchase depends on it (because it does).
- **Deadline:** 1 week.

Step 2: Content Creation Commando
- **Task:** Produce content that guides your leads closer to the sale. Value-packed and on-point.
- **Deadline:** Ongoing.

Step 3: Email Automation Army
- **Task:** Set up email sequences that nurture leads day and night. Sleep is for the weak.
- **Deadline:** 2 weeks.

Section 10.4: Conversion Conquest

Step 1: Conversion Point Cleanup
- **Task:** Optimize every step where a lead can turn into a sale. No excuses.
- **Deadline:** 2 weeks.

Step 2: A/B Test Assault
- **Task:** Test everything. Then test it again. If it can be improved, it's not good enough yet.
- **Deadline:** Ongoing.

Step 3: Post-Conversion Paradise

- **Task:** Keep customers happy and engaged even after they've bought. Upsell, cross-sell, and sell some more.
- **Deadline:** Ongoing.

Section 10.5: Loyalty Legion

Step 1: Loyalty Program Launch
- **Task:** Design a loyalty program that turns one-time buyers into lifetime fans.
- **Deadline:** 1 month.

Step 2: Feedback Frontline
- **Task:** Set up a system for collecting and acting on customer feedback. Listen, adapt, and overcome.
- **Deadline:** Ongoing.

Step 3: Personalization Power Play
- **Task:** Make every customer feel like your only customer. Personalize everything.
- **Deadline:** Ongoing.

Section 10.6: Feedback Fire-Up

Step 1: Feedback Loop Formation
- **Task:** Create airtight feedback loops for every stage of the funnel. If there's a leak, plug it.
- **Deadline:** 2 weeks.

Step 2: Improvement Impact Zone
- **Task:** Identify and prioritize funnel tweaks based on feedback. Impact over effort.
- **Deadline:** 1 week.

Step 3: Change Champion
- **Task:** Roll out changes and keep a hawk's eye on the results. Adapt or die.

- **Deadline:** Ongoing.

Section 10.7: Funnel Finale

Step 1: Integration Invasion
- **Task:** Make sure every tweak and test feeds back into a unified funnel strategy. Cohesion is king.
- **Deadline:** Ongoing.

Step 2: Experimentation Empire
- **Task:** Encourage a culture of testing and learning. The status quo is the enemy.
- **Deadline:** Ongoing.

Step 3: Optimization Odyssey
- **Task:** Commit to never-ending funnel optimization. The journey doesn't end; it evolves.
- **Deadline:** Forever.

There you have it—a blueprint to funnel mastery that's all killer, no filler. Follow these steps, and watch your conversions, loyalty, and growth skyrocket. The clock's ticking. Let's get... it... done!

Chapter 11 Pre-Breakdown: No Fluff, Just Facts

Section 11.1: Analytics - Your Business's Crystal Ball

Listen up, because if you're not knee-deep in analytics, you're flying blind. This isn't about fancy graphs and numbers; it's about using cold, hard data to make smarter decisions. Whether it's understanding your cash flow or figuring out your customers' next move, analytics is your secret weapon.

Insights You Can't Ignore:
- **Performance Check:** Use analytics to measure everything from sales spikes to the success of your latest marketing campaign. If you're not tracking it, how do you know if it's working?
- **Customer Deep Dive:** Get into the nitty-gritty of what your customers want, when they want it, and how they want it served. Analytics isn't just nice to have; it's your roadmap to customer satisfaction.
- **Trend Spotting:** Stay ahead of the curve by identifying market trends before they explode. Analytics gives you a front-row seat to what's next.
- **Efficiency Expert:** Find the leaks in your operations and plug them with data-driven solutions. Every process can be optimized, and analytics shows you how.

Section 11.2: KPIs - The Scoreboard of Success

If you're not keeping score with KPIs, you're just playing a pickup game in the business world. KPIs are your scoreboard, telling you if you're winning or just playing the game.

Metrics That Matter:
- **Revenue Growth:** Are you making more money than last month, last quarter, last year? If not, why?
- **Customer Costs:** How much does it cost you to get a new customer in the door and keep them there?
- **Lifetime Value:** How much is each customer worth over time? Are you investing in keeping them around?
- **Satisfaction Scores:** Are your customers happy warriors for your brand or looking for the nearest exit?
- **Conversion Rates:** How good are you at turning window shoppers into buyers?

Section 11.3: Your Data Analysis Toolbox

In the age of data, using Excel spreadsheets is like bringing a knife to a gunfight. You need the big guns of analytics tools to slice through the data jungle.

Tools That Don't Mess Around:
- **Google Analytics:** The Swiss Army knife for digital marketing data. If it's happening online, Google Analytics is on it.
- **Tableau:** Turns your data into a visual feast. If you can't see the patterns with Tableau, you're not looking.
- **Power BI:** Microsoft's answer to "Show me the money!" in data form.
- **SAS & Adobe Analytics:** For when you're serious about digging deep into data and customer insights.

Section 11.4: Data - The Map to Treasure

Interpreting data isn't about reading tea leaves; it's about finding the treasure map in the numbers. The businesses that get it right use data to chart their course to undiscovered riches.

Interpretation That Pays Off:
- **Descriptive Diving:** What happened? This is your business's rearview mirror.
- **Diagnostic Detective Work:** Why did it happen? Put on your Sherlock Holmes hat and find out.
- **Predictive Power:** What's likely to happen next? Get your crystal ball polished with predictive analytics.
- **Prescriptive Pathways:** What should we do about it? Data doesn't just highlight problems; it offers solutions.

Section 11.5: Continuous Improvement - The Never-Ending Quest

The game of business isn't won in a sprint; it's a never-ending marathon of improvement. Use analytics to keep pushing forward, optimizing every step, and leaving competitors in your dust.

Keep Moving Forward:
- **Plan-Do-Check-Act:** The business world's loop of life. Plan your moves, do the deed, check the results, and act on what you've learned.
- **Lean and Mean:** Cut the fluff. If it doesn't add value, it's dead weight. Lean analytics keeps you nimble.
- **Six Sigma:** Chase perfection, and you might just catch excellence. It's all about minimizing mistakes and maximizing quality.

Section 11.6: Overcoming Data Decision Dilemmas

Data-driven decision-making is the Holy Grail, but the path is littered with obstacles. From data overload to analysis paralysis, navigating the data landscape requires cunning and strategy.

Strategies That Deliver:
- **Tame the Data Beast:** Too much data? Focus on what matters. Quality trumps quantity every time.
- **Skill Up:** Not everyone's a data scientist, but a little training goes a long way. Knowledge is power.
- **Break Down Silos:** Data doesn't belong in a vault. Share the wealth across departments for a united front.

Section 11.7: Embracing Analytics - The Path to Business Nirvana

At the end of the day, analytics isn't just part of the business; it is the business. It's the difference between guessing and knowing, between hoping and winning.

Final Words of Wisdom:
- **Data Literacy:** Make data your second language. The future belongs to the fluent.
- **Invest in Tools:** The right tools don't just make the job easier; they make the impossible possible.
- **Adopt and Adapt:** Be ready to pivot on a dime. The market waits for no one, and analytics is your best advisor.

Analytics isn't just about collecting data; it's about creating a future where every decision is informed, every strategy is sound, and every investment pays off. Dive in, the data's fine.

Chapter 11: Buckle up, nerds! Time to READ. विजय की ओर! (Vijay ki or!)

- Hindi, with the spirit of a Bollywood hero.

Section 11.1: The Role of Analytics in Business Strategy

In the modern business landscape, the strategic use of data analytics has become a cornerstone for organizations aiming to maintain competitive advantage, drive growth, and enhance operational efficiency. This section explores the pivotal role of data analytics in measuring business performance and how analytics can be leveraged for strategic decision-making and adaptation.

Key Insights: Importance of Data Analytics in Measuring Business Performance

Data analytics offers a comprehensive view of an organization's operational, financial, and customer engagement metrics, providing invaluable insights that are critical for:

1. **Performance Measurement:** Analytics enables businesses to quantify their performance against key indicators such as revenue growth, customer acquisition costs, retention rates, and return on investment (ROI). These metrics offer a clear picture of where the business stands in achieving its strategic objectives.
2. **Customer Insights:** Through the analysis of customer data, businesses can gain deep insights into customer behavior, preferences, and trends. This understanding is crucial for tailoring offerings, enhancing customer experiences, and identifying new market opportunities.
3. **Market Trends:** Analytics helps businesses stay ahead of market trends and shifts by analyzing patterns in industry data. This foresight allows for timely strategic adjustments to capitalize on emerging opportunities or mitigate potential threats.
4. **Operational Efficiency:** By analyzing operational data, businesses can identify inefficiencies and areas for improvement within their processes. This can lead to

cost savings, improved productivity, and enhanced service delivery.

Strategic Use of Data: Leveraging Analytics for Decision-Making and Adaptation

1. **Data-Driven Strategy Formation:** Utilize analytics to inform the development of strategic plans and initiatives. By basing strategies on data rather than intuition, businesses can ensure their decisions are grounded in reality and aligned with market demands.
2. **Adaptive Decision-Making:** In an ever-changing business environment, the ability to adapt quickly is key to survival and growth. Analytics provides the agility needed for rapid decision-making by offering real-time insights into performance and market conditions.
3. **Predictive Analytics:** Beyond analyzing past and present data, predictive analytics can forecast future trends and behaviors. This enables businesses to proactively adjust their strategies in anticipation of future developments.
4. **Customer Segmentation and Personalization:** Use analytics to segment customers based on various criteria and tailor marketing efforts and product offerings to

match the specific needs and preferences of each segment.

5. **Optimization of Marketing and Sales:** Analytics can significantly enhance the effectiveness of marketing and sales efforts by identifying the most profitable channels, optimizing marketing spend, and increasing conversion rates.

6. **Risk Management:** Through the analysis of historical data and market trends, businesses can identify potential risks and develop strategies to mitigate them before they impact the organization.

The strategic integration of data analytics into business operations is not merely an option but a necessity for companies seeking to navigate the complexities of the modern market. By emphasizing the importance of data analytics in measuring performance and leveraging analytics for strategic decision-making and adaptation, businesses can enhance their agility, operational efficiency, and ultimately, their competitiveness in the marketplace. The role of analytics in business strategy marks a paradigm shift towards more informed, responsive, and customer-centric business practices, paving the way for sustainable growth and success.

Section 11.2: Key Performance Indicators (KPIs) for Success

Key Performance Indicators (KPIs) serve as the navigational instruments for businesses, offering measurable values that reflect the performance and success of an organization in achieving key business objectives. This section delves into the critical task of identifying and defining KPIs across different business operations and explores case studies of businesses that have harnessed the power of KPIs to drive growth and improvement.

Defining KPIs: Identifying Critical Metrics Across Business Operations

1. **Revenue Growth:** Measures the increase in a company's sales over a specific period, indicating the effectiveness of sales and marketing strategies.
2. **Customer Acquisition Cost (CAC):** Calculates the total cost of acquiring a new customer, including all marketing and sales expenses, crucial for understanding the efficiency of customer acquisition strategies.
3. **Customer Lifetime Value (CLTV):** Estimates the total revenue a business can expect from a single customer

account throughout their relationship, highlighting the importance of customer retention strategies.

4. **Net Promoter Score (NPS):** Gauges customer satisfaction and loyalty by measuring the likelihood of customers to recommend a company's products or services to others.

5. **Conversion Rate:** The percentage of visitors who take a desired action, such as making a purchase, crucial for assessing the effectiveness of sales funnels and marketing campaigns.

6. **Operational Efficiency Ratios:** Metrics such as inventory turnover, employee productivity, and production costs, which are vital for monitoring the efficiency of business operations.

7. **Return on Investment (ROI):** Measures the gain or loss generated on an investment relative to the amount of money invested, essential for evaluating the profitability of different investments.

KPI Case Studies: Businesses Leveraging KPIs for Growth

- **E-commerce Platform's CLTV Improvement:** An e-commerce company focused on increasing its CLTV by implementing targeted upselling and cross-selling strategies based on customer purchase history analytics. By closely monitoring CLTV as a KPI, the company optimized its marketing efforts, resulting in a 25% increase in average customer lifetime value within a year.

- **Tech Startup's CAC Reduction:** A tech startup utilized detailed tracking of its CAC to identify the most cost-effective marketing channels. By reallocating its budget towards these channels and improving its onboarding process, the startup significantly reduced its CAC while maintaining a steady growth rate in customer acquisition.

- **Manufacturing Firm's Operational Efficiency:** A manufacturing firm introduced KPIs related to production costs and employee productivity to pinpoint inefficiencies in its operations. Through data-driven adjustments to its production processes and workforce management, the firm achieved a 15% reduction in operational costs, enhancing overall profitability.

Identifying and meticulously tracking KPIs is fundamental to the strategic management of a business, enabling leaders to make informed decisions based on quantifiable data. The successful implementation of KPIs, as demonstrated in the case studies, illustrates their value in driving growth, enhancing operational efficiency, and improving customer satisfaction. For businesses aiming to thrive in today's competitive landscape, the strategic use of KPIs is not merely beneficial but essential. By continuously measuring, analyzing, and acting upon these critical indicators, businesses can ensure their operations are aligned with their strategic goals, paving the way for sustained success and improvement.

Section 11.3: Tools for Effective Data Analysis

In the digital age, the ability to analyze vast amounts of data accurately and efficiently is not just an advantage but a necessity for businesses seeking to optimize their operations and strategy. This section provides an overview of leading analytics tools that have become indispensable in deriving actionable insights from data. Additionally, it offers guidance on selecting the most appropriate analytics tools tailored to specific business needs, ensuring that organizations can navigate the complexities of data analysis with precision and effectiveness.

Analytics Tools Review: Leading Solutions for Business Applications

1. **Google Analytics:** An essential tool for digital marketing analysis, Google Analytics offers comprehensive insights into website traffic, user behavior, and conversion metrics. Its integration capabilities with other Google services make it a versatile option for businesses of all sizes.
2. **Tableau:** Renowned for its powerful data visualization capabilities, Tableau allows businesses to create interactive and shareable dashboards. It supports data analysis from various sources, making complex data more accessible and understandable.
3. **Microsoft Power BI:** Power BI is a business analytics solution that enables organizations to visualize data and share insights across the company or embed them in an app or website. Its strong integration with Microsoft products makes it a popular choice for businesses already using the Microsoft ecosystem.
4. **SAS Analytics:** Offering advanced analytical capabilities, SAS Analytics is suited for businesses looking for sophisticated data analysis, predictive modeling, and

machine learning capabilities. It is widely used in industries such as banking, healthcare, and retail.

5. **Adobe Analytics:** Focused on customer journey analytics, Adobe Analytics provides detailed insights into customer interactions across various channels. It is particularly beneficial for businesses focused on optimizing customer experiences.

6. **Salesforce Analytics:** Embedded within the Salesforce platform, Salesforce Analytics extends CRM capabilities with custom reports and dashboards, AI-driven insights, and predictive analytics, making it ideal for sales and customer relationship management.

Choosing the Right Tools: Guidance for Selecting Analytics Tools

1. **Identify Your Business Needs:** Begin by clearly defining the specific insights you seek to gain from your data. Consider factors such as the size of your data sets, the complexity of analysis required, and the primary objectives of your data analysis efforts.

2. **Evaluate Tool Capabilities:** Assess whether a tool's features align with your analytics needs. Look for functionalities such as real-time analysis, data

visualization, integration with existing systems, and scalability.

3. **Consider Ease of Use:** The tool should be accessible to the team members who will use it most frequently. User-friendly interfaces and comprehensive support resources can enhance productivity and reduce the learning curve.

4. **Review Integration Options:** The ability to seamlessly integrate with other tools and systems within your business is crucial. Compatibility can prevent data silos and ensure a unified approach to data analysis.

5. **Analyze Cost vs. Benefit:** Evaluate the cost of the tool against the value it brings to your business. Consider both the initial investment and ongoing expenses such as subscriptions, training, and maintenance.

6. **Trial and Feedback:** Many tools offer trial periods that allow you to test their capabilities. Use this opportunity to gather feedback from end-users and assess the tool's effectiveness in meeting your analytical needs.

Choosing the right analytics tools is a critical decision that can significantly influence a business's ability to understand and act upon its data. By carefully reviewing available options and aligning them with specific business requirements, organizations can harness the power of data analytics to inform strategic decisions, uncover new opportunities, and drive sustained growth. The key is to approach this selection process with a clear understanding of your objectives, a thorough evaluation of each tool's capabilities, and a commitment to investing in the resources that will most effectively meet your analytical needs.

Section 11.4: Interpreting Data for Actionable Insights

In today's data-driven business environment, the ability to interpret data to extract actionable insights is paramount. This section explores various data interpretation techniques that can transform raw data into strategic intelligence, driving informed decision-making and competitive advantage. It also presents real-world examples of how businesses have successfully turned data insights into strategic actions, setting a blueprint for leveraging data analytics effectively.

Data Interpretation Techniques: Analyzing Data for Business Insights

1. **Descriptive Analytics:** This foundational technique involves summarizing historical data to understand changes over time. It helps businesses identify trends, patterns, and anomalies in their operations, sales, and customer behavior.
2. **Diagnostic Analysis:** Going beyond what happened, diagnostic analysis seeks to understand why it happened. Techniques such as correlation analysis and root cause analysis can pinpoint the factors driving outcomes.
3. **Predictive Analytics:** Leveraging statistical models and machine learning, predictive analytics forecasts future trends and behaviors. This allows businesses to anticipate market shifts, customer needs, and potential risks.
4. **Prescriptive Analytics:** The most advanced form of data analysis, prescriptive analytics, suggests actions businesses can take to achieve desired outcomes. It combines insights from descriptive, diagnostic, and predictive analytics to recommend strategic decisions.
5. **Segmentation Analysis:** This technique divides data into segments based on shared characteristics. Businesses can use segmentation to tailor marketing

efforts, product development, and customer service strategies to specific customer groups.

6. **Sentiment Analysis:** By analyzing customer feedback, reviews, and social media conversations, sentiment analysis gauges public opinion about a brand, product, or service. This insight can inform marketing strategies, product improvements, and customer engagement approaches.

Turning Data into Strategy: Real-World Business Applications

- **Retail Chain's Inventory Optimization:** A retail chain used predictive analytics to forecast demand for products across different regions and seasons. By aligning inventory levels with predicted demand, the chain reduced stockouts and overstock situations, optimizing inventory costs and improving customer satisfaction.
- **Financial Services Firm's Risk Assessment:** Leveraging machine learning models, a financial services firm analyzed customer transaction data to identify patterns indicative of fraudulent activity. This prescriptive approach allowed the firm to implement

more effective fraud prevention measures, reducing losses and enhancing customer trust.

- **Healthcare Provider's Patient Care Improvement:** A healthcare provider used descriptive and diagnostic analytics to analyze patient data, identifying common factors leading to readmissions. By understanding these trends, the provider implemented targeted interventions to improve patient care and reduce readmission rates.

- **E-commerce Platform's Personalized Marketing:** An e-commerce platform used segmentation and sentiment analysis to understand customer preferences and sentiment towards various product categories. This data informed personalized marketing campaigns, significantly increasing conversion rates and customer loyalty.

Interpreting data for actionable insights is a critical capability that can significantly impact a business's strategic direction and operational efficiency. By employing a combination of data interpretation techniques, organizations can uncover hidden patterns, predict future trends, and make informed decisions that drive growth and innovation. The examples highlighted demonstrate the transformative potential of data analytics when insights are effectively translated into strategic action. As businesses continue to navigate an increasingly complex and data-rich environment, the ability to turn data into strategy will remain a key differentiator in achieving long-term success.

Section 11.5: The Iterative Process of Business Improvement

In the rapidly evolving business landscape, continuous improvement is not just a strategy but a necessity for survival and growth. This section delves into the models for iterative business improvement based on analytics and outlines strategies for adapting business practices to gleaned analytical insights. It underscores the importance of a dynamic, data-driven approach to refining processes, enhancing customer experiences, and optimizing performance over time.

Continuous Improvement Models Based on Analytics

1. **The PDCA (Plan-Do-Check-Act) Cycle:** Originating from quality management, the PDCA cycle provides a systematic approach to problem-solving and process improvement. Businesses can apply this model to plan

changes based on data analysis, implement these changes, measure the outcomes, and act on the insights to refine further or implement the strategy broadly.

2. **Lean Analytics:** Rooted in the Lean Startup methodology, Lean Analytics focuses on measuring and optimizing business processes with a keen eye on value creation and waste reduction. By identifying key metrics (or one metric that matters at different stages), businesses can rapidly prototype, test, and iterate on ideas based on customer feedback and data analysis.

3. **Six Sigma:** Six Sigma is a data-driven approach aimed at near-perfection in business process performance. By applying statistical methods to identify and eliminate defects or inefficiencies, businesses can improve quality and consistency in their operations.

4. **Data-Driven Decision Making (DDDM):** DDDM involves making decisions based on data analysis and interpretation rather than intuition. By integrating DDDM into their culture, businesses ensure that every decision is informed by relevant and timely data, facilitating continuous improvement.

Adaptation Strategies Based on Analytical Insights

1. **Customer Experience Optimization:** Use customer behavior data and feedback to continually refine the customer journey, addressing pain points and enhancing touchpoints to improve satisfaction and loyalty.
2. **Product and Service Innovation:** Analyze market trends, customer feedback, and competitive insights to inform the development of new products or the improvement of existing offerings, ensuring they meet evolving customer needs.
3. **Operational Efficiency:** Apply insights from process analytics to streamline operations, reduce costs, and improve productivity. This might involve automating repetitive tasks, optimizing supply chains, or redesigning workflows for better efficiency.
4. **Marketing and Sales Alignment:** Utilize sales data and marketing analytics to refine targeting strategies, personalize communications, and optimize sales funnels. This alignment ensures that marketing efforts directly contribute to sales objectives.
5. **Risk Management:** Leverage predictive analytics to identify potential risks before they materialize. By analyzing historical data and market trends, businesses can devise strategies to mitigate risks and avoid costly setbacks.

The iterative process of business improvement, underpinned by continuous analytical review, allows organizations to remain agile, responsive, and competitive. By embracing models such as PDCA, Lean Analytics, Six Sigma, and fostering a culture of data-driven decision-making, businesses can ensure that improvement is not a one-time initiative but a continuous journey. Adaptation strategies informed by analytical insights enable businesses to pivot when necessary, seize new opportunities, and maintain a trajectory of growth and excellence. In the modern business environment, where change is the only constant, the iterative process of improvement is the mainstay of sustainable success.

Section 11.6: Overcoming Challenges in Data-Driven Decision Making

Data-driven decision-making (DDDM) is a pivotal component of modern business strategy, enabling organizations to make objective, informed choices based on empirical evidence. However, navigating the path to effective DDDM can be fraught with challenges and pitfalls. This section explores common obstacles in the journey towards data-driven culture and proposes strategic approaches to surmount these hurdles, ensuring businesses can leverage data to its fullest potential.

Common Pitfalls in Data-Driven Decision Making

1. **Data Overload:** With the vast amounts of data available to businesses, it's easy to become overwhelmed. The challenge lies in identifying what data is relevant and actionable.
2. **Quality and Accuracy Issues:** Poor data quality and inaccurate data can lead to misguided decisions. Ensuring data integrity is paramount but often challenging.
3. **Lack of Comprehensive Analytics Skills:** The gap in analytics expertise can hinder the ability to interpret data correctly and extract valuable insights.
4. **Siloed Data:** Data stored in silos across different departments can prevent a unified view of information, leading to fragmented decision-making.
5. **Resistance to Change:** Organizational culture that favors intuition or tradition over data-driven approaches can impede the adoption of DDDM.

6. **Failure to Act on Insights:** Collecting and analyzing data is one thing; the real challenge is often in implementing changes based on those insights.

Mitigation Strategies: Navigating Through Challenges

1. **Implement Data Management Best Practices:** Develop a clear data governance strategy to manage data overload and ensure high data quality. This includes establishing clear data collection, storage, and analysis protocols.
2. **Invest in Training and Development:** Bridge the analytics skills gap by investing in training for existing staff and hiring data specialists. Creating a culture of continuous learning can empower teams to leverage data more effectively.
3. **Foster Cross-Departmental Collaboration:** Break down data silos by promoting interdepartmental collaboration and integrating data platforms. A unified data ecosystem allows for a holistic analysis and more cohesive decision-making.
4. **Cultivate a Data-Driven Culture:** Address resistance to change by championing the value of DDDM at all levels of the organization. Success stories and demonstrable

benefits from data-driven decisions can help shift cultural perceptions.

5. **Adopt Agile Decision-Making Processes:** Ensure that insights lead to action by adopting more agile decision-making processes. This includes being open to experimentation, learning from failures, and quickly adapting strategies based on new data.
6. **Utilize Advanced Analytics and AI:** Leverage advanced analytics tools and artificial intelligence to manage complex data sets, predict trends, and generate actionable insights. These technologies can automate the heavy lifting of data analysis, making it more accessible to decision-makers.

Overcoming the challenges in data-driven decision making requires a multifaceted strategy that addresses technical, cultural, and operational hurdles. By focusing on data management best practices, investing in analytics capabilities, fostering collaboration, and promoting a culture receptive to change, organizations can navigate the complexities of DDDM. The journey towards a fully integrated data-driven approach is continuous, demanding ongoing commitment to improvement and adaptation. However, the rewards—enhanced strategic agility, improved operational efficiency, and superior competitive advantage—signify its critical importance in the digital age.

Section 11.7: Embracing Analytics for Business Evolution

As we culminate Chapter 11 of this book, it is imperative to underscore the transformative power of analytics in sculpting the trajectory of business success. This concluding section synthesizes the essence of the analytical journey, emphasizing the pivotal role of data-driven insights in fostering organizational growth, innovation, and resilience.

Key Takeaways: The Transformative Power of Analytics

1. **Informed Decision-Making:** Analytics equips businesses with the empirical evidence required to make informed decisions, moving beyond intuition to a more objective, data-driven approach.
2. **Strategic Agility:** The ability to swiftly adapt to market changes, customer preferences, and competitive dynamics is significantly enhanced by leveraging real-time data and predictive insights.

3. **Customer-Centricity:** Analytics enables a deeper understanding of customer behavior, preferences, and needs, allowing businesses to tailor their offerings, enhance customer experiences, and build lasting relationships.
4. **Operational Efficiency:** Through the identification of inefficiencies and optimization opportunities, analytics drives operational improvements, cost reduction, and productivity enhancements.
5. **Risk Management:** Data analytics aids in anticipating potential risks, enabling proactive measures to mitigate impact and navigate uncertainties more effectively.
6. **Innovation and Growth:** By uncovering trends, gaps, and opportunities, analytics serves as a catalyst for innovation, guiding the development of new products, services, and business models.

Call to Action: Adopting a Data-Driven Approach

The journey towards integrating analytics into the fabric of business operations is both a strategic imperative and a competitive necessity. Businesses are urged to:

- **Prioritize Data Literacy:** Cultivate a culture where data literacy is valued and fostered, ensuring team members across the organization can interpret and leverage data effectively.

- **Invest in Analytics Infrastructure:** Allocate resources towards building or enhancing your analytics infrastructure, including tools, technologies, and talent, to harness the full potential of data.
- **Embrace a Culture of Experimentation:** Foster an environment where experimentation is encouraged, allowing for innovation and learning from data-driven trials and iterations.
- **Implement Continuous Learning:** Stay abreast of advancements in analytics methodologies and technologies. Continuous learning and adaptation are key to maintaining relevance and competitiveness.
- **Align Analytics with Business Objectives:** Ensure that your analytics initiatives are closely aligned with strategic business objectives, driving measurable impact and value creation.
- **Champion Data Governance:** Develop robust data governance policies to ensure data quality, security, and privacy, forming the backbone of a trustworthy analytics program.

The embrace of analytics signifies a commitment to continuous improvement, strategic foresight, and a resilient, adaptable business model. As organizations navigate the complexities of the modern market, the integration of a comprehensive, data-driven approach stands as a beacon of progress, innovation, and enduring success. Encouraging businesses to harness the power of analytics is not just a call to action—it is a call to evolution, a mandate to transcend traditional boundaries and redefine the parameters of success in an increasingly data-centric world.

Chapter 11: Step-By-Step How to "Get... It... Done!"

Embrace the Numbers or Get Left Behind

Kickoff: Analytics Boot Camp

Step 1: Analytics Audit - Cut the Excuses

- **Action:** Dive deep. What's your analytics game look like? Weak? Non-existent? Time to level up.
- **By When:** This week.
- **Straight Talk:** Find the gaps, then plan to fill them. Yesterday.

Step 2: Goal-Setting - Aim or Miss

- **Action:** What's the target? More sales? Smoother ops? Nail it down.
- **By When:** Next week.
- **Straight Talk:** Vague goals equal vague results. Be sharp.

Step 3: Plan of Attack - No More Flying Blind

- **Action:** Map it. What tools? Which data? How to track? Get specific.
- **By When:** Two weeks.

- **Straight Talk:** A plan without details is just a wish. Get real.

The KPI Crusade

Step 1: KPI Hunt - What Actually Matters?

- **Action:** Pick KPIs that hit home. Vanity metrics are for amateurs.
- **By When:** This week.
- **Straight Talk:** Choose the KPIs you'd bet your salary on. That serious.

Step 2: Tracking Setup - No More Guessing

- **Action:** Get the systems up. Yesterday's news is old news.
- **By When:** Next week.
- **Straight Talk:** If you're not tracking in real-time, you're losing.

Step 3: Actionable Insights - Adapt or Die

- **Action:** Regular check-ins on KPIs. Adjust fire as needed.
- **By When:** Ongoing.
- **Straight Talk:** Use it or lose it. Data's not just to look pretty.

Tool Time: Choose Wisely

Step 1: Tech Recon - No More Dinosaur Tech

- **Action:** What's out there? What fits? Do the homework.
- **By When:** This week.
- **Straight Talk:** Stop using the tech equivalent of a flip phone.

Step 2: Integration Operation - Get It Together

- **Action:** Make the chosen tools part of your DNA.
- **By When:** Two weeks.
- **Straight Talk:** New tools, same old silos? You've solved nothing.

Step 3: Insight Mining - Strike Gold

- **Action:** Dig into that data. Find the gold.
- **By When:** Ongoing.
- **Straight Talk:** If insights were easy, everyone would have them. Dig deeper.

From Data to Dollars

Step 1: Skill Up - No More Amateurs

- **Action:** Your team needs to know their stuff. Train them.
- **By When:** This month.
- **Straight Talk:** Data illiteracy is a business death sentence.

Step 2: Decision Time - No More Gut Feelings
- **Action:** Use the data. Make smarter moves.
- **By When:** Ongoing.
- **Straight Talk:** Your gut's good for digesting food, not making business decisions.

Step 3: Continuous Evolution - Never Settle
- **Action:** Always be iterating. What worked today might not tomorrow.
- **By When:** Forever.
- **Straight Talk:** The market waits for no one. Keep moving.

Culture Shift: Data-Driven or Bust
Step 1: Break Down Walls - Share or Perish
- **Action:** Data silos are the enemy. Tear them down.
- **By When:** ASAP.
- **Straight Talk:** Hoarding data is like hoarding toilet paper. Pointless and annoying.

Step 2: Live by Data - Make It Your Religion
- **Action:** Data-driven decisions at all levels. No exceptions.
- **By When:** From now till the end.

- **Straight Talk:** If you're not using data, you're just another business casualty.

Wrap-Up: Analytics isn't just for the geeks; it's your lifeline. Get with the program, integrate those insights, and make moves that count. This isn't just about surviving; it's about thriving. Let's get... it... done!

Chapter 12 Pre-Breakdown: No Fluff, Just Facts

Section 12.1: Failure – Your Secret Weapon

Forget sugarcoating. Every disaster you've faced is a goldmine. Those flops? They're not just mess-ups; they're your map to not screwing up again. Let's get real about turning those faceplants into your comeback story.

- **Tech Misfire:** Remember when a tech giant missed the mark? They shot for the stars but forgot to check if anyone wanted to go to space. **Takeaway:** Match your moonshots with what the crowd actually wants.
- **Retail Ghost Town:** That retail behemoth that snubbed online shopping? They're a cautionary tale in not listening. **Takeaway:** Your customers are talking. Start listening or start packing.
- **Overreach and Burn:** Expansion is great until you're expanding into places that don't want you. **Takeaway:** Know your turf before you plant your flag.
- **Diversify with Caution:** Jack of all trades, master of none? Not a great look. **Takeaway:** Stick to your guns. If you're going to branch out, make sure it's not a wild swing.

Section 12.2: Adaptation is Your Superpower

Some businesses are like chameleons, blending and thriving. They see a wall, they don't headbutt it; they find a way around it. Here's how they do it:

- **Cloud Conversion:** That software giant didn't just jump on the cloud bandwagon; they built the wagon. **Takeaway:** Spot the next big wave and surf it before it breaks.
- **Retail's Digital Rebirth:** That old-school retailer that went digital and killed it? They got that you can't fight the future. **Takeaway:** Online is not the enemy; it's the evolution.
- **Green is the New Black:** That food company that went all-in on organic? They knew green would make them gold. **Takeaway:** Sustainability isn't just good for the earth; it's great for business.
- **EV or Bust:** Cars that don't guzzle gas but still turn heads? That's one automaker's bet, and it's paying off. **Takeaway:** Lead the charge on change, and the market will follow.

Section 12.3: Innovate or Die Trying

Innovation isn't just throwing stuff at the wall and seeing what sticks. It's about changing the game. Here's how the big guns do it:

- **Smartphone Saga:** That one smartphone that changed everything? It wasn't just a phone; it was a revolution in your pocket. **Takeaway:** Build something that turns the everyday into the extraordinary.
- **E-commerce Empire:** That retail giant online didn't just sell stuff; they redefined shopping. **Takeaway:** Make buying so easy that going to the store feels like a chore.
- **Drive Electric:** The car company that bet big on electric when everyone else was hedging? They're not just

making cars; they're crafting the future. **Takeaway:** Don't follow where the path may lead; go where there's no path and leave a trail.

Section 12.4: Engage or Go Extinct

Customer engagement isn't about spamming their inbox. It's about making them feel like part of the tribe. Here's the playbook:
- **Tech's Seamless World:** That tech giant's ecosystem isn't just products; it's a lifestyle. **Takeaway:** Make your brand an experience, not just a purchase.
- **Retail's Rewards Revolution:** That retailer's loyalty program isn't a card; it's a club. **Takeaway:** Make them feel special, and they'll stick like glue.
- **Hospitality's Personal Touch:** That hotel chain doesn't just offer a bed; they offer a dream. **Takeaway:** Treat every customer like they're the only one.
- **Automotive's Aftercare:** That car brand's service doesn't end with the sale; it's just the beginning. **Takeaway:** Keep wooing them long after they've bought in.

Section 12.5: Marketing Magic

A killer marketing campaign doesn't just catch eyes; it captures hearts. Here's how legends are made:
- **Real-Time Genius:** That snack brand that won the blackout? They weren't just quick; they were clever. **Takeaway:** Be the brand that knows how to party, even when the lights go out.

- **Beauty's New Face:** That beauty campaign that showed real people? It wasn't just ads; it was a movement. **Takeaway:** Show the world as it is, and they'll see you as the hero.
- **User-Generated Gold:** That campaign that got everyone shooting their shots? It wasn't just content; it was community. **Takeaway:** Turn your customers into your creators.

Section 12.6: Digital or Bust

Digital transformation isn't a buzzword; it's your bread and butter. Here's how you don't get left in the digital dust:
- **Banking on Blockchain:** That bank that went blockchain wasn't just tech-savvy; they were trust-building. **Takeaway:** Use tech to solve problems, not just to show off.
- **Retail's Omnichannel Oasis:** That retailer that blended online and offline? They didn't just adapt; they anticipated. **Takeaway:** Be everywhere your customers are, even before they know they need you.
- **Manufacturing's Smart Shift:** That factory that went smart? They weren't just cutting costs; they were cutting edge. **Takeaway:** Automate the mundane, innovate the extraordinary.

Section 12.7: Future-Proof or Face Oblivion

Wrapping it up, here's the deal: Learn from the legends, dodge the duds, and always be two steps ahead. Your business isn't just a business; it's a legacy. Start building it like one.

- **Adaptability:** Like water, my friends. Be ready to flow or crash through, whatever it takes.
- **Customer King:** Know them, wow them, keep them. It's that simple and that hard.
- **Purpose-Driven:** Solve real problems, and they'll throw money at you to solve theirs.
- **Data-Driven:** If you're not measuring, you're guessing. Stop guessing.
- **Sustainability and Ethics:** Do good, and the good comes back. Karma's a business model.
- **Tech-Forward:** If you're not riding the wave of the latest tech, you're swimming against the tide.

There you have it. No fluff, just the hard truths about winning in business. Now, go get it.

Chapter 12: Buckle up, nerds! Time to READ. Para sa Tagumpay! (For Success!)

- Filipino, because winning is more fun in the Philippines.

Section 12.1: Lessons from Failure

The road to business success is often paved with failures. Each misstep carries potent lessons that, when properly analyzed and understood, can significantly alter a company's strategic trajectory for the better. This section explores insightful case studies of business failures, delving into the critical lessons learned and discussing how these moments of failure became pivotal turning points for strategic reevaluation and eventual success.

- **Adaptability:** Like water, my friends. Be ready to flow or crash through, whatever it takes.
- **Customer King:** Know them, wow them, keep them. It's that simple and that hard.
- **Purpose-Driven:** Solve real problems, and they'll throw money at you to solve theirs.
- **Data-Driven:** If you're not measuring, you're guessing. Stop guessing.
- **Sustainability and Ethics:** Do good, and the good comes back. Karma's a business model.
- **Tech-Forward:** If you're not riding the wave of the latest tech, you're swimming against the tide.

There you have it. No fluff, just the hard truths about winning in business. Now, go get it.

Chapter 12: Buckle up, nerds! Time to READ. Para sa Tagumpay! (For Success!)

- Filipino, because winning is more fun in the Philippines.

Section 12.1: Lessons from Failure

The road to business success is often paved with failures. Each misstep carries potent lessons that, when properly analyzed and understood, can significantly alter a company's strategic trajectory for the better. This section explores insightful case studies of business failures, delving into the critical lessons learned and discussing how these moments of failure became pivotal turning points for strategic reevaluation and eventual success.

Insightful Failures: Analyzing Business Missteps

1. **Technology Misalignment:** A leading tech company once ventured into the mobile market with a product that was significantly ahead of its time. The failure stemmed from a lack of market readiness and insufficient infrastructure. Lesson Learned: Innovation must align with market capacity and customer readiness to ensure adoption.

2. **Ignoring Customer Feedback:** A once-dominant retail giant failed to adapt to the digital revolution, largely ignoring customer preferences for online shopping and more personalized services. Lesson Learned: Customer feedback is invaluable; ignoring it can lead to obsolescence.

3. **Overexpansion:** A popular restaurant chain rapidly expanded its operations globally without a solid understanding of local markets, leading to massive financial losses. Lesson Learned: Sustainable growth requires careful planning and an understanding of local consumer behaviors.

4. **Product Diversification Without Focus:** A renowned software company diversified into hardware without a clear strategy or focus, resulting in products that

confused consumers and diluted brand identity. Lesson Learned: Diversification needs to be strategic and focused to bolster, not dilute, brand strength.

Turning Points: Strategic Reevaluation Post-Failure

- **Pivot to Customer-Centric Innovation:** The tech company that failed in the mobile market leveraged its learnings to later introduce products that were not only technologically advanced but also aligned with consumer trends and infrastructure developments.
- **Digital Transformation:** The retail giant's failure prompted a strategic overhaul, leading to significant investments in e-commerce, digital marketing, and data analytics to better meet customer expectations.
- **Localized Market Strategies:** The restaurant chain reevaluated its expansion strategy, opting for a more localized approach that considered cultural preferences and eating habits, which eventually stabilized its operations.
- **Refocused Core Competencies:** The software company retracted its unsuccessful foray into hardware and refocused on its core competencies, leveraging its

strengths in software to regain market leadership and trust.

Failures, though challenging, offer invaluable lessons that can redefine business strategies and pave the way for future successes. By thoroughly analyzing where things went wrong, businesses can identify underlying issues, reevaluate their strategies, and make pivotal changes. This process of learning from failure and adapting accordingly is crucial for businesses aiming to thrive in a constantly evolving market. The case studies highlighted underscore the importance of resilience, adaptability, and the continuous pursuit of alignment with market needs and customer expectations. Turning failures into lessons and strategic turning points is an essential skill for any business committed to long-term growth and innovation.

Section 12.2: Success Stories of Adaptation and Growth

In the tumultuous landscape of modern business, the ability to adapt to market changes and internal challenges is not just an asset; it's a necessity for survival and growth. This section highlights businesses that have exemplified agility and innovation, successfully navigating through adversity to achieve remarkable growth. By dissecting the strategies that propelled these companies forward, we can distill valuable insights for businesses striving to carve their paths to success.

Adaptation Successes: Navigating Through Change

1. **Technology Firm's Pivot to Cloud Computing:** A global technology firm, initially focused on traditional software products, recognized the burgeoning potential of cloud computing early on. By pivoting its business model towards cloud services, the company not only secured its market position but also opened new revenue streams, leading to unprecedented growth.
2. **Retail Chain's Digital Transformation:** Facing the brink of irrelevance due to the rise of e-commerce, a traditional brick-and-mortar retail chain reinvented itself by embracing digital technologies. Through the integration of online and offline experiences, the retailer managed to enhance customer engagement, driving a significant increase in sales.
3. **Food and Beverage Company's Sustainability Shift:** In response to growing consumer demand for

sustainable and healthy products, a leading food and beverage company overhauled its product lineup to include organic and eco-friendly options. This strategic adaptation not only boosted its brand image but also attracted a new segment of environmentally conscious consumers.

4. **Automotive Manufacturer's Electrification Strategy:** An established automotive manufacturer successfully transitioned from traditional combustion engines to electric vehicles (EVs) in anticipation of future mobility trends. This forward-thinking approach allowed the company to lead the EV market, capitalizing on the growing demand for sustainable transportation solutions.

Growth Strategies: Lessons from Successful Adaptations

- **Visionary Leadership:** The cornerstone of successful adaptation lies in visionary leadership that can anticipate future trends and steer the company in the right direction.
- **Customer-Centric Innovation:** Understanding and responding to customer needs is crucial. The companies

that thrive are those that continuously innovate to meet and exceed customer expectations.

- **Agility and Flexibility:** The ability to quickly pivot in response to market changes is a defining trait of adaptive businesses. Implementing flexible processes and a culture that embraces change is vital.
- **Strategic Investment in Technology:** Leveraging the latest technologies to enhance products, services, and customer experiences can significantly differentiate a company from its competitors.
- **Sustainability and Social Responsibility:** Aligning business practices with sustainability and ethical considerations resonates with today's consumers and can open new markets.
- **Continuous Learning and Improvement:** Successful companies foster a culture of continuous learning, ensuring that they remain competitive and relevant in a fast-evolving business environment.

The success stories of businesses that have masterfully adapted to change underscore the importance of agility, innovation, and strategic foresight in today's business landscape. These narratives not only inspire but also offer practical lessons and strategies for businesses aiming to navigate the complexities of market dynamics and internal challenges. Embracing adaptation as a core component of business strategy is essential for achieving sustained growth and building resilience against the inevitable shifts of the business world.

Section 12.3: Innovations That Changed the Market

In the relentless pursuit of progress, innovation stands as the beacon that guides industries into new eras. This section delves into the remarkable case studies of businesses whose innovations not only redefined their markets but also set new benchmarks for their industries, creating ripple effects that reshaped competitive landscapes and consumer expectations.

Market Innovators: Trailblazers of Industry

1. **The Smartphone Revolution:** The introduction of the smartphone by a tech giant revolutionized not just the telecommunications sector but also the way people interact with technology, integrating computing power, connectivity, and multimedia capabilities into a single device. This innovation paved the way for a new

ecosystem of apps and services, transforming various industries including retail, entertainment, and finance.

2. **E-commerce Platforms:** A leading online retailer redefined the retail industry by introducing an e-commerce platform that offered unparalleled convenience, selection, and customer service. This innovation not only disrupted traditional retail but also catalyzed the growth of online shopping globally, forcing retailers to adapt or risk obsolescence.

3. **Electric Vehicles (EVs):** An automotive company's commitment to electric vehicles sparked a revolution in the auto industry, challenging the dominance of internal combustion engines and accelerating the shift towards sustainable transportation. This move not only positioned the company as a leader in EV technology but also prompted traditional automakers to accelerate their own EV initiatives.

4. **Cloud Computing:** The advent of cloud computing by a tech corporation transformed the IT landscape, enabling businesses of all sizes to access computing resources and services on-demand. This innovation democratized technology, fostering agility, scalability, and innovation across industries.

Impact Analysis: The Ripple Effects of Market Innovations

- **Consumer Behavior:** These innovations significantly altered consumer behavior and expectations, emphasizing convenience, sustainability, and connectivity. Businesses across sectors are now compelled to innovate continuously to meet these evolving demands.
- **Industry Standards:** Innovations such as these often set new industry standards, compelling competitors to innovate or adopt similar technologies to remain relevant. This has led to rapid advancements and the emergence of new industry paradigms.
- **Regulatory and Ethical Considerations:** Groundbreaking innovations often challenge existing regulatory frameworks and raise ethical considerations, prompting discussions around data privacy, environmental sustainability, and market monopolies.
- **Economic Impact:** By creating new markets and opportunities, these innovations have contributed significantly to economic growth, job creation, and the emergence of new business models.
- **Global Reach:** The global adoption of these innovations underscores the interconnectedness of modern markets,

where a significant breakthrough in one region can have far-reaching implications worldwide.

The innovations that have reshaped markets underscore the transformative power of visionary ideas and relentless execution. These case studies not only highlight the potential for innovation to drive growth and change but also underscore the importance of adaptability, foresight, and resilience in an ever-evolving business landscape. As industries continue to evolve, the lessons drawn from these market innovators will remain invaluable for businesses aiming to lead rather than follow in the march towards the future.

Section 12.4: Effective Customer Engagement Models

In the realm of modern business, the art of customer engagement has evolved into a critical determinant of success. This section showcases businesses renowned for their exceptional customer engagement and loyalty programs, unraveling the strategies and practices that have cemented their status as leaders in fostering deep, enduring connections with their customers.

Engagement Excellence: Benchmark Businesses

1. **Tech Giant's Ecosystem Loyalty:** A leading technology company has masterfully created an integrated ecosystem that encourages loyalty by seamlessly connecting various products and services. Customers invested in this ecosystem find value not just in individual products but in the collective experience, making it harder to switch to competitors.
2. **Retail Loyalty Program Innovation:** A multinational retail corporation revolutionized customer loyalty through a program that offers personalized discounts, priority service, and exclusive access to new products. This program uses data analytics to tailor benefits, enhancing customer satisfaction and retention.
3. **Hospitality Industry's Personalized Experiences:** A luxury hotel chain is distinguished by its commitment to personalized guest experiences. By leveraging customer data, the chain can customize every aspect of a guest's stay, from room preferences to dining, ensuring a memorable and unique experience that drives repeat business.
4. **Automotive Customer Care Excellence:** An automotive brand set the benchmark for customer

engagement through an unparalleled after-sales service program. This includes regular updates, maintenance tips, and direct support, fostering a sense of belonging and loyalty among car owners.

Model Strategies: The Foundations of Success

- **Personalization:** Tailoring interactions and offerings based on individual customer preferences and behaviors is key. This requires sophisticated data analysis and a commitment to understanding each customer's unique needs.
- **Consistency Across Channels:** Providing a consistent, high-quality customer experience across all touchpoints, whether online, in-store, or through customer service, builds trust and satisfaction.
- **Community Building:** Encouraging the formation of customer communities around a brand or product can significantly enhance loyalty. This can be achieved through social media, exclusive events, or online forums.
- **Feedback Loops:** Implementing mechanisms to collect and act on customer feedback demonstrates a commitment to continuous improvement and customer satisfaction.

- **Rewarding Loyalty:** Developing comprehensive loyalty programs that offer real value to customers encourages repeat business and word-of-mouth promotion.
- **Emotional Connection:** Beyond transactions, successful engagement models foster an emotional connection with the brand, turning customers into brand advocates.
- **Innovation:** Continuously innovating the customer experience keeps engagement fresh and exciting, setting the brand apart from competitors.

The businesses highlighted in this section exemplify the pinnacle of customer engagement and loyalty, achieved through strategic personalization, exceptional service, and innovative loyalty programs. Their success stories underscore the importance of viewing customer engagement as a holistic, ongoing process that spans the entirety of the customer journey. For businesses aspiring to elevate their customer engagement, these models offer valuable insights and practices that can be adapted and implemented to suit their unique contexts and customer bases. In the competitive landscape of today, where customer expectations are ever-evolving, embracing these principles of engagement excellence is not just beneficial—it's essential for sustained growth and success.

Section 12.5: Transformative Marketing Campaigns

The landscape of marketing is replete with campaigns that have not only captured the public's imagination but also dramatically shifted brand perception and market share. This section delves into some of the most groundbreaking marketing campaigns, highlighting the strategic planning, innovative execution, and significant outcomes that have left indelible marks on their industries.

Campaign Highlights: Marketing that Moves Markets

1. **The Dawn of Real-Time Marketing:** A leading beverage company capitalized on a major live event's blackout, crafting an instantaneous, witty social media post that became the talk of the night. This pioneering use of real-time marketing showcased the power of agility and relevance in capturing audience attention.
2. **Empowerment Through Advertising:** A beauty brand transformed its image from traditional beauty products to champions of real beauty through a campaign that

used real women of various shapes, sizes, and ethnicities instead of models. This campaign not only elevated brand perception but also sparked global conversations about beauty standards.

3. **Leveraging User-Generated Content:** A technology giant encouraged users to create and share content using their product, leading to a massive influx of user-generated content that showcased the product's versatility and user engagement, effectively turning customers into brand ambassadors.

4. **Sustainability as a Selling Point:** An outdoor clothing and gear company launched a campaign urging consumers to reconsider purchasing needs, emphasizing the brand's commitment to sustainability and responsible consumption. This paradoxical marketing approach enhanced brand loyalty and attracted a broad, eco-conscious customer base.

Behind the Scenes: Crafting Campaigns that Resonate

- **Strategic Planning:** These campaigns began with deep market research and strategic planning, identifying unique opportunities to engage with audiences in meaningful ways. Understanding audience values, trends, and behaviors was key to crafting messages that resonate.

- **Creative Execution:** Creativity and innovation were at the heart of these campaigns. Whether through leveraging new technologies, platforms, or concepts, each campaign broke away from conventional advertising norms to capture attention and engage audiences.

- **Measurable Outcomes:** The impact of these campaigns was profound, leading to increased brand awareness, elevated brand perception, and, in many cases, significant market share growth. Beyond metrics, these campaigns also achieved deeper emotional connections with audiences, contributing to long-term loyalty and advocacy.

- **Adaptability and Learning:** Post-campaign analyses were crucial in understanding the effectiveness of strategies, allowing brands to adapt and refine future marketing efforts. Lessons learned from these campaigns have often set new standards in marketing excellence.

The transformative marketing campaigns highlighted in this section illustrate the profound impact that strategic, creative, and well-executed marketing can have on brand perception and market dynamics. These campaigns serve as inspiring benchmarks for how to engage audiences in an increasingly cluttered and evolving marketplace. By understanding the behind-the-scenes planning and execution that contributed to their success, businesses can glean valuable insights into developing their own groundbreaking marketing strategies. In the end, these campaigns underscore the power of marketing not just to sell, but to inspire, engage, and effect genuine change.

Section 12.6: Pioneers in Digital Transformation

The digital era has ushered in unprecedented changes across all sectors, compelling businesses to adapt or face obsolescence. This section explores the journey of digital trailblazers who not only embraced digital transformation but also set new benchmarks within their industries. Through detailed case studies, we examine the strategies, technologies, and outcomes of their digital evolution, offering insights into the blueprint for successful transformation.

Digital Trailblazers: Leading the Charge in Innovation

1. **Financial Services Transformation:** A global bank embraced digital transformation by integrating AI and blockchain technology to streamline operations and enhance customer service. This move not only improved efficiency and security but also revolutionized the customer experience through personalized, real-time banking services.
2. **Retail Reinvention:** Facing the challenge of online competition, a traditional retailer pivoted to an omnichannel strategy, leveraging data analytics and digital technologies to unify the online and in-store experience. This approach boosted sales, improved inventory management, and significantly enhanced customer loyalty.
3. **Manufacturing Industry 4.0:** An automotive manufacturer adopted Industry 4.0 principles, incorporating IoT, machine learning, and smart automation into its production lines. This digital overhaul increased production flexibility, reduced waste, and allowed for real-time monitoring and predictive maintenance.

4. **Healthcare Digitalization:** A healthcare provider implemented electronic health records (EHR), telemedicine, and AI-driven diagnostic tools, transforming patient care by improving access, personalizing treatment plans, and enhancing outcomes through data-driven insights.

Transformation Tactics: Navigating the Digital Shift

- **Strategic Planning:** Successful digital transformation begins with a clear vision and strategic plan that aligns with business goals and customer needs. This involves assessing current capabilities, identifying digital gaps, and prioritizing initiatives that offer the highest value.
- **Customer-Centric Approach:** At the heart of digital transformation is the need to enhance the customer experience. Businesses that lead in digital transformation use technology to gain a deeper understanding of their customers and deliver personalized, convenient, and seamless experiences.
- **Agile Implementation:** Embracing an agile methodology for digital projects allows businesses to iterate rapidly, test new ideas, and adapt strategies

based on feedback and results. This flexibility is crucial in the fast-paced digital landscape.
- **Technology Investment:** Investing in the right technologies is key to enabling digital transformation. This includes cloud computing for scalability, AI and analytics for insights, and cybersecurity measures to protect data and build trust.
- **Culture and Leadership:** Transformative change requires buy-in at all levels of the organization, from executive leadership fostering a culture of innovation to employees adapting to new digital workflows and mindsets.
- **Measuring Success:** Establishing clear metrics and KPIs to measure the impact of digital initiatives ensures that businesses can track progress, optimize strategies, and demonstrate value.

The pioneers of digital transformation have set the stage for a new era of business, where agility, innovation, and customer-centricity are paramount. Their journeys underscore the importance of embracing change, leveraging technology, and fostering a culture of continuous improvement. For businesses looking to navigate their own digital transformations, these case studies serve as both inspiration and a roadmap, highlighting that the path to digital excellence is both a challenge and an opportunity to redefine success in the digital age.

Section 12.7: Synthesizing Insights for Future Strategy

As we conclude Chapter 12 of this book, it's crucial to distill the essence of the transformative journeys, strategic pivots, and innovative campaigns we've explored. These narratives not only serve as a testament to the dynamic nature of the market but also offer a treasure trove of insights and lessons that can guide businesses towards enhanced success and resilience. This section encapsulates the core learnings from the case studies presented and issues a call to action for businesses to integrate these insights into their strategic frameworks.

Key Takeaways: Lessons from the Frontlines of Business Innovation

1. **Adaptability is Key:** The ability to pivot and adapt in response to market shifts, technological advancements, or consumer behavior changes is paramount. The case

studies underscored the significance of agility in sustaining and amplifying success.

2. **Customer-Centricity Drives Engagement:** Deeply understanding and responding to customer needs, preferences, and values fosters stronger engagement, loyalty, and advocacy. Tailoring experiences and communications to customer insights can set a brand apart.

3. **Innovation Should Be Purposeful:** Whether through product development, marketing campaigns, or digital transformation, innovation that addresses real needs, solves problems, or enhances experiences is most effective. Purpose-driven innovation resonates with audiences and yields lasting impacts.

4. **Data is a Strategic Asset:** Leveraging data analytics to inform decision-making, personalize customer interactions, and optimize operations is a critical competitive advantage. Data-driven insights can illuminate opportunities and guide strategic direction.

5. **Sustainability and Ethics Matter:** Incorporating sustainability and ethical considerations into business practices and value propositions appeals to modern consumers and can elevate brand perception and market position.

6. **Leverage Technology Strategically:** The judicious application of technology—be it through digital marketing, e-commerce platforms, or cloud computing—can dramatically enhance operational efficiency, customer engagement, and innovation capacity.

Call to Action: Leveraging Lessons for Strategic Advantage

Businesses are encouraged to absorb and apply the lessons gleaned from these case studies to their strategic planning and execution. To navigate the complexities of today's market and carve a path toward future success, businesses should:

- Cultivate a Culture of Adaptability: Encourage flexibility, continuous learning, and innovation at all organizational levels. Being prepared to pivot quickly can make all the difference in capitalizing on new opportunities or mitigating risks.
- **Deepen Customer Insights:** Invest in understanding your customers through data analytics, direct feedback, and market research. A nuanced understanding of your audience can inform more effective engagement strategies.

- **Embrace Purposeful Innovation:** Align innovation initiatives with clear objectives that meet customer needs, drive value, and differentiate your brand. Innovation for its own sake is less likely to yield meaningful results.
- **Harness Data for Strategic Decision-Making:** Develop robust data analytics capabilities to inform strategic decisions, optimize performance, and personalize customer experiences. Data should be a cornerstone of strategic planning.
- **Prioritize Sustainability and Ethics:** Integrate sustainability and ethical practices into your business model. These considerations are increasingly influencing consumer choices and can strengthen your brand's reputation and loyalty.

The insights from the case studies presented in this chapter illuminate a path forward for businesses seeking to thrive in an ever-evolving marketplace. By internalizing these lessons and integrating them into strategic planning, businesses can enhance their adaptability, innovation, customer engagement, and overall resilience. The future of business success lies in the ability to synthesize insights from past successes and failures, applying them to forge strategies that are robust, responsive, and aligned with the values of today's consumers.

Chapter 12: Step-By-Step How to "Get... It... Done!"

Section 12.1: Failures to Fortunes

Step 1: Failure Post-Mortem

- **Just Do It:** Rip off the Band-Aid. Look at where you tanked, why, and how it stung.
- **Deadline:** 1 week.
- **Real Talk:** No sugarcoating. Find the ugly truths.

Step 2: Strategy Rehab

- **Just Do It:** Fix your strategy like it's a leaky pipe. Plug the holes with what you learned.
- **Deadline:** 2 weeks.
- **Real Talk:** It's surgery time. Cut the fluff, keep the stuff.

Step 3: Disaster-Proofing

- **Just Do It:** Craft your "Oh, no, not again" plan.
- **Deadline:** 1 week.
- **Real Talk:** Make a plan so solid it'd survive a zombie apocalypse.

Section 12.2: Success Story Stealing

Step 1: Success Heist

- **Just Do It:** Hunt down businesses that turned lemons into limousines.

- **Deadline:** 1 week.
- **Real Talk:** Be a copycat, but make it fashion.

Step 2: Adapt or Die

- **Just Do It:** Make their win your win but with your signature on it.
- **Deadline:** 2 weeks.
- **Real Talk:** Clone it, own it, hone it.

Step 3: Evolution or Extinction

- **Just Do It:** Keep an eye on your new moves. Are they soaring or snoring?
- **Deadline:** Continuous.
- **Real Talk:** Adapt like you're on "Survivor." Outwit, outplay, outlast.

Section 12.3: Innovate or Evaporate

Step 1: Innovation Safari

- **Just Do It:** Spot the big game changers in your jungle.
- **Deadline:** 1 week.
- **Real Talk:** Find the wheel inventors, not the wheel spinners.

Step 2: Purpose-Driven Innovation

- **Just Do It:** Innovate where it hurts so good.
- **Deadline:** 3 weeks.

- **Real Talk:** Solve actual problems. Don't just add bells and whistles.

Step 3: Trial by Fire
- **Just Do It:** Unleash your brainchild and see if it flies or flops.
- **Deadline:** Continuous.
- **Real Talk:** Be ready to pivot faster than a politician.

Section 12.4: Engage or Be Enraged

Step 1: Engagement Autopsy
- **Just Do It:** Tear apart your current "how we make them love us" tactics.
- **Deadline:** 1 week.
- **Real Talk:** Find the dead zones and the no-go zones.

Step 2: Swipe Right on Best Practices
- **Just Do It:** Steal like an artist from the masters of heart-stealing.
- **Deadline:** 2 weeks.
- **Real Talk:** Make it fit like it was always meant to be there.

Step 3: Love Potion Brewing
- **Just Do It:** Whip up ways to make your customers never want to leave.
- **Deadline:** Continuous.

- **Real Talk:** Get them addicted (legally).

Section 12.5: Marketing on Steroids
Step 1: Campaign Deep Dive
- **Just Do It:** Dissect campaigns that actually got people excited.
- **Deadline:** 1 week.
- **Real Talk:** What made them tick, stick, and click?

Step 2: Your Marketing Masterpiece
- **Just Do It:** Craft a campaign so good it feels illegal.
- **Deadline:** 3 weeks.
- **Real Talk:** Make sure it's on-brand but with a side of "whoa."

Step 3: Launch and Stalk
- **Just Do It:** Set it free, then watch like a hawk.
- **Deadline:** Continuous.
- **Real Talk:** Be ready to twist, tweak, and turn on a dime.

Section 12.6: Digital Domination
Step 1: Digital Reality Check
- **Just Do It:** How digitally savvy are you really? Be brutally honest.
- **Deadline:** 1 week.
- **Real Talk:** Spot your digital duds and studs.

Step 2: Go Digital or Go Home
- **Just Do It:** Map your digital glow-up.
- **Deadline:** 3 weeks.
- **Real Talk:** Focus on what will catapult you, not just keep you afloat.

Step 3: Deploy and Decipher
- **Just Do It:** Roll out the red carpet for your digital strategy.
- **Deadline:** Continuous.
- **Real Talk:** Embrace change like it's your long-lost friend.

Section 12.7: Strategy on Steroids
Step 1: Insight Hoarding
- **Just Do It:** Round up every golden nugget of insight from this chapter.
- **Deadline:** 1 week.
- **Real Talk:** What's going to catapult you past the competition?

Step 2: Strategy Synthesis
- **Just Do It:** Fuse these insights into your master plan.
- **Deadline:** 2 weeks.
- **Real Talk:** Make your strategy smarter, sharper, sexier.

Step 3: Culture Shift

- **Just Do It:** Cultivate a workplace that thrives on insights and innovation.
- **Deadline:** Continuous.
- **Real Talk:** Make being insight-driven your brand.

Wrap-Up: There you go, a blueprint for those ready to roll up their sleeves and dive headfirst into the fray. Let's not just do things; let's make things happen. Time to move from planning to action, from dreaming to doing. Let's get... it... done!

Chapter 13 Pre-Breakdown: No Fluff, Just Facts

Section 13.1: Getting Ready to Roll

The Deal: Strategy's nothing without action. It's crunch time, and here's how you make sure your grand plans don't end up as just fancy PowerPoint slides.

Quick Wins:

- **Roadmap It:** Break down the master plan into bite-sized tasks. Assign, set deadlines, and get a project management tool so you're not managing this on sticky notes.
- **Timelines and Resources:** Be real about how long stuff takes and what you need to get it done. Overoptimism is your enemy.
- **Talk, Monitor, Repeat:** Keep everyone in the loop and keep your eyes on the prize. If things go sideways, you want to know yesterday.

Section 13.2: Team Spirit on Steroids

The Deal: Your team's gotta be all in. If they're not buying what you're selling, you're going nowhere fast.

Quick Wins:

- **Open Mic:** Share the vision, ask for input, and actually listen. Regularly.

- **Skill Up:** Identify gaps, then train, workshop, and upskill. People can't deliver if they don't know how.
- **Props Where Props Are Due:** Recognize and reward. A little "thank you" goes a long way.

Section 13.3: Tech to the Rescue

The Deal: The right tech can make your life a lot easier. Wrong tech, and it's a headache you don't need.

Quick Wins:

- **Tech Audit:** Figure out what you need, then find the tech that fits, not the other way around.
- **Test Drive:** Pilot it before you commit. If it's a flop, no big deal. Next!
- **Teach Your People:** Roll out new tech with training sessions. If they can't use it, it's just expensive digital decor.

Section 13.4: Hurdle Jumping

The Deal: Obstacles? Guaranteed. Here's how you dodge, tackle, or jump over them.

Quick Wins:

- **Change Management:** Get ahead of the pushback. Involve, inform, and support.
- **Plan B (and C):** Stuff happens. Have contingencies.

- **Lead the Charge:** Leaders gotta lead. Be visible, be vocal, be there.

Section 13.5: Keeping Score and Shifting Gears

The Deal: You can't manage what you don't measure. And you can't improve if you're not ready to pivot.

Quick Wins:

- **KPIs:** What does success look like? Define it, measure it, track it.
- **Review Rhythms:** Regular check-ins on progress. No surprises.
- **Feedback Loops:** Listen, learn, adjust. Rinse and repeat.

Section 13.6: Playing the Long Game

The Deal: It's a marathon, not a sprint. Sustainability and adaptability are your best friends.

Quick Wins:

- **Sustainability Built-In:** Make it part of the strategy from the get-go.
- **Stay Alert:** Keep an eye on the horizon. What's next? Be ready.
- **Never Stop Learning:** Encourage curiosity and innovation. Complacency kills.

Section 13.7: Strategy Meets Street

The Deal: It's go-time. Strategy's on paper; execution's on the ground. Make it happen.

Quick Wins:

- **All In:** Commitment is key. Half-hearted efforts yield zero results.
- **Agile, Not Fragile:** Be ready to move with the punches. Adapt, overcome.
- **Leadership Front and Center:** Lead by example. Drive the change, celebrate the wins, navigate the losses.

Wrap-Up: There you have it. Strategy to execution, no fluff. Your move.

Chapter 13: Buckle up, nerds! Time to READ. ابسم الله!

(Bismillah!) - Arabic for "In the name of God!" Often said at the beginning of an endeavor for blessings and success.

Section 13.1: Laying the Groundwork for Implementation

Transitioning from strategic planning to actionable implementation is a critical phase in any business's growth trajectory. This initial step determines the effectiveness and efficiency of strategy execution, setting the pace for achieving set objectives. Here, we outline the foundational elements necessary for a seamless transition to action, ensuring that businesses are well-prepared to navigate the complexities of implementation.

Key Insights: Preparing for Strategic Implementation

The journey from plan to action involves meticulous preparation, where strategic foresight meets operational readiness. Understanding the scope of the strategy, its impact on various facets of the business, and the resources required for execution is paramount. This phase lays the groundwork for the actualization of strategic goals, necessitating a clear, detailed, and feasible plan of action.

Actionable Strategies: Building a Robust Implementation Framework

Develop a Detailed Implementation Roadmap:
- Break down the strategic plan into actionable steps, assigning specific tasks, deadlines, and responsible parties for each segment of the plan.
- Use project management tools to visualize the roadmap, track progress, and maintain alignment with strategic objectives.

Set Realistic Timelines:
- Establish timelines that reflect the complexity of tasks, the availability of resources, and potential challenges that may arise during implementation.
- Allow for flexibility in timelines to accommodate unforeseen delays or adjustments, ensuring that the overall strategic goals remain achievable.

Allocate Resources Effectively:

- Conduct a thorough resource analysis to identify the financial, human, and technological resources required to implement the strategy.
- Secure the necessary resources in advance, ensuring they are allocated efficiently to support the various stages of implementation.

Establish Clear Communication Channels:
- Maintain open and effective communication across all levels of the organization to ensure that team members are informed, engaged, and aligned with the implementation process.
- Use regular updates, meetings, and feedback sessions to foster collaboration and address any issues promptly.

Monitor Progress and Adapt as Needed:
- Implement a robust monitoring system to track the progress of the implementation against the established roadmap and timelines.
- Be prepared to make strategic adjustments based on performance data, feedback, and changing market conditions, ensuring the strategy remains relevant and effective.

Cultivate a Culture of Accountability and Support:

- Foster a culture where team members take ownership of their roles in the implementation process, encouraging accountability and dedication to achieving strategic objectives.
- Provide the necessary support, training, and resources to empower teams to execute their tasks effectively.

Laying the groundwork for implementation is a crucial step that determines the success of strategic initiatives. By establishing a clear implementation roadmap, setting realistic timelines, and effectively allocating resources, businesses can ensure a smooth transition from planning to action. Emphasizing communication, monitoring, adaptation, and a supportive culture further enhances the likelihood of achieving strategic goals. This foundational phase is not just about preparation; it's about setting the stage for sustainable growth and long-term success in the competitive market landscape.

Section 13.2: Building a Supportive Team Culture

In the journey from strategic vision to tangible success, the role of a supportive team culture cannot be overstated. This chapter section illuminates the critical nature of aligning team culture with strategic goals, ensuring that every member of the organization is rowing in the same direction. It further explores actionable strategies for empowering teams to not only embrace change but also to take ownership of the implementation process, thereby enhancing the likelihood of achieving collective objectives.

Cultural Alignment: The Bedrock of Strategic Success

The congruence between team culture and strategic goals forms the bedrock upon which successful implementation rests. A culture that is aligned with an organization's strategic objectives fosters an environment where team members are motivated, engaged, and committed to the collective vision. Such alignment ensures that organizational behaviors, from decision-making processes to daily operations, support the strategic direction and facilitate its realization.

Empowering Teams: Strategies for Cultivating Ownership and Adaptability

Communicate with Transparency:

- Foster a culture of openness by communicating strategic goals, the reasons behind them, and the roles individuals play in achieving these objectives. Transparency builds trust and ensures that team members understand the bigger picture and their part in it.

Encourage Participation and Feedback:
- Create channels for team members to offer insights and feedback on the strategy and its implementation. Participation fosters a sense of ownership and values each member's contribution, driving engagement and innovation.

Provide Training and Development:
- Equip teams with the skills and knowledge needed to navigate the changes brought about by strategic implementation. Ongoing training and development opportunities signal an investment in team members' growth and adaptability.

Recognize and Reward Contributions:
- Acknowledge and reward efforts and achievements that contribute to strategic goals. Recognition programs, whether formal or informal, reinforce desired behaviors and

outcomes, motivating teams and individuals alike.

Foster a Culture of Learning and Resilience:
- Encourage a mindset of continuous learning and resilience in the face of challenges. Celebrate both successes and failures as opportunities for growth, reinforcing the notion that setbacks are part of the path to innovation and improvement.

Lead by Example:
- Leadership should embody the cultural values and strategic alignment they wish to see throughout the organization. Leading by example is a powerful motivator and sets the tone for expected behaviors and attitudes.

Build Supportive Structures and Processes:
- Implement structures and processes that support the strategic goals and facilitate their implementation. This includes setting up cross-functional teams, streamlining communication, and ensuring that operational processes are in harmony with strategic objectives.

Building a supportive team culture is not a one-off task but a continuous effort that evolves alongside strategic goals and market demands. By aligning team culture with strategic objectives and empowering teams to take ownership of the implementation process, organizations can create a dynamic, resilient workforce capable of navigating challenges and capitalizing on opportunities. This synergy between culture and strategy is a formidable lever for organizational success, driving innovation, engagement, and achievement of strategic ambitions in the competitive landscape of the market.

Section 13.3: Leveraging Technology for Efficient Execution

In the era of digital transformation, leveraging technology has become a cornerstone for executing business strategies with efficiency and precision. This section delves into the strategic integration of tech-enabled solutions into business operations, aiming to enhance the execution of strategic initiatives. Furthermore, it provides a comprehensive guide on selecting the appropriate technological tools and platforms, ensuring they align with and support the organization's strategic goals.

Tech-Enabled Solutions: Streamlining Strategy Implementation

The adoption of technology in business operations offers a plethora of advantages, including automation of manual processes, enhanced data analysis capabilities, and improved communication across departments. Technologies such as cloud computing, big data analytics, AI, and machine learning not only optimize operational efficiency but also provide valuable insights that can inform strategic decisions and implementation efforts.

1. Automation for Efficiency: Utilizing automation tools can significantly reduce the time and resources spent on routine tasks, allowing teams to focus on activities that add strategic value. For example, CRM and ERP systems automate customer relationship and resource management processes, respectively, aligning operations closely with strategic objectives.
2. Data Analytics for Informed Decisions: Advanced analytics platforms enable businesses to sift through large volumes of data to uncover patterns, trends, and insights. This capability is crucial for validating strategic assumptions and measuring the impact of strategic initiatives.
3. Collaboration Tools for Team Alignment: Cloud-based project management and collaboration tools like Asana,

Trello, and Slack facilitate seamless communication and coordination among teams, ensuring that everyone is aligned with the strategic goals and implementation timelines.

Tool Selection: Choosing the Right Technological Support

Selecting the right technological tools is vital for the successful execution of business strategies. The process involves understanding the specific needs of the organization, evaluating the functionality and scalability of potential tools, and considering the integration capabilities with existing systems.

1. Assess Organizational Needs: Begin by identifying the specific challenges and bottlenecks in the strategy implementation process that technology can address. This might include inefficiencies in data management, communication hurdles, or a lack of real-time analytics.
2. Evaluate Tool Functionality: Research and evaluate tools based on their features, ease of use, and ability to meet the identified needs. Prioritize solutions that offer customization options to tailor the tool to your specific strategic initiatives.
3. Consider Scalability and Integration: Choose tools that can scale with your business growth and easily integrate

with existing systems to ensure a smooth adoption process and minimize disruption to operations.

4. Trial and Feedback: Implement trial periods for shortlisted tools, gathering feedback from end-users to ensure the selected technology adequately supports the team's needs and strategic objectives.

5. Ongoing Evaluation and Adaptation: Technology evolves rapidly, necessitating regular reviews of the tools in use. Stay informed about new solutions that could further enhance strategic execution and be prepared to adapt your tech stack as needed.

Leveraging technology for the efficient execution of business strategies is not just about digital adoption but about strategically aligning technological tools with organizational goals. By carefully selecting and implementing tech-enabled solutions, businesses can significantly enhance their capacity for strategic implementation, ensuring agility, precision, and a competitive edge in the market. This approach not only streamlines operations but also empowers teams to innovate and drive the organization towards its strategic objectives with confidence and clarity.

Section 13.4: Overcoming Implementation Challenges

The path from strategic planning to successful implementation is fraught with challenges that can derail even the most well-conceived strategies. This section identifies common obstacles businesses encounter during the implementation phase and provides actionable solutions and best practices to navigate these challenges effectively, ensuring that strategic initiatives remain on track.

Common Obstacles: Identifying the Roadblocks to Success

1. Resistance to Change: One of the most significant hurdles is the natural resistance to change within an organization. Employees may be reluctant to adopt new processes, technologies, or ways of thinking, particularly if the benefits of the change are not clearly communicated.
2. Lack of Resources: Adequate resources, including time, budget, and personnel, are crucial for implementation. A common challenge is the underestimation of the resources required, leading to overextended teams and budget constraints.

3. Poor Communication: Ineffective communication can lead to misunderstandings, misaligned priorities, and a lack of coordination among teams, hindering the progress of implementation efforts.
4. Inadequate Planning: Insufficient detail in the planning phase can result in unclear roles, responsibilities, and timelines, making it difficult to execute the strategy effectively.
5. Lack of Leadership Support: Without strong leadership commitment and support, strategic initiatives can lose momentum and direction, ultimately failing to achieve their objectives.

Navigating Challenges: Strategies for Smooth Implementation

Facilitate Change Management:
- Address resistance by involving team members in the planning process, ensuring they understand the reasons behind changes and the benefits they bring.
- Implement change management practices, including training, support, and communication

strategies, to ease the transition and foster buy-in.

Ensure Adequate Resource Allocation:
- Conduct a thorough resource analysis at the planning stage to identify the needs of the implementation process accurately.
- Secure commitments for the necessary resources in advance and manage them effectively throughout the implementation.

Strengthen Communication Channels:
- Develop a comprehensive communication plan that outlines how updates, changes, and achievements will be communicated across the organization.
- Utilize various communication tools and platforms to ensure messages reach all stakeholders clearly and promptly.

Refine Planning and Execution Details:
- Break down the strategic plan into detailed action items with specific timelines, assigned responsibilities, and defined outcomes.
- Use project management software to track progress, manage tasks, and maintain visibility across all implementation activities.

Cultivate Leadership and Support:
- Engage leadership at all levels to champion the strategy and its implementation, providing the necessary support and resources.
- Establish a steering committee or task force to oversee the implementation process, address challenges promptly, and ensure alignment with strategic goals.

Overcoming the challenges of strategy implementation requires a proactive and structured approach. By acknowledging common obstacles and applying targeted strategies to address them, businesses can enhance their capacity to execute strategic initiatives effectively. Through change management, resource allocation, clear communication, detailed planning, and strong leadership support, organizations can navigate the complexities of implementation, keeping projects on track and driving towards successful outcomes.

Section 13.5: Measuring Progress and Adjusting Course

The execution of a strategic plan is an evolving process, necessitating continuous monitoring and the flexibility to make adjustments as needed. This section explores the critical aspects of measuring the progress of strategic implementation and the iterative process of making adjustments to stay aligned with overarching strategic objectives.

Monitoring Success: Setting the Metrics for Strategic Achievement

The foundation of effective strategic implementation lies in the establishment of clear, measurable metrics and Key Performance Indicators (KPIs) that reflect the strategic goals of the organization. These metrics serve as benchmarks for success, enabling businesses to assess the effectiveness of their strategies and identify areas for improvement.

1. **Identify Relevant Metrics and KPIs:** Start by defining the metrics that are most relevant to the strategic objectives. These could range from financial performance indicators, such as revenue growth and profit margins, to operational metrics, like customer satisfaction scores and employee engagement levels.
2. **Implement Monitoring Systems:** Utilize data analytics tools and dashboards to track these metrics in real-time,

providing a clear view of progress towards strategic goals. This infrastructure supports data-driven decision-making and ensures that insights are readily available for review.
3. **Benchmark Against Industry Standards:** Comparing performance against industry benchmarks can offer additional insights into the organization's relative position in the market, highlighting strengths to build upon and areas requiring attention.

Iterative Adjustments: The Key to Strategic Flexibility

The dynamic nature of business environments necessitates an approach to strategic implementation that accommodates regular review and adjustment. This iterative process ensures that strategies remain relevant and aligned with both internal and external changes.

1. **Schedule Regular Review Sessions:** Establish a schedule for regular strategic review meetings, involving key stakeholders across the organization. These sessions should assess progress against KPIs, review external market developments, and evaluate the effectiveness of current strategies.

2. **Foster an Agile Mindset:** Cultivate a culture that values flexibility and agility, encouraging teams to adapt and pivot strategies based on performance data and market feedback. This mindset is crucial for responding to unforeseen challenges and seizing new opportunities.
3. **Implement a Feedback Loop:** Encourage continuous feedback from employees, customers, and other stakeholders. This feedback can provide invaluable insights into the practical aspects of strategy execution and areas where adjustments may be necessary.
4. **Adjust and Communicate Changes:** When data indicates that a change in course is needed, make the necessary adjustments to the strategy promptly. Equally important is the clear communication of these changes and their rationale to all stakeholders to ensure continued buy-in and alignment.

Measuring progress and making iterative adjustments are indispensable components of successful strategic implementation. By establishing clear metrics and KPIs, regularly reviewing progress, fostering an agile approach to strategy execution, and effectively communicating changes, businesses can navigate the complexities of the modern market. This continuous cycle of measurement and adjustment not only ensures alignment with strategic goals but also positions the organization to respond proactively to changes in the business environment, securing long-term success and competitive advantage.

Section 13.6: Ensuring Long-Term Sustainability

In the dynamic landscape of business, ensuring the long-term sustainability of strategic initiatives is paramount. This section delves into the strategies for embedding sustainability and continuous improvement within the strategic implementation process, alongside providing actionable tips for future-proofing these initiatives against unpredictable market shifts and emerging challenges.

Sustainability Planning: Embedding Durability in Strategy

Sustainability in the context of business strategy refers to the capacity to maintain and adapt strategic initiatives over time, ensuring they continue to deliver value and drive growth in the face of changing market conditions. This requires a forward-looking approach, where sustainability considerations are integrated from the outset of the planning and implementation processes.

1. **Integrate Sustainability Principles:** Begin by embedding sustainability principles into the core of strategic objectives. This includes considerations for environmental stewardship, social responsibility, and economic viability, ensuring that strategies contribute positively to the organization's triple bottom line.
2. **Build Resilience into Operations:** Design operational processes with flexibility and resilience in mind, allowing for rapid adaptation to changes without compromising strategic integrity. This may involve diversifying supply chains, investing in scalable technologies, or developing versatile skill sets within the workforce.
3. **Promote a Culture of Continuous Improvement:** Encourage a culture that values ongoing learning and iterative improvement. This involves regular review cycles, open feedback mechanisms, and the willingness to pivot or evolve strategies in response to new insights or changing circumstances.

Future-Proofing: Preparing for Tomorrow's Challenges

Future-proofing strategic initiatives requires anticipation of potential market shifts and the proactive management of emerging risks. It's about creating strategies that are robust, adaptable, and capable of navigating the future landscape of business.

1. **Conduct Scenario Planning:** Regularly engage in scenario planning exercises to envision various future states of the market and assess how different strategic initiatives might perform under these conditions. This helps in identifying potential risks and opportunities ahead of time.
2. **Leverage Data and Analytics:** Utilize advanced data analytics and market intelligence tools to stay informed about trends and emerging challenges. This data-driven approach supports informed decision-making and strategic agility.
3. **Invest in Innovation:** Maintain a commitment to innovation, both in terms of products/services and internal processes. Encourage experimentation and the exploration of new business models, technologies, and markets to stay ahead of competitive and environmental curves.

4. **Strengthen Stakeholder Relationships:** Build strong relationships with all stakeholders, including customers, employees, suppliers, and the community. These relationships can provide valuable support, insights, and flexibility in times of change or challenge.
5. **Review and Revise Regularly:** Make strategic review and revision an integral part of the business cycle. By regularly assessing the alignment of strategies with current and anticipated market conditions, organizations can adjust course as needed to maintain strategic relevance and effectiveness.

Ensuring the long-term sustainability of strategic initiatives is a complex but essential component of business success. By integrating sustainability planning, promoting a culture of continuous improvement, and adopting future-proofing practices, organizations can develop strategies that not only withstand the test of time but also adapt and thrive in the face of future challenges. This holistic approach to strategic implementation fosters resilience, agility, and sustained growth, securing a competitive advantage in the ever-evolving market landscape.

Section 13.7: Bridging Strategy and Execution

The culmination of strategic planning and its execution forms the bedrock of organizational success. This final section of Chapter 13 emphasizes the indispensable link between devising strategic plans and their tangible implementation within the business environment. It underscores the necessity for businesses to not only envision their goals with clarity and precision but also to commit to a systematic, agile methodology for actualizing these visions into concrete outcomes.

Key Takeaways: The Essence of Strategy-Execution Alignment

1. **Integrated Approach:** The seamless integration of strategy and execution is paramount. A strategic plan, irrespective of its brilliance, is futile without the mechanisms for effective implementation. It is the execution that transforms strategic visions into realities, driving the organization towards its desired state.
2. **Agility and Discipline:** Agility in responding to market dynamics and discipline in adhering to strategic plans are not mutually exclusive but rather complementary

forces. Businesses must foster an environment where strategic agility is balanced with the discipline to stay the course, making informed adjustments as necessary.

3. **Continuous Improvement:** The journey from strategy to execution is iterative, not linear. Continuous improvement, based on real-time feedback and performance metrics, ensures that strategies evolve in alignment with both internal growth and external market changes.

4. **Leadership and Culture:** Effective execution is deeply rooted in leadership commitment and organizational culture. Leaders must champion the strategy, embodying the change they wish to see, while cultivating a culture that is receptive to change, innovation, and collaboration.

5. **Measurement and Accountability:** Establishing clear metrics for success and holding individuals and teams accountable for their contributions are critical. Regularly measuring progress against these metrics ensures that the organization remains focused and aligned with its strategic objectives.

Call to Action: Committing to Strategic Realization

Businesses are urged to embrace a disciplined yet flexible approach to bridging the gap between strategic planning and execution. This entails:

- **Committing to Execution:** Embrace the execution of strategies with the same enthusiasm and rigor as their planning. Understand that the true value of a strategy lies in its realization.
- **Fostering an Agile Mindset:** Cultivate an organizational culture that is agile, resilient, and adaptable, enabling swift navigation through the complexities of the business landscape.
- **Empowering Teams:** Equip teams with the necessary resources, authority, and support to implement strategies effectively. Encourage ownership and accountability at all levels.
- **Leveraging Technology:** Utilize technological tools and platforms to streamline processes, enhance communication, and provide actionable insights, supporting efficient and effective execution.
- **Prioritizing Continuous Learning:** Commit to ongoing learning and adaptation, using insights gained from both successes and setbacks to refine and enhance future strategies.

The bridge between strategy and execution is where organizational aspirations meet reality. By committing to a disciplined, agile approach to turning strategic visions into actionable realities, businesses can navigate the complexities of the market, seize opportunities for growth, and achieve sustained success. The journey is continuous, demanding a relentless focus on alignment, execution excellence, and the willingness to adapt and evolve.

Chapter 13 Simplified: Actionable Guide for Busy Execs

Hey execs, whether you're the go-getter, the laid-back type, or at your wit's end, here's a no-nonsense, cut-the-crap guide to making Chapter 13 work for you. Let's get your strategy from paper to practice, with some deadlines to keep you honest. Ready? Let's dive in.

Section 13.1: Laying the Groundwork for Implementation

1. Chart Your Course:
- **Task:** Break down your grand strategy into bite-sized tasks. Assign who does what by when.
- **Deadline:** 1 week.
- **Action:** Whip out those project management apps. Time to get visual and trackable.

2. Time and Resources:
- **Task:** Set timelines that don't make you laugh (or cry). Figure out what you need and get it.
- **Deadline:** 3 days.
- **Action:** Resource roundup. Get everything and everyone in place, stat.

3. Communication is Key:
- **Task:** Decide how you'll keep everyone in the loop and how you'll watch the plan's progress.
- **Deadline:** 2 days.
- **Action:** Set up your war room. Weekly check-ins are now your thing.

Section 13.2: Building a Supportive Team Culture

1. Open Up:
- **Task:** Share your master plan and ask for input. Yes, really listen.
- **Deadline:** Immediate.
- **Action:** Schedule a team meeting. Yesterday.

2. Skill Up:
- **Task:** Identify skills gaps and fill them. Make learning a part of the job.
- **Deadline:** 2 weeks.
- **Action:** Get those training sessions on the calendar.

3. Say Thanks:
- **Task:** Recognize the hard work. Make your team feel like rockstars.
- **Deadline:** Ongoing.
- **Action:** Spot rewards, shout-outs, maybe even a trophy or two.

Section 13.3: Leveraging Technology for Efficient Execution

1. Tech Needs:
- **Task:** Pinpoint where technology can make your life easier.
- **Deadline:** 1 week.
- **Action:** Audit your tech stack. Fill in the gaps.

2. Choose Wisely:
- **Task:** Pick tools that actually help, not just look pretty.
- **Deadline:** 1 week for selection, 2 weeks for trials.
- **Action:** Trial run, then full steam ahead.

3. Train the Troops:

- **Task:** Make sure your team can actually use the new toys.
- **Deadline:** 3 weeks.
- **Action:** Training sessions galore. Make it fun, if possible.

Section 13.4: Overcoming Implementation Challenges

1. Face Resistance Head-On:
- **Task:** Deal with the naysayers and fill the gaps.
- **Deadline:** Continuous.
- **Action:** Bring everyone on board. Find resources, fast.

2. Plan Better:
- **Task:** Make your plan foolproof. Then communicate like there's no tomorrow.
- **Deadline:** 1 week.
- **Action:** Clarify every detail, then blast it out on all channels.

3. Lead Like You Mean It:
- **Task:** Show you're all in. Cultivate a team that owns it.
- **Deadline:** Now and always.
- **Action:** Walk the talk. Make accountability the norm.

Section 13.5: Measuring Progress and Adjusting Course

1. KPIs and Eyes on the Prize:
- **Task:** Know what success looks like. Keep tabs on it.
- **Deadline:** 1 week for KPI setup, ongoing monitoring.
- **Action:** Dashboard everything. Live by it.

2. Review and Adapt:
- **Task:** Regularly check if you're still on the right track.
- **Deadline:** Monthly reviews.
- **Action:** Be ready to pivot. Agility is your new best friend.

3. Loop It:
- **Task:** Feedback is your goldmine. Use it to improve.
- **Deadline:** Continuous.
- **Action:** Adjust based on feedback. Communicate changes clearly.

Section 13.6: Ensuring Long-Term Sustainability

1. Weave Sustainability Into Your DNA:
- **Task:** Make sustainability core to your strategy, not an afterthought.
- **Deadline:** Start now, refine forever.
- **Action:** Scenario planning and innovation investments.

2. Future-Proofing:
- **Task:** Stay ahead of curveballs the market might throw at you.
- **Deadline:** Ongoing.
- **Action:** Use analytics, build relationships, stay alert.

3. Never Stop Learning:
- **Task:** Keep evolving. Stagnation is your enemy.
- **Deadline:** Every day.
- **Action:** Promote a culture of curiosity and continuous improvement.

Section 13.7: Bridging Strategy and Execution

1. Execution with Passion:
- **Task:** Dive into execution with the energy of a startup on launch day.
- **Deadline:** Every. Single. Day.
- **Action:** Align daily grind with big-picture goals.

2. Flexibility Meets Discipline:

- **Task:** Be as flexible as a gymnast with the discipline of a monk.
- **Deadline:** Balance daily.
- **Action:** Adapt but stay the course. Fine-tune as you go.

3. Lead and Measure:
- **Task:** Drive the strategy home. Celebrate the wins.
- **Deadline:** Celebrate small wins weekly; major milestones, quarterly.
- **Action:** Keep score, cheer loudly, rinse and repeat.

There you have it, execs. Cut through the clutter, follow these steps, and let's see your business not just survive but thrive. And remember, procrastination is the enemy of execution. Time to roll up those sleeves!

Chapter 14 Pre-Breakdown: No Fluff, Just Facts

Hey, execs – the vigilant, the lazy, and the fed-up. It's time to cut through the noise. Here's the straight talk on Chapter 14, your no-BS guide to mastering the ever-evolving beast that is customer and client engagement. Grab your coffee (put down the whiskey), and let's get into it.

Section 14.1: What's Hot in Customer Engagement

The Deal: The digital world is spinning faster than ever. If you're not keeping up with AI, personalized experiences, and sustainable practices, you're basically driving a horse and buggy on the autobahn.

Quick Wins:
- **Digitalization and Personalization:** Get cozy with AI and data analytics. It's not just for tech nerds; it's your ticket to offering what your customers didn't know they needed.
- **Omnichannel Experiences:** Your customers are everywhere. Be like Visa – be everywhere they want to be, seamlessly.
- **Sustainability:** It's cool to care now. Show your customers you're not just about the green in your wallet.

Section 14.2: CRM Isn't Just a Fancy Acronym

The Deal: CRM technology is on steroids now, thanks to AI and blockchain. If your CRM system is still stuck in the early 2000s, you've got homework.

Quick Wins:
- **Upgrade Your CRM:** Look into AI and blockchain to make your CRM smarter and safer. Yes, it's a bit of work. Yes, it's worth it.
- **Training:** Don't just throw new tools at your team. Train them. Or watch those tools collect digital dust.
- **Compliance:** Privacy laws are like in-laws – ignore them at your peril. Make sure your CRM practices are up to snuff.

Section 14.3: AI and ML Aren't Just Buzzwords

The Deal: AI and ML can make your customer engagement smarter, but only if you're smart about using them. Don't be the company that uses a chainsaw when a scalpel is needed.

Quick Wins:
- **Personalize Like a Pro:** Use AI for tailored marketing and support. Just keep it creepy-free.
- **Ethics and Bias:** Keep your AI ethical. Nobody likes a biased bot.
- **Upskilling:** AI might change some jobs. Prepare your team for the shift. Upskill, reskill, and keep the human in human resources.

Section 14.4: Social Media – The Beast You Can't Ignore

The Deal: Social media is your gateway to customers' hearts and minds. But it's a wild beast – unpredictable and ever-changing.

Quick Wins:

- **Content is King:** Embrace visual and interactive content. If it's not on Instagram, did it even happen?
- **Listen Up:** Use social listening tools. It's like eavesdropping, but for business.
- **Service with a Smile:** Amp up your customer service on social. Be quick, be witty, and solve problems.

Section 14.5: Privacy – More Than Just a Good Fence

The Deal: In the age of data breaches, your stance on privacy can make or break customer trust. Don't be the company that plays fast and loose with personal info.

Quick Wins:
- **Privacy Policy Makeover:** Make it readable. Make it compliant. Make it a priority.
- **Security Upgrades:** Invest in encryption and other fun security measures. Make hackers weep.
- **Transparency:** Be open about how you use data. Honesty is still the best policy.

Section 14.6: Green is the New Black

The Deal: Sustainability isn't a trend; it's a necessity. Show your customers you give a damn about the planet, and they'll show you some love back.

Quick Wins:
- **Eco-friendly Practices:** Find ways to go green in your operations. Even small changes count.

- **Communicate:** Brag a little. Let your customers know about your sustainability efforts.
- **Innovate:** Offer sustainable products or services. Green can be profitable.

Section 14.7: Stay Sharp, Stay Ahead

The Deal: The future doesn't wait. Keep your finger on the pulse of emerging trends and technologies, or risk getting left behind.

Quick Wins:
- **Future Workshops:** Regularly brainstorm with your team about the next big thing. Keep the ideas flowing.
- **Innovation Lab:** Dedicate resources to experimentation. Fail fast, learn faster.
- **Strategic Reviews:** Regularly revisit your strategies. Adaptation is key to survival.

Wrap-Up: Listen, whether you're leading the charge, barely keeping up, or just plain over it, these insights are your roadmap to not just surviving but thriving in the chaos of today's market. Get off your ass and make it happen. Your business – and your legacy – depends on it.

Chapter 14: Buckle up, nerds! Time to READ. Til Triumph!

-Scandinavian flair for those who conquer with style and a Viking ship.

Section 14.1: Emerging Trends in Customer Engagement

Understanding the transformative landscape of customer engagement is imperative for businesses aiming to thrive in a rapidly evolving market. The emergence of digital technologies and shifting consumer expectations has given rise to new trends that are reshaping the interaction between businesses and their clientele. This section delves into these emerging trends, providing insight into how they are sculpting the future of customer engagement across various industries. Moreover, it offers strategic approaches for businesses to adapt and leverage these trends to foster deeper, more meaningful relationships with their customers.

Market Evolution: Insight into Emerging Trends

The current market evolution is significantly influenced by digitalization, personalized experiences, and sustainability concerns. One notable trend is the increasing reliance on data analytics and artificial intelligence (AI) to understand and predict customer behavior. These technologies enable businesses to deliver personalized experiences at scale, a key demand among today's consumers. Furthermore, there is a growing emphasis on creating seamless omnichannel experiences, allowing customers to interact with brands through multiple platforms yet receive a consistent level of service.

Sustainability and ethical business practices have also emerged as critical factors in customer engagement. Consumers are increasingly favoring brands that demonstrate a commitment to environmental stewardship and social responsibility. This shift necessitates businesses to not only focus on profit but also consider the impact of their operations on the planet and society.

Another trend reshaping the landscape is the rise of experiential marketing. Instead of traditional advertising, companies are investing in creating memorable experiences that resonate with their target audience on a deeper level. These experiences, whether online or offline, are designed to foster a stronger emotional connection between the brand and its customers.

Adapting to Trends: Enhancing Customer Relationships

To harness these emerging trends effectively, businesses must adopt a proactive and adaptive approach. Firstly, integrating advanced analytics and AI into their operations can provide them with actionable insights into customer preferences and behaviors. This integration enables the delivery of highly personalized experiences, a key differentiator in today's competitive market.

Embracing omnichannel strategies is another crucial adaptation. By ensuring a cohesive brand experience across all platforms, businesses can meet customers where they are, enhancing accessibility and convenience. This approach not only strengthens customer relationships but also boosts loyalty and retention.

Companies should align their values and operations with the growing demand for sustainability and ethical practices. This alignment can involve adopting eco-friendly practices, engaging in community initiatives, or transparently communicating the social impact of their products and services. Such efforts can significantly enhance brand perception and customer engagement.

Investing in experiential marketing can provide businesses with a unique opportunity to engage with their audience in meaningful ways. By creating experiences that elicit positive emotions and memories, companies can build a loyal community of advocates, driving both engagement and growth.

The emerging trends in customer engagement present both challenges and opportunities for businesses. By understanding these trends and strategically adapting their approaches, companies can not only navigate the evolving market landscape but also forge stronger connections with their customers, setting the stage for sustained success in the future.

Section 14.2: Innovations in Client Relationship Management

The domain of Client Relationship Management (CRM) has witnessed a paradigm shift, courtesy of technological and methodological innovations. These advancements are not just reshaping the tools and platforms businesses use but are also redefining the very ethos of client interactions and management strategies. This section embarks on an exploration of these innovations, delineating their impact on CRM practices. Furthermore, it outlines strategic approaches for businesses to seamlessly integrate these innovations into their CRM frameworks, thereby enhancing client engagement and achieving unparalleled business growth.

Innovative CRM: Technological and Methodological Transformations

At the forefront of this transformation is the integration of Artificial Intelligence (AI) and Machine Learning (ML) into CRM systems. These technologies offer predictive analytics, enabling businesses to anticipate client needs and preferences with remarkable accuracy. This foresight allows for the customization of services and communication, fostering a more personalized relationship with clients.

Blockchain technology has also made its mark, offering unprecedented security and transparency in client transactions. By facilitating secure, tamper-proof systems, blockchain technology builds trust, a cornerstone of any client-business relationship. Moreover, the advent of cloud-based CRM solutions has revolutionized data accessibility, allowing for real-time updates and collaboration across global teams, ensuring that client needs are addressed promptly and efficiently.

On the methodological front, the shift towards value-based engagement models stands out. Businesses are moving away from transactional interactions, focusing instead on creating value for clients through advisory and consultancy roles. This approach not only deepens client relationships but also positions businesses as indispensable partners in their clients' success.

Implementation of Innovations: Strategies for Effective Integration

Adopting these innovations requires a strategic approach, beginning with a comprehensive assessment of existing CRM systems and processes. Businesses must identify gaps and areas for improvement, ensuring that the integration of new technologies aligns with their overall business objectives.

Training and development play a critical role in the successful implementation of these innovations. Employees must be equipped with the necessary skills and knowledge to leverage new CRM tools and methodologies effectively. This involves not only technical training but also a cultural shift towards client-centricity and adaptability.

Businesses must adopt a phased approach to implementation, starting with pilot programs to test the efficacy of new technologies and methodologies. This allows for the identification of potential challenges and adjustments to strategies before a full-scale rollout.

Data governance and compliance are also crucial considerations. As businesses collect and analyze more client data, they must ensure adherence to data protection regulations, safeguarding client privacy and maintaining trust.

The innovations transforming CRM offer businesses unprecedented opportunities to enhance client relationships. However, the successful integration of these innovations requires careful planning, training, and adherence to ethical standards. By embracing these changes, businesses can set new benchmarks in client engagement, driving growth and success in an increasingly competitive market.

Section 14.3: The Role of AI and Machine Learning

The integration of Artificial Intelligence (AI) and Machine Learning (ML) into the sphere of client and customer engagement represents a significant leap forward in how businesses understand and interact with their audiences. This section explores the expanding role of these technologies in delivering personalized experiences that cater to the unique needs and preferences of each client or customer. It also delves into the ethical considerations and challenges that accompany the implementation of AI in customer and client relations, ensuring that businesses navigate this new terrain with responsibility and foresight.

AI Integration: Personalizing Client and Customer Experiences

AI and ML technologies have become pivotal in analyzing vast amounts of data to derive actionable insights, enabling businesses to tailor their offerings and communications with unprecedented precision. Through predictive analytics, companies can anticipate customer needs and preferences, often before the customers themselves are aware of them. This proactivity in personalization enhances customer satisfaction and loyalty, as clients feel understood and valued on an individual level.

AI-powered chatbots and virtual assistants have transformed customer service, providing instant, 24/7 responses to inquiries and support requests. These AI solutions can learn from each interaction, continuously improving their ability to resolve issues and provide information, thereby elevating the overall customer experience.

In the realm of marketing, AI and ML enable hyper-targeted campaigns that reach individuals with messages that resonate with their specific interests and behaviors. This not only improves the effectiveness of marketing efforts but also increases the efficiency of resource allocation by focusing on high-conversion opportunities.

Ethical Considerations: Navigating the Implementation of AI

The deployment of AI and ML in client and customer engagement, while offering numerous benefits, also raises important ethical considerations. Privacy concerns are at the forefront, as the collection and analysis of personal data are fundamental to the functioning of these technologies. Businesses must ensure they are not only compliant with data protection regulations but also transparent with customers about how their data is being used and protected.

Bias in AI algorithms presents another significant challenge. If not carefully monitored and corrected, biases in data can lead to discriminatory outcomes, unfairly targeting or excluding certain groups. Ensuring AI systems are fair and impartial is crucial to maintaining trust and integrity in business practices.

The issue of human displacement by AI technologies cannot be overlooked. While AI can enhance efficiency and decision-making, it also poses the risk of replacing jobs, necessitating strategies to manage workforce transitions and retraining programs.

AI and ML are transforming the landscape of client and customer engagement, offering personalized experiences that were once beyond reach. However, the ethical implementation of these technologies requires careful consideration of privacy, bias, and workforce impact. By addressing these challenges head-on, businesses can harness the power of AI to not only achieve commercial success but also foster trust and loyalty among their clients and customers.

Section 14.4: The Impact of Social Media Dynamics

The digital age has ushered in a paradigm shift in how businesses engage with clients and customers, with social media playing a pivotal role in this transformation. This section scrutinizes the evolving dynamics of social media and their profound impact on client and customer engagement strategies. It also delineates best practices for leveraging these platforms to forge stronger, more meaningful relationships with audiences.

Social Media Shifts: Influencing Engagement Strategies

The landscape of social media is in constant flux, driven by technological advancements, changing user preferences, and the emergence of new platforms. This dynamic environment presents both challenges and opportunities for businesses aiming to connect with their audience.

One significant shift is the rise of visual and interactive content. Platforms like Instagram, Snapchat, and TikTok have popularized ephemeral, video-based content, compelling businesses to adopt more visually engaging and authentic storytelling approaches. This trend underscores the growing preference for experiences that are not only informative but also entertaining and relatable.

Another notable change is the increasing importance of social listening and analytics. With the vast amount of data generated on social media, businesses have unprecedented access to insights into consumer behavior, preferences, and sentiments. Leveraging this data allows for more targeted and effective engagement strategies, enabling businesses to respond proactively to trends and feedback.

Social media has evolved into a primary channel for customer service. Consumers increasingly turn to social platforms to seek support, share their experiences, and engage in dialogue with brands. This public forum demands a higher level of responsiveness and transparency from businesses, turning customer service into a significant aspect of social media strategy.

Strategic Social Media Use: Building Stronger Relationships

To capitalize on the opportunities presented by social media, businesses must adopt strategic approaches that align with their brand values and audience expectations. Creating authentic, high-quality content that resonates with the target audience is foundational. This involves not only understanding the audience's interests and needs but also keeping pace with the latest content trends and platform features.

Engagement is another critical component. Beyond broadcasting messages, businesses should foster a two-way dialogue with their audience, encouraging interaction through comments, shares, and direct messages. This approach not only enhances brand visibility but also builds a sense of community and loyalty among followers.

Influencer partnerships can also amplify reach and credibility. Collaborating with influencers who share the brand's values and have a genuine connection with their followers can lead to more authentic and effective endorsements.

Measuring the impact of social media activities is essential. Utilizing analytics tools to track engagement rates, conversion metrics, and ROI helps businesses refine their strategies and allocate resources more effectively.

The changing dynamics of social media necessitate a flexible and informed approach to client and customer engagement. By embracing innovation, prioritizing authenticity, and engaging in meaningful interactions, businesses can leverage social media platforms to not only reach their audience but also build lasting relationships that drive growth and success.

Section 14.5: Data Privacy and Trust

Data is often described as the new oil, its management, particularly regarding privacy, has become a pivotal factor influencing client and customer trust. This section examines the escalating importance of data privacy and its profound impact on the relationship between businesses and their audiences. Furthermore, it articulates strategic measures that organizations can adopt to bolster transparency and trust, addressing privacy concerns proactively in their operations.

Privacy Concerns: The Bedrock of Client and Customer Trust

There has been an exponential increase in the volume of personal data collected by businesses recently. From browsing habits to purchase history, this information is invaluable for companies seeking to personalize experiences and streamline their services. However, this data collection has also heightened privacy concerns among consumers, wary of how their information is used, shared, or potentially compromised.

Recent high-profile data breaches and misuse incidents have cast a spotlight on the importance of data privacy, making it a critical issue for consumers. Trust in a brand can be significantly eroded by perceived mishandling of personal information, leading to a loss of loyalty and business. Consequently, data privacy has ascended from a legal compliance requirement to a strategic business imperative, central to building and maintaining customer and client trust.

Building Trust: Strategies for Enhancing Transparency

To navigate this landscape, businesses must adopt a multifaceted approach centered on transparency, security, and ethical data practices. Establishing clear, accessible privacy policies that explain how data is collected, used, and protected is a foundational step. These policies should not only comply with regulatory requirements but also be communicated in a way that is easy for the average consumer to understand.

Implementing robust data security measures is another crucial strategy. This involves not just technological solutions like encryption and secure data storage, but also ongoing employee training to mitigate human error, often a weak link in data security.

Engaging in transparent communication is essential, especially in the event of a data breach. Companies must promptly inform affected parties and regulatory bodies, outlining the breach's scope, the measures taken in response, and how they plan to prevent future incidents. This openness can help mitigate damage to trust and reputation.

Businesses can differentiate themselves by adopting a privacy-first approach, viewing data protection as a competitive advantage rather than a compliance burden. This can involve practices like data minimization, collecting only what is necessary, and giving customers control over their data through consent mechanisms and easy-to-use privacy settings.

Engaging in third-party audits and certifications can provide an external validation of a company's data privacy and security practices, offering reassurance to clients and customers about the seriousness with which their data is treated.

As privacy concerns continue to loom large in the minds of consumers, the businesses that succeed will be those that prioritize the ethical management of personal data. By fostering transparency, implementing stringent security measures, and adopting a privacy-first culture, businesses can build a foundation of trust that not only mitigates risk but also enhances customer loyalty and brand reputation in the long term.

Section 14.6: Sustainable Practices in Relationship Management

The integration of sustainability into the core strategies of businesses has become a critical factor in building and maintaining long-term relationships with clients and customers. This section illuminates the growing role of sustainability in relationship management and outlines practical steps that organizations can take to weave sustainable practices into their engagement strategies. In doing so, it aims to showcase how businesses can not only contribute positively to the environment and society but also enhance their brand loyalty and trust among their clientele.

Sustainability Focus: Enhancing Client and Customer Bonds

Sustainability, once considered a niche interest, has burgeoned into a global movement, with consumers increasingly making choices that align with their values and concerns for the planet. This shift has prompted businesses to reconsider their operations, products, and services through the lens of environmental and social responsibility. The role of sustainability in relationship management extends beyond mere compliance or marketing; it is about forging deeper connections with individuals who seek to support companies that reflect their ethical standards.

Clients and customers are more likely to develop a strong, lasting relationship with brands that demonstrate a genuine commitment to sustainability. This commitment can manifest in various forms, such as reducing carbon footprints, employing fair labor practices, or supporting community initiatives. Such actions not only contribute to a better world but also engender trust and loyalty, as they resonate with the values of an increasingly conscientious consumer base.

Implementing Sustainability: Steps Towards Greener Relationship Management

The path to integrating sustainability into relationship management involves several key steps, each contributing to a comprehensive strategy that aligns with broader business goals.

1. **Assessment and Goal Setting:** Begin with a thorough assessment of current practices to identify areas where sustainability efforts can have the most impact. Set clear, measurable goals for improvement, whether in reducing

waste, lowering energy consumption, or sourcing materials ethically.
2. **Incorporation into Core Values:** Embed sustainability into the company's core values and mission statement. This alignment ensures that sustainable practices are not peripheral efforts but integral to the business's identity and operations.
3. **Transparent Communication:** Share your sustainability goals, initiatives, and progress openly with your clients and customers. Transparency fosters trust and demonstrates a genuine commitment to environmental and social responsibility.
4. **Engage and Collaborate:** Involve clients and customers in sustainability initiatives. This could be through community projects, sustainability-focused events, or feedback mechanisms that allow them to contribute ideas and preferences.
5. **Innovate for Sustainability:** Leverage technology and innovation to develop more sustainable products and services. This not only reduces environmental impact but also meets the growing consumer demand for green options.
6. **Regular Review and Adaptation:** Sustainability is an evolving field. Regularly review practices and impacts,

adapting strategies to reflect new technologies, regulations, and consumer expectations.

Integrating sustainability into relationship management is not just about responding to a trend. It's about recognizing the interconnectedness of business practices, environmental stewardship, and societal well-being. By adopting sustainable practices, businesses can forge stronger, more meaningful relationships with their clients and customers, setting a foundation for long-term success and mutual benefit.

Section 14.7: Navigating the Future Landscape

As we culminate our exploration of the dual approach to client and customer engagement in "Mastering the Market," it is imperative to encapsulate the anticipated trends that are poised to redefine this landscape. This section serves to recapitulate these trends, underscoring their potential impact on the intricate web of client-customer relations. Furthermore, it extends a call to action to businesses, urging them to proactively align with these emerging paradigms to ensure their competitive edge and relevance in an ever-evolving market.

Key Takeaways: Anticipated Trends and Their Impacts

The trajectory of customer and client engagement is unmistakably veering towards personalization, driven by the advancements in AI and machine learning. These technologies stand as the vanguard in tailoring experiences that resonate on an individual level, fostering a new era of engagement characterized by depth and relevance. Similarly, the role of social media continues to morph, presenting novel avenues for interaction and service delivery, while the integration of sustainability into business models is no longer optional but a requisite for fostering long-term loyalty and trust.

Data privacy and ethical considerations have emerged as paramount, with businesses that champion transparency and security distinguishing themselves in the marketplace. The innovations in client relationship management, particularly those leveraging technological breakthroughs, have set new standards in efficiency and effectiveness, compelling businesses to adopt or risk obsolescence.

Call to Action: Staying Ahead of the Curve

In light of these insights, businesses are called upon to embrace a forward-looking stance, ensuring they are not merely reactive but proactive in integrating these trends into their strategic planning. The imperative to innovate, adapt, and evolve has never been more critical. Companies must invest in understanding and implementing AI and machine learning technologies, not just as tools for operational efficiency but as the cornerstone of personalized client and customer experiences.

The strategic use of social media must evolve beyond traditional marketing and communication, becoming a dynamic platform for engagement, service, and community building. Sustainability should be woven into the fabric of business operations and ethos, reflecting a genuine commitment to environmental stewardship and social responsibility.

Privacy and data protection require unwavering attention, with policies and practices that not only comply with regulatory demands but also exceed them, building a foundation of trust that is indispensable in today's digital age. Lastly, the adoption of innovative CRM solutions should be viewed as an ongoing journey, one that is continually refined to meet the changing needs and expectations of clients and customers.

Navigating the Future

The landscape of client and customer engagement is undeniably complex and challenging. Yet, within this complexity lies unparalleled opportunity for businesses willing to lead with innovation, integrity, and insight. By staying abreast of these trends and adapting strategies accordingly, businesses can not only navigate the future landscape with confidence but also shape it, crafting experiences that resonate, inspire, and endure.

This book underscores a pivotal truth: the future of business is not just about transactions; it's about connections. Deep, meaningful, and sustainable connections that are cultivated with every interaction, decision, and innovation. The journey ahead is both exciting and exigent, beckoning businesses to chart a course that is responsive, responsible, and revolutionary.

Chapter 14: Step-By Step How to "Get... It... Done!"

Let's cut to the chase, execs! Whether you're on top of your game, dragging your feet, or about to throw in the towel, it's time to shake things up. Here's your no-nonsense, get-it-done guide to Chapter 14. Time's ticking, so let's dive in!

Section 14.1: Emerging Trends in Customer Engagement

Objective: Get ahead by tapping into the latest trends. Impress your customers, don't just exist.

1. Market Research (1 hour):
- **Task:** Dig into digitalization, personalized experiences, and green practices. Google is your friend, or throw some cash at a consultant if you're feeling fancy.
- **Goal:** Identify 3 top trends. No dilly-dallying!

2. Technology Integration (1 week):
- **Task:** Pick an AI tool. Start small, think big. Personalized emails, anyone?
- **Goal:** Launch a mini-project. Measure the response. Adjust fire as needed.

3. Omnichannel Strategy Development (2 weeks):
- **Task:** Map your customer's journey like you're plotting a treasure hunt. Where's the X?
- **Goal:** Plug holes, smooth transitions. Make buying from you as easy as scrolling through memes.

4. Sustainability Initiatives (1 month):
- **Task:** Go green or go home. Audit your operations; find where you can cut the carbon.

- **Goal:** Implement one eco-friendly change. Brag about it online.

5. Experiential Marketing Campaign (2 months):
- **Task:** Brainstorm an event or campaign that'll get people talking. Think outside the box.
- **Goal:** Create and launch. Aim for Instagram-worthy.

Section 14.2 to 14.7: Speed-Run Through CRM Innovation to Future-Proofing

CRM Revamp (1 month):
- Assess, train, pilot, and check compliance. Make your CRM work harder than you do.

AI & ML Integration (3 months):
- Pick a spot for AI magic. Set ethical rules. Help your team adapt. Don't let robots take over; use them to boost your human touch.

Social Media Shake-Up (1 month):
- Overhaul your content strategy. Use social listening like the NSA. Amp up your DM game.

Data Privacy Overhaul (2 weeks):
- Update that privacy policy. Secure your data like it's Fort Knox. Launch a "We Protect You" campaign.

Sustainability as Strategy (3 months):
- Report, engage, innovate. Make Mother Earth your business partner.

Future-Proof Your Empire (Ongoing):
- Workshops, innovation labs, and strategic reviews. Stay ready, so you don't have to get ready.

Now, listen up! This isn't about ticking boxes; it's about revolutionizing how you engage with those who keep your lights on - your clients and customers. Roll up those sleeves, set your timers, and let's make some waves. Remember, inaction is the only real failure. Let's do this!

Chapter 15: Farewell, nerds! Time to READ. FOR THE LAST TIME!

Section 15.1: Recap of Key Strategies

In the journey through "Mastering the Market: A Dual Approach to Client and Customer Engagement," we've traversed a landscape rich with strategies, innovations, and insights pivotal for businesses seeking to thrive in today's dynamic market. This final chapter synthesizes the essence of these discussions, offering a consolidated overview of the critical strategies and insights that constitute the core of effective market mastery through dual engagement. The aim is to equip businesses with a distilled compendium of wisdom for easy reference and application in their quest for excellence in client and customer engagement.

Strategic Overview: Mastering Dual Engagement

The book has underscored the indispensability of personalized experiences, facilitated by the strategic integration of AI and machine learning, in cultivating deeper client and customer relationships. These technologies not only enable the customization of interactions but also empower businesses with predictive insights, fostering a proactive rather than reactive approach to engagement.

Social media's evolving role has been highlighted as a double-edged sword; while offering unparalleled opportunities for direct engagement and brand building, it demands a nuanced understanding and strategic utilization to navigate its complexities effectively.

Sustainability has emerged as a non-negotiable element of modern business strategy. In an era marked by environmental consciousness and social responsibility, integrating sustainable practices has proven to be a key driver of long-term loyalty and trust among clients and customers.

The critical importance of data privacy and ethical considerations in building and maintaining trust cannot be overstated. As businesses collect and leverage vast quantities of personal information, adopting transparent, secure, and ethical data practices is fundamental to sustaining confidence and integrity in client and customer relationships.

Consolidated Insights: Lessons for Application

From the discussions presented, several consolidated insights emerge as beacons for businesses aiming to excel in the dual engagement landscape:

1. **Adaptability and Innovation:** Staying ahead in the market requires a commitment to continuous learning and adaptation, leveraging emerging technologies and trends to enhance engagement strategies.
2. **Authenticity and Transparency:** These are the pillars upon which trust is built. Businesses must strive for genuine interactions and open communication, making transparency in operations, sustainability efforts, and data handling a priority.
3. **Customer-Centricity:** Placing the client and customer at the heart of business strategies is non-negotiable. Understanding their needs, preferences, and values enables businesses to create offerings and experiences that resonate deeply.
4. **Strategic Integration of Technology:** The judicious application of AI, machine learning, and social media

analytics can dramatically elevate the quality of engagement, offering personalized, timely, and relevant interactions.

5. **Ethical Leadership:** In navigating the challenges of privacy, data security, and sustainability, ethical leadership is paramount. Businesses that lead with integrity will not only navigate these challenges successfully but also set new standards in their industries.

"Mastering the Market" offers a holistic guide to navigating the complexities of client and customer engagement in the modern era. By embracing the strategies and insights outlined, businesses can position themselves to thrive, building robust, enduring relationships that are the hallmark of market leaders.

Section 15.2: Implementing a Unified Engagement Approach

In navigating the intricate web of client and customer engagement, businesses face the formidable challenge of integrating diverse strategies into a unified approach. This section aims to provide actionable guidance on synthesizing the strategies explored throughout "Mastering the Market" into a cohesive framework. It also offers insights into maintaining balance and focus amid the implementation of these multifaceted strategies, ensuring businesses can effectively engage their clients and customers without losing sight of their core objectives.

Unified Strategies: Creating a Cohesive Engagement Framework

The foundation of a unified engagement approach lies in the alignment of business objectives with engagement strategies. This entails a holistic understanding of the business's goals, target audience, and the unique value proposition it offers. Integrating personalized experiences through AI and machine learning should be balanced with the authentic human touch, ensuring that technology enhances rather than replaces the nuances of personal interaction.

Social media strategies should be aligned with the overall communication and branding efforts, utilizing these platforms not just for promotion but as channels for genuine interaction and feedback. Sustainability initiatives must be integrated into the business model and communicated transparently, demonstrating a commitment to ethical practices that resonate with client and customer values.

Data privacy and ethical considerations are the underpinning of trust in any engagement strategy. A unified approach requires robust data governance frameworks that are transparently communicated to clients and customers, assuring them of their data's security and ethical use.

Balanced Execution: Maintaining Focus Amid Diverse Strategies

Implementing a unified engagement approach necessitates a balanced execution, which can be achieved through several key practices:

1. **Strategic Prioritization:** Identify and focus on strategies that offer the highest impact relative to your business goals and customer expectations. This prioritization ensures that resources are allocated efficiently, maximizing the return on investment.
2. **Cross-functional Collaboration:** Foster collaboration across different departments to ensure a seamless integration of strategies. Marketing, sales, customer service, and IT departments, among others, should work in harmony to deliver a consistent and cohesive customer experience.

3. **Continuous Monitoring and Adaptation:** Implement a system for continuously monitoring the effectiveness of engagement strategies. Use data analytics to gain insights into customer behavior and preferences, allowing for timely adjustments to strategies as market dynamics evolve.
4. **Employee Training and Empowerment:** Equip employees with the necessary skills and knowledge to execute the unified engagement strategy effectively. Empower them to make decisions that align with the overarching engagement goals, fostering a culture of accountability and innovation.
5. **Customer Feedback Loop:** Establish mechanisms for collecting and analyzing customer feedback. This direct input from clients and customers is invaluable for refining engagement strategies and ensuring they remain aligned with audience needs and expectations.

Implementing a unified engagement approach is a dynamic process that requires strategic foresight, agile execution, and continuous refinement. By adhering to the principles of unified strategies and balanced execution, businesses can navigate the complexities of client and customer engagement, driving sustainable growth and building enduring relationships in the competitive market landscape.

Section 15.3: Cultivating a Culture of Continuous Learning

The ability of an organization to adapt and grow continuously is not just an asset but a necessity. This section delves into the critical importance of fostering a culture of continuous learning within organizations, offering a roadmap for leaders looking to embed adaptability and proactive learning at the heart of their teams. Additionally, it outlines effective strategies for encouraging knowledge sharing and collaborative learning, ensuring that the collective intelligence of the organization is harnessed and amplified.

Learning Organization: The Bedrock of Adaptability

A learning organization is one that actively cultivates the pursuit of knowledge and the application of new insights across all levels of the company. Such an organization recognizes that the only constant in the market is change itself and prepares its members to not only respond to changes but to anticipate and lead them. This proactive stance on learning enables businesses to stay ahead of emerging trends, adapt strategies in real time, and innovate continuously.

The importance of cultivating a culture of continuous learning cannot be overstated. It empowers employees, enhances organizational agility, and fosters an environment where innovation thrives. Employees who are encouraged to learn and grow will be more engaged, more productive, and better equipped to contribute to the organization's success.

Knowledge Sharing: Strategies for Collaborative Learning

Encouraging knowledge sharing and collaborative learning within an organization involves creating an environment where information flows freely and where every employee feels valued as both a contributor and a learner. The following strategies can help achieve this:

1. **Create Learning Communities:** Establish forums, interest groups, or communities of practice where employees can share insights, challenges, and successes. These communities should cut across hierarchical lines to foster a sense of equality and open exchange.
2. **Leverage Technology for Learning:** Utilize digital platforms, such as intranets or specialized learning

management systems, to make resources accessible to all employees. Online forums and collaboration tools can also facilitate knowledge sharing among remote teams.

3. **Encourage Mentorship and Coaching:** Pairing less experienced employees with mentors or coaches can accelerate learning and knowledge transfer. This relationship benefits both parties, as mentors refine their leadership skills while mentees gain from their experience.

4. **Recognize and Reward Knowledge Sharing:** Implement recognition programs that reward individuals and teams for contributing to the learning environment. Acknowledgment can take many forms, from formal awards to simple public acknowledgment in meetings.

5. **Embed Learning into Everyday Activities:** Make learning an integral part of daily work by encouraging employees to set aside time for it, integrating learning objectives into project plans, and reviewing what was learned after completing tasks or projects.

6. **Foster a Safe Environment for Experimentation:** Encourage an atmosphere where trying new things and even failing is seen as part of the learning process. This

approach will empower employees to take initiative and innovate without fear of reprisal.

Cultivating a culture of continuous learning is paramount for organizations aiming to master the market dynamics of client and customer engagement. By prioritizing adaptability, encouraging knowledge sharing, and fostering collaborative learning, businesses can not only navigate the challenges of today's market but also anticipate and shape the trends of tomorrow. This commitment to learning and growth is what will differentiate the market leaders from the followers in the relentless pursuit of excellence.

Section 15.4: Leveraging Feedback for Growth

In the pursuit of mastering the market through dual engagement of clients and customers, feedback emerges not merely as a tool for assessment but as a cornerstone for strategic evolution and growth. This section reiterates the pivotal role of feedback loops in refining business strategies and provides a structured approach to transforming feedback into actionable steps that drive strategic enhancement. Through this lens, feedback is not only a mechanism for gauging satisfaction but also a dynamic resource for continuous improvement and innovation.

Feedback Utilization: The Engine for Refinement and Evolution

Feedback loops serve as critical channels for insight, offering direct perspectives from those most affected by a business's products, services, and overall strategies. Whether it comes from clients, customers, employees, or other stakeholders, feedback provides a mirror reflecting the efficacy of business operations and the alignment of offerings with market needs. Establishing systematic processes for collecting, analyzing, and acting upon feedback ensures that businesses remain responsive, agile, and aligned with their audience's evolving preferences.

The significance of feedback loops extends beyond reactive adjustments; they are instrumental in identifying opportunities for innovation, uncovering latent needs, and preempting potential market shifts. By embracing feedback as a continuous input into the strategic planning process, businesses can cultivate a culture of learning and adaptability, essential for long-term success in dynamic markets.

Actionable Feedback: From Insights to Strategy

Transforming feedback into actionable steps entails a structured approach to ensure that insights lead to meaningful enhancements. The following guide outlines the process for leveraging feedback for strategic growth:

1. **Systematic Collection:** Implement diverse channels for feedback collection, such as surveys, focus groups, social media monitoring, and direct customer interactions. Utilizing multiple sources enriches the feedback pool, providing a more comprehensive view of experiences and perceptions.
2. **Thorough Analysis:** Analyze feedback to identify patterns, trends, and areas of concern or opportunity. This analysis should differentiate between symptomatic issues and underlying causes, ensuring that actions address root causes rather than just surface-level symptoms.
3. **Prioritization of Feedback:** Not all feedback will have the same impact on strategic goals. Prioritize feedback based on its potential to influence key business outcomes, align with strategic objectives, and improve customer or client satisfaction.

4. **Development of Action Plans:** For prioritized feedback, develop specific, measurable, achievable, relevant, and time-bound (SMART) action plans. These plans should outline the steps needed to address the feedback, including resource allocation, responsible parties, and timelines.
5. **Implementation and Monitoring:** Execute the action plans with clear communication about the changes being made and why. Monitor the implementation process closely to ensure adherence to timelines and objectives, adjusting as necessary based on ongoing feedback and outcomes.
6. **Feedback Loop Closure:** Inform stakeholders, especially those who provided the feedback, about the actions taken in response. Closing the feedback loop enhances trust and demonstrates a genuine commitment to continuous improvement.
7. **Continuous Improvement Cycle:** Integrate feedback-driven changes into the business's continuous improvement cycle. Regularly review the impact of these changes on performance and satisfaction, using new insights to inform future strategies.

Leveraging feedback for growth is a strategic imperative for businesses committed to mastering the market. By systematically collecting, analyzing, and acting on feedback, organizations can refine their strategies, enhance their offerings, and strengthen their relationships with clients and customers. This proactive and responsive approach to feedback not only drives immediate improvements but also lays the foundation for sustained innovation and competitive advantage.

Section 15.5: Staying Ahead of Market Dynamics

In the intricate dance of business strategy, the ability to stay agile and responsive to the ever-shifting landscape of market dynamics is not merely advantageous—it is essential. This section delves into the criticality of market adaptability, illustrating how businesses can maintain a posture of readiness and agility. Furthermore, it provides a strategic blueprint for future-proofing businesses against the inevitable tides of market shifts, ensuring sustained relevance and competitiveness.

Market Adaptability: The Agile Response to Market Dynamics

Market adaptability refers to the capability of a business to quickly respond to changes in the market environment—be it through innovation, modification of strategies, or pivoting business models. This agility is crucial in a world where technological advancements, consumer preferences, and competitive landscapes evolve at an unprecedented pace. The necessity of staying agile stems from the volatile, uncertain, complex, and ambiguous (VUCA) nature of modern markets, where yesterday's strategies may no longer be tomorrow's solutions.

Adaptable businesses are characterized by their proactive stance, leveraging real-time data and analytics to anticipate market trends and adjust their strategies accordingly. This dynamic approach allows them to seize opportunities, mitigate risks, and navigate through challenges with resilience and foresight.

Future Preparedness: Strategies for Future-Proofing the Business

Future-proofing a business against upcoming market shifts involves a multifaceted strategy, focused on building flexibility, fostering innovation, and cultivating a forward-looking culture. The following strategies provide a roadmap for businesses aiming to stay ahead of market dynamics:

1. **Invest in Continuous Learning and Development:** Cultivate a culture of continuous learning within the organization, encouraging employees to stay abreast of industry trends, technological advancements, and emerging market needs. This investment in human capital enhances the organization's adaptability and innovative capacity.
2. **Leverage Technology and Data Analytics:** Utilize advanced technologies and data analytics to gain insights into market trends, customer behavior, and competitive activities. This information becomes the foundation for informed decision-making and strategic agility.
3. **Diversify Offerings and Markets:** Diversification reduces dependency on a single market or product line, spreading risk and increasing resilience against market fluctuations. Exploring new markets and developing a

broad range of products or services can safeguard the business against unforeseen disruptions.

4. **Foster an Innovative Ecosystem:** Encourage a culture of innovation where new ideas are valued and experimentation is rewarded. Innovation should permeate every aspect of the business, from product development to customer engagement strategies.
5. **Build Strategic Partnerships:** Collaborate with other businesses, research institutions, or startups to pool resources, share knowledge, and co-create solutions. Strategic partnerships can provide access to new technologies, markets, and insights, amplifying the business's capacity to adapt and innovate.
6. **Implement Agile Methodologies:** Adopt agile methodologies in project management and business operations to enhance flexibility and responsiveness. Agile practices allow businesses to iterate quickly, adapt plans based on feedback, and deliver value continuously.

Staying ahead of market dynamics is an ongoing process that requires vigilance, agility, and a commitment to continuous improvement. By embracing adaptability as a core business strategy and implementing measures to future-proof against market shifts, businesses can navigate the complexities of the modern market with confidence. The journey towards mastering market dynamics is both challenging and rewarding, offering opportunities for growth, innovation, and long-term success.

Section 15.6: Encouraging Innovation and Adaptability

In the arena of modern business, innovation and adaptability are not merely advantageous attributes but essential components of sustained growth and competitiveness. This section illuminates the pivotal role of innovation in propelling businesses forward and outlines a comprehensive framework for embedding adaptability and innovation into the very fabric of organizational DNA. Through fostering an environment where innovation thrives and adaptability is second nature, businesses can navigate the complexities of the market with agility and foresight.

Innovation Culture: The Catalyst for Sustained Growth

Innovation, in its essence, is the lifeblood of business growth and competitiveness. It entails not just the introduction of new products or services but the reinvention of business processes, the exploration of new markets, and the adoption of novel business models. A culture of innovation encourages continuous questioning, experimentation, and a willingness to challenge the status quo. This culture is characterized by a pervasive mindset that views challenges as opportunities for improvement and growth.

The role of innovation in sustaining business competitiveness cannot be overstated. It enables businesses to stay ahead of market trends, meet evolving customer needs, and differentiate themselves from competitors. Moreover, an innovation-driven culture attracts and retains top talent, individuals who are eager to contribute to a dynamic and forward-thinking organization.

Adaptability Framework: Embedding Innovation into Organizational DNA

Creating an organization that is inherently adaptable and innovative requires a structured approach. The following framework provides strategic pillars for embedding these qualities into the organizational DNA:

1. **Leadership Commitment:** Leadership must unequivocally support and actively participate in innovation initiatives. This includes providing strategic

direction, allocating resources, and setting an example of openness to new ideas and approaches.

2. **Strategic Flexibility:** Develop a strategy that incorporates flexibility, allowing the organization to pivot in response to market changes or emerging opportunities. This involves scenario planning, risk management, and maintaining a portfolio of initiatives that can be adapted or scaled as needed.

3. **Empowerment and Collaboration:** Empower employees at all levels to contribute ideas and take initiative. Foster a collaborative environment that breaks down silos and encourages cross-functional teams to work together on innovation projects.

4. **Continuous Learning and Development:** Invest in the continuous learning and development of the workforce. Encourage employees to acquire new skills and knowledge that can drive innovation, and provide platforms for sharing insights and learning across the organization.

5. **Reward and Recognition Systems:** Implement reward systems that recognize and celebrate innovation and risk-taking, even when efforts do not always lead to success. This reinforces the value placed on experimentation and learning.

6. **Processes and Tools:** Integrate processes and tools that support innovation, from idea management systems to agile project management methodologies. These tools should facilitate the rapid development and testing of ideas.

7. **Culture of Openness and Feedback:** Cultivate a culture that values openness, feedback, and constructive criticism. Encourage dialogue and learning from both successes and failures, viewing each as an opportunity for growth and improvement.

Fostering a culture of innovation and adaptability is essential for businesses aiming to thrive in today's dynamic market landscape. By embedding these principles into the organizational DNA, companies can not only navigate the present challenges but also shape the future, driving sustained growth and maintaining a competitive edge. The journey towards innovation and adaptability is ongoing, requiring commitment, resilience, and a willingness to continuously evolve.

Section 15.7: Final Thoughts: Building a Legacy of Engagement

As we draw the curtains on this book, it is imperative to reflect on the essence of what it means to not only navigate the market today but to build a legacy that endures. This final section aims to inspire businesses to see beyond the immediate horizon of profits and performance metrics, to a future where deep, meaningful engagement with clients and customers forms the cornerstone of lasting success. It is a call to action for readers to apply the strategies and insights from this guide to forge relationships that transcend transactions, fostering loyalty and driving sustainable growth.

Legacy Building: The Art of Meaningful Engagement

Building a legacy of engagement is about creating connections that are both enduring and enriching. It's about crafting experiences that resonate, communicating values that align with those of your clients and customers, and demonstrating an unwavering commitment to their success and satisfaction. This legacy is built on the pillars of trust, integrity, and innovation, where every interaction is an opportunity to reinforce the strength of the relationship.

A legacy of engagement transcends the boundaries of conventional business metrics to embed your brand deeply in the lives of those you serve. It means becoming an integral part of your clients' and customers' stories, where your contributions to their success are remembered and valued. This form of legacy is not measured in quarters or fiscal years but in the lasting impact you have on the markets you serve and the communities you touch.

Call to Action: Crafting Lasting Relationships for Sustainable Growth

The journey through "Mastering the Market" has laid out a blueprint for achieving excellence in client and customer engagement. The insights and strategies shared within these pages are more than theoretical concepts; they are practical tools waiting to be wielded in the hands of visionary leaders and dedicated teams.

1. **Embrace Adaptability and Innovation:** In a world that never stands still, your ability to adapt and innovate is your greatest asset. Let the pursuit of excellence through innovation be the hallmark of your brand, always seeking new ways to engage, inspire, and serve.

2. **Foster a Culture of Continuous Learning:** Building a legacy requires a foundation of knowledge and insight. Cultivate a culture where learning is continuous, and every challenge is seen as an opportunity to grow and improve.
3. **Leverage Feedback for Growth:** View feedback as the compass that guides your journey towards excellence. Embrace it, learn from it, and use it to refine your strategies and offerings.
4. **Prioritize Genuine Connections:** In the digital age, personal connections matter more than ever. Prioritize genuine engagement with your clients and customers, building relationships based on trust, respect, and mutual value.
5. **Act with Integrity and Purpose:** Let your actions reflect your values. Build your legacy on the foundation of integrity, operating with a clear sense of purpose and responsibility towards those you serve and the world you inhabit.

In closing, the path to mastering the market and building a lasting legacy is both challenging and rewarding. It is a journey marked by constant learning, innovation, and an unwavering commitment to excellence in engagement. As you move forward, let the insights from this book guide your strategies, inspire your actions, and help you create enduring relationships that drive sustainable growth.

Chapter 15: Wrapping It Up with a Bang - The "Let's Not Make This Awkward" Finale

Welcome to the end of the road, folks - Chapter 15. You've been through the wringer, from decoding the digital jungle to turning your business into an eco-warrior. Now, it's time to tie it all up with a pretty bow and maybe even a cherry on top. Let's recap the gold nuggets and lay down the action plan that'll make your competitors weep (or, at least, give them something to think about).

Section 15.1: The TL;DR of Dominating Dual Engagement

We've covered more ground than a marathon runner here, from AI high-fives to making green the new black in business. Here's the espresso shot of what matters:

- **Personalized Experience:** Thanks to our pals, AI and machine learning, we're not just shooting in the dark. We're crafting experiences so personal; your customers will think you're mind readers.
- **Social Media Tightrope:** It's a wild world out there, but get it right, and it's your oyster. Wrong, and well, let's not go there.
- **Going Green:** If you're not thinking about sustainability, you're living in the past. Modern businesses are as much about saving the world as they are about profit.
- **Trust Is Everything:** With great data comes great responsibility. Handle it with care, or it'll bite you in the back.

Section 15.2: The "Mixtape" of Engagement Strategies

Here's how to blend all these tunes into a chart-topping hit:

- **Harmony Between Tech and Touch:** Like peanut butter and jelly, AI and the human element together are unbeatable. Find that sweet spot.
- **Singing on Social:** Your strategy here should be like a hit song – catchy, on-point, and impossible to ignore.
- **Eco-Friendly Grooves:** Make sustainability part of your brand's rhythm. It's not just nice; it's necessary.
- **Data With Dignity:** Treat personal info like a secret diary. Lock it up tight and only peek when absolutely necessary.

Section 15.3: Keeping the Band Together

Adaptability and innovation aren't just buzzwords; they're your backstage passes to staying relevant. Encourage your team to think big, make mistakes, and keep pushing boundaries. Remember, the only bad idea is the one you didn't share.

Section 15.4: The Feedback Loop - Your Encore

Feedback is like an encore; it keeps the show going and lets you know what hits to play next. Embrace it, act on it, and watch how it transforms your business. It's not just noise; it's the sound of opportunity knocking.

Section 15.5: Future-Proofing - The Sequel

Staying ahead isn't about having a crystal ball; it's about being ready to dance even when the music changes. Keep your eyes open, your ears to the ground, and never stop learning. The market waits for no one, so keep your sneakers laced and ready to move.

Section 15.6: Innovation - Not Just a Buzzword

Inject innovation into your business's DNA like it's caffeine. Encourage wild ideas, celebrate successes (and failures), and always ask, "What's next?" Your business should be as dynamic as a startup that's had too much coffee.

Section 15.7: The Mic Drop

You didn't just read a book; you embarked on a journey to revolutionize your business. Now, it's time to take these lessons, mix them with your secret sauce, and cook up something legendary. Build those relationships, make your mark, and let's create a legacy that's not just about profit but about making a dent in the universe.

And there you have it, the grand finale. Now, go forth and conquer. The market's your stage, and it's time for your solo. Drop the mic; you've got this.

The legacy you build today will define your success tomorrow. Let it be a legacy of deep engagement, meaningful impact, and enduring value. The future is yours to shape. It has been a pleasure and my personal honor to serve you and your business.

Made in the USA
Middletown, DE
28 April 2024

53595573R00308